G000270845

BIG CAESARS AND
LITTLE CAESARS

BIG CAESARS AND LITTLE CAESARS

How They Rise and How They Fall — From Julius Caesar to Boris Johnson

FERDINAND MOUNT

BLOOMSBURY CONTINUUM
LONDON • OXFORD • NEW YORK • NEW DELHI • SYDNEY

BLOOMSBURY CONTINUUM
Bloomsbury Publishing Plc
50 Bedford Square, London, WC1B 3DP, UK
29 Earlsfort Terrace, Dublin 2, Ireland

BLOOMSBURY, BLOOMSBURY CONTINUUM and the Diana logo are trademarks of
Bloomsbury Publishing Plc

First published in Great Britain 2023
Paperback 2024

Copyright © Ferdinand Mount, 2023

Ferdinand Mount has asserted his right under the Copyright, Designs and Patents Act, 1988,
to be identified as Author of this work

For legal purposes the Picture Credits and Acknowledgements on pp. 293–5 constitute an
extension of this copyright page

All rights reserved. No part of this publication may be reproduced or transmitted in any form or
by any means, electronic or mechanical, including photocopying, recording, or any information
storage or retrieval system, without prior permission in writing from the publishers

Bloomsbury Publishing Plc does not have any control over, or responsibility for, any third-party
websites referred to or in this book. All internet addresses given in this book were correct at the
time of going to press. The author and publisher regret any inconvenience caused if addresses
have changed or sites have ceased to exist, but can accept no responsibility for any such changes

A catalogue record for this book is available from the British Library

Library of Congress Cataloguing-in-Publication data has been applied for

ISBN: PB: 978-1-3994-0972-8; eBook: 978-1-3994-0973-5; ePDF: 978-1-3994-0968-1

2 4 6 8 10 9 7 5 3 1

Typeset by Deanta Global Publishing Services, Chennai, India
Printed and bound in Great Britain by CPI Group (UK) Ltd, Croydon CR0 4YY

To find out more about our authors and books visit www.bloomsbury.com and sign up
for our newsletters

'Upon what meat doth this our Caesar feed
That he is grown so great?'

JULIUS CAESAR, ACT I, SCENE II

'I am meant to be in charge. I am the Führer. I'm the
king who takes the decisions.'

BORIS JOHNSON, 2020

Praise for Big Caesars and Little Caesars

'Highly informative and hugely entertaining […] a reminder that dictators have long been, and continue to be, a threat to democracy.'

Forbes

'The power of this needle-sharp book lies in the acuity of its observations and in its ability to zoom out and see modern politicians in broader context, bringing something both fresh and timeless to an otherwise well-worn subject.'

The Guardian

'Wry, informative but deadly – a great book.'

Will Hutton

'Mount's prose is enjoyable and some of the vignettes are a delight. [The Caesars] make for compelling reading.'

The Sunday Times

'Mount's prose is vivid, erudite and highly opinionated… [he] dissects all these villains in entertaining style… his range of historical reference points is impressive.'

Irish Independent

'Pass deep historical knowledge through the silkiest of minds and deliver the product onto the page with the most fluent of pens, and you find the combination of gifts which make Ferdie Mount pre-eminent among the political commentariat of our day. He has created a book that will endure in 50 years' time when students of British Politics will still struggle to understand how the supposedly most mature political system in the world could have placed Boris Johnson in Downing Street for three years. This is the volume they will have to read first.'

Peter Hennessy

'Always absorbing and often bitterly funny, Ferdinand Mount's survey traces with characteristic panache an unedifying line of populist opportunists from classical times down to the shoddy and sinister figures of Johnson and Trump. His eloquent concluding call for the restoration and safeguarding of parliamentary authority has never been more urgently needed.'

Roy Foster, Emeritus Professor of Irish History at the University of Oxford

'A wonderfully wry field guide to autocrats. With tremendous wit and wisdom, the former head of Margaret Thatcher's policy unit identifies the qualities particular to dictators – and warns against consigning such people to history. […] Mount, learned to the pink tips of his ears, knows so much, and what he didn't before, he has found out.

Mount's considerable journalistic skills deployed here in the cause of concision, the pricking of pomposity and, sometimes, his own outrage. […] He is especially good on Johnson […] Mount is beautifully wry in this book, on top of everything else.'

Observer

'Mount is an entertaining guide to dictatorship.'

Book of the week, The Times

'…a fast-paced and impassioned essay.'

Sunday Telegraph

'[Mount] is one of the best contemporary essayists in English. He writes elegantly with an occasional brutal turn of phrase.'

The Tablet

'Delicious work, beautifully and acerbically written by a cultured man of a kind achingly rare in our world of intellectual short cuts and tawdry soundbites.'

Wall Street Journal

'A thoughtful and cogent account of the Johnson premiership.'

Literary Review

'Those interested in how someone such as Boris Johnson could have been responsible for what was possibly the greatest foreign-policy own-goal in Great Britain's history would do well to read Mount's book.'

Foreign Policy

Contents

Prologue

Caesars are back, big Caesars and little Caesars, in big countries and little countries, in advanced nations and backward nations. The world seems to be full of self-proclaimed Strong Men strutting their stuff, or waiting in the wings, or licking their wounds and plotting a comeback after their humiliating fall. Right up to the last minute, we really believed that it couldn't happen here, or now. How can these uncouth figures with their funny hair, their rude manners and their bad jokes take such a hold on the popular imagination? How can anyone bear to listen to their endless resentful rants? Surely he (it's mostly a he, but not always) can't get away with it? People will see through him before it's too late. He's so obviously a con artist, a charlatan, a little corporal from God knows where. It's not even as if he bothers to conceal his intentions. He wants to be king of the world, and he lets us know it. How on earth can we fall for his tawdry gimmicks?

In any case, surely our institutions are too strong to crumble under such a trumpery assault? Our liberties are too well dug in. The voters are educated now, and too sophisticated to be caught by any passing demagogue. Besides – and this is the high-flown academic argument – the Caesar is a throwback. He has been consigned to the dustbin of history. The evolution of modern democratic societies cannot be reversed. Francis Fukuyama taught us in *The End of History* (1992) that there is no alternative to liberal democracy. We may experience setbacks and temporary breakdowns of constitutional order, unpleasant little spurts of nationalism or religious conflict may erupt here and there, but the long-term direction of travel is clear and securely established. We had reserved seats on a smooth passage to modernity, many of us in first class.

Well, that's how the comfortable classes thought 20 or 30 years ago, after the fall of the Berlin Wall, if we thought at all. We don't think like that any more. The road ahead now seems bumpy, unpredictable, often laden with menace. Neither the 'liberal' nor the 'democratic' part of liberal democracy seems quite so secure. On the contrary, modern Caesars, ruling by rough methods and with scant regard for liberal pieties – or any pieties at all – have settled themselves in power with remarkably little resistance. Of the 91 dictators down the ages portrayed in Iain Dale's new study, 29 have come to power in the past 30 years – that is, since Fukuyama's essay was published.

This is an uncomfortable prospect. It was assumed that the discrediting of fascism, and then of communism, and the lack of any alternative ideology, had left the field clear for liberal democracy, because liberal democracy now had no plausible competitors. But the little Caesars of today seem to get along quite nicely without any proper ideology worth the name. For what consistent line have Donald Trump, Vladimir Putin, Recep Erdoğan, Viktor Orbán, Jair Bolsonaro, Narendra Modi, President Xi and even Boris Johnson been operating on, beyond a shouty sort of nationalism and a carefully advertised hostility to immigrants – a mixture familiar to us from ancient times? The great Pericles himself instituted a law barring anyone who was not a pure-born Athenian from claiming citizenship (his own foreign-born wife fell foul of the law).

But why should this surprise us so much? Dictators of one sort or another have been an ever-lurking threat throughout history. They interrupted and betrayed the constitutional traditions of ancient Greece and the Roman Republic: Peisistratos, Critias and the Thirty Tyrants in Athens: Sulla, Marius and Julius Caesar in Rome. As early as the time of Thucydides and Plato, the word *tyrannos* had mutated from a neutral term for 'king' into our modern pejorative sense of 'tyrant'. Absolutist rulers broke up the constitutional city states of medieval Germany and Italy, and brought in their train time-serving sycophants who rewrote history to justify their actions. Witness Machiavelli's craven sucking up to the Medici after they grabbed power, though nothing could be quite as repellent as Machiavelli's adulation of Cesare Borgia. Only by smoothing history into a linear narrative with a beginning, a middle and an end can we avoid being aware of the recurring disruptive threat of the would-be Caesar.

How do these Caesars gain power? What are their vital ingredients? How do they normalize their breaches with constitutional tradition? To answer questions like these, we must free ourselves from the comforting illusions of historicism – the sort of illusion by which we have seen Cromwell smoothed into our parliamentary tradition in total defiance of almost everything he did. The first thing that every would-be Caesar understands is that patterns are there to be smashed. And we must understand that too.

Students of dictatorship often like to make subdivisions of the species. They draw a distinction between 'authoritarian' regimes and 'totalitarian' ones. Authoritarian rulers, though they may be corrupt and brutal, we are told, content themselves with grabbing and hoarding as much power over their subjects' lives as they need to stay in power and get their own way. By contrast, totalitarian regimes aspire to control every waking moment of their luckless subjects' lives. Under President Reagan, this distinction was even erected into a foreign policy, 'the Kirkpatrick doctrine', after Reagan's feisty ambassador to the UN, Jeane Kirkpatrick. The United States, she argued, could do business with the authoritarians and help them to evolve towards democracy in return for a solid alliance with America; as FDR had said of the Nicaraguan dictator Anastasio Somoza back in 1939, 'He may be a son of a bitch, but he's our son of a bitch.' By contrast, according to Kirkpatrick, totalitarian regimes like the Soviet Union were too stable and entrenched to be budged; they could only be confronted.

This turned out in practice to be a decidedly dubious rule of thumb. American entanglements in the Philippines, Nicaragua and Guatemala, not to say Chile, had calamitous results, whereas the notion that the USSR was incapable of transformation was shattered in 1989. The danger of typecasting regimes in this way is that we may miss how far in practice the regime differs from the archetype: the suffering inflicted by authoritarian regimes like Pinochet's may actually be worse than that inflicted by totalitarian regimes such as the USSR over the same period; conversely, the degree of total control over the economy exerted by, say, the Nazi regime may be less all-encompassing than the stereotype depicts. It was some time before it dawned on analysts that in fact Nazi Germany had been less mobilized for war than Great Britain.

This inquiry has a rather different preoccupation: to identify the tricks and techniques common to all Caesars, big and little. As far as possible, I want to show how they all operate along the same spectrum. It is admittedly a huge spectrum; the Caesars range in intensity from overblown bully boys and con artists to mass murderers of unspeakable wickedness. But again and again, we shall find piquant resemblances in the ways by which all these Caesars and would-be Caesars set out to acquire power, and the ways in which they strive to hang on to and, where possible, enhance that power. To be clear: when I talk of 'big' Caesars, I do not mean that they are of greater moral or physical stature. On the contrary, many have been monsters, not to mention also physically stunted; what I mean is that their violence, their law-breaking, their lying, are on a huge, often limitless scale. Little Caesars go only as far as they need to: in breaking the law or introducing new repressive laws, in telling lies, in fixing elections or controlling the judges. 'Tinpot dictators' says it nicely.

As we go along, we are repeatedly confronted by a discomfiting thought: that Caesars may pop up in any country and under all sorts of political and economic circumstances. Just as there turns out to be no inexorable law of development which leads to socialism, so there is no law of development which makes a Caesar impossible. For more than two centuries, we have been bewitched by tapestries of progress proposed by the most seductive embroiderers: by the Marquis de Condorcet before the French Revolution, by Hegel and Marx in the nineteenth century, and so on into our own time by those who have assumed liberal democracy to be the end point of history, of whom Francis Fukuyama has been only the most alluring exponent. None of these patterns is looking especially persuasive just now.

I make no apology for two features of this book. The first is that it will jump about in a way that may disconcert some readers. We shall, for example, swing between describing how Julius Caesar broke open the Treasury in the Temple of Saturn, in order to fund his war against Pompey, to describing how Donald Trump declared a National Emergency in order to divert funds voted by Congress for other purposes, and use the money to fund the Mexican Wall which Congress had repeatedly refused to pay for. The point is not simply to note the piquant similarity between these two monstrous grabs of funds belonging to the state but, more generally, to illustrate how the would-be Caesar is inevitably drawn to break the law to gain his ends. Again, we shall jump from Boris Johnson's repressive Five Acts of 2022 to Lord Liverpool's repressive Six Acts of 1819, to demonstrate how governments under pressure from rebel movements resort to a flurry of ill thought-out and reactionary laws to demonstrate how tough they are being.

Secondly, the text has quite a few illustrations, more perhaps than is usual in a book about politics. This is because the Caesar creates his own visual culture and basks in it. The Emperor Augustus had the text of his boastful brief autobiography *Res Gestae Divi Augusti* carved in bronze or stone and then erected in public spaces all across the Empire; you can still see today surviving fragments of this huge exercise in global PR.

Modern replica of the *Res Gestae* outside the Museum of the Ara Pacis, Rome.

Ever since, the Caesar has been a pioneer in the use of new media: from the inventions of printing and photography, through the development of public advertising, then the cinema, radio and television to, finally, perhaps most potent of all, social media, which gives him unrivalled direct access to every voter. His delight in the visual image is no accident. The Caesar thrives in the moment; he is the enemy of long-winded statutes and codes of law and practice, and the king of the photo opportunity. He is an endless source of stunts, gestures, masquerades; he may appear in the guise of a Greek god or a Roman emperor, or of a construction worker or a fighter pilot, never resting in his efforts to convince the public that life is simply more vibrant, more fun when he is around. His verbal messages are deliberately simple, aimed at the lowest common denominator in his audience (a point hammered home *ad nauseam* in *Mein Kampf*). These communications, 'comms' as we now call them, also necessarily involve a good deal of distortion of the truth. Many pages of this book are about lying.

Caesar as construction worker.

But the book is also about how Caesars fail, about why coups flop, and how Caesars can be unhorsed, either by their own overreaches or by resolute and ingenious opponents banding together. This is not a pessimistic book; it is a hymn to vigilance. So in Part I, we consider the idea of Caesarism, how it has come into fashion and gone out again, and why. Then in Part II, we look at the conditions and techniques which help a Caesar to gain power and retain it. But in Part III, we look at the other side, examining in some detail half-a-dozen attempted coups which came to a sticky end. And we examine some of the reasons for those failures. In Part IV, we venture into the holy of holies, the chambers of parliaments and senates. The idea is to underline the essential principle at the heart of the argument: that these institutions of constitutional government are not mere practical conveniences. They are what John Locke called them three centuries ago: 'the soul that gives form, life and unity to the Commonwealth'. And their day is not done yet. Within the past two years, the United States Congress has twice impeached a froward President who broke the law and then refused to accept the verdict of the voters. In the UK Parliament, Conservative MPs have deposed a Prime Minister who

repeatedly broke every rule of conduct. In Brazil, the voters threw out
the overweening Jair Bolsonaro. If we live in a new age of Caesars,
we also live in an age of Caesar-toppling. No Caesar is immortal, or
immune to age and ill-health. Every Caesar sets out to cultivate the
'illusion of permanence', just as the British Raj did in India. That illusion may hold sway right up to the last minute before the whole show
disintegrates. All we can safely predict is that new Caesars will arise,
and that they in their turn will fall. If history is any guide at all, this
won't be the last time that the voters or their elected representatives
in Parliament will be called on to perform the painful duty of turfing
out their self-proclaimed and once adored saviour.

But we should not imagine that getting rid of a Caesar in itself
will return us automatically to the status quo ante. These ill-starred
comets leave a long trail of debris: social and economic dislocation,
corrupted legal systems, broken relations with other nations, bitter and
unreconciled losers, widespread demoralization and bewilderment.

Which is why we must do our best to head the would-be Caesar off
at the pass. We need to be alert to the flaws of an upcoming Caesar:
his relentless egotism, his lack of scruple, his thoughtless brutality, his
cheesy glitz. But we need also to appreciate the countervailing virtues
of parliaments and senates when they are at their best (which is not
always, by any means): their capacity to resolve stubborn conflicts,
their willingness to entertain second thoughts, their tenacity in
ironing out the details of complex legislation, their ability to speak
for every part of the nation, in extremis to overthrow incompetent
or tyrannical rulers; above all, their dedication to deliberation and
debate. Lyndon Baines Johnson was an imperfect human being, but
no American President has achieved more. He carried through the
Great Society – the Civil Rights Act, Medicare and Medicaid, the war
on poverty. As leader of the Senate, he was an unrivalled wheeler-
dealer. Throughout his political career, he took as his motto Isaiah
1.18: 'Come now, and let us reason together.' It is hard to improve
on that advice.

PART I

THE IDEA OF A CAESAR

Why Is He There?

Oliver Cromwell statue outside Westminster Hall.

It is the first figure you meet as you cross the road to the Houses of Parliament. He is all on his own, there's no other statue near him: 'Oliver Cromwell, 1599–1658', with his sword in one hand, hefty Bible in the other and the British lion recumbent at his feet. The sculptor, Hamo Thornycroft, was a graceful neoclassical artist, and possessed of great personal charm. (Henry James and the critic Edmund Gosse were besotted with him; when asked, Lytton Strachey said that Gosse was 'hamosexual'.) Here, though, Thornycroft has done his best to follow Cromwell's famous instructions to Sir Peter Lely two centuries earlier: 'Mr Lely, I desire you would use all your skill to paint my picture truly like me, and not flatter me at all; but remark all these roughnesses, pimples, warts and everything as you see me; otherwise I will never pay a farthing for it.' The result here is not quite such a blotchy plug-ugly as in Lely's portrait but, for all Thornycroft's skill, Cromwell still looks more like a nightclub bouncer than a national hero.

The question, though, and it's a question that is still alive today, is: what's he doing here? Why does Cromwell get such pride of place? After all, the one thing every schoolboy knows is that Cromwell is famous for smashing up Parliament and seizing the mace. The contemporary accounts of this and his other clashes with Parliament are vivid and alarming. 'Come, come, I will put an end to your prating,' is how he begins, before walking up and down the House like a madman, and kicking the ground with his feet. 'You are no Parliament,' he cries out. 'I say you are no Parliament, I will put an end to your sitting. Call them in, call them in.' The Serjeant opens the doors and two files of musketeers tramp into the House. While they are taking up their positions, the Lord General is still stumping up and down, abusing MPs who catch his eye. 'You, sir, are a drunkard, and some of you are whoremasters' (looking at Henry Marten and Sir Peter Wentworth). Then Cromwell points to the Speaker up in his chair: 'Fetch him down.' The Speaker is the famous William Lenthall, who was to be Speaker for most of the twenty years of the Long Parliament. When Lenthall doesn't budge, Cromwell shouts, 'Put him out,' and Thomas Harrison, one of the regicides and later to be hanged, drawn and quartered at Charing Cross (Pepys describes him as 'looking as cheerfully as any man could do in that condition'), goes to persuade him. 'I will not come down unless I am pulled out,' says Lenthall, but eventually consents to take Harrison's hand, and he is marched out through a line of 200 soldiers without the mace, which normally accompanies the Speaker's procession. 'Take away that bauble,' says Cromwell – or is it, 'What shall we do with this bauble?' At all events, the soldiers carry off the mace and dump it in Cromwell's quarters in the Cockpit, where he gives one of those fake-rueful debriefings great men give after something hasn't gone entirely to plan: 'When I went there, I did not think to have done this. But perceiving the spirit of God so strong upon me, I would not consult flesh and blood.'[1]

The Dissolution of the Rump on 20 April 1653 effectively ended the Commonwealth and opened the way for Oliver Cromwell to become Lord Protector eight months later. It remains one of the most memorable and terrifying scenes in English history. The rough words of command, the coarse personal abuse, the utter disrespect of custom and ceremony – this is Cromwell. It always was. The capacity for abrupt violence, the words and actions in terrifying sync: this is his shtick, his forte, his USP. And he stayed the same, through to the end.

His last dissolution was as abrupt as his first. On 4 February 1658, seven months before his death, he arrived unannounced in a hackney carriage at Westminster Hall – the Thames was too icebound to go by water – and told his startled son-in-law, Charles Fleetwood, that he intended to dissolve Parliament once again. Think hard about it first, Fleetwood pleaded, for it was a decision of great consequence. 'You are a milksop,' Cromwell replied, no more willing to consult flesh and blood on this occasion than he had been five years earlier. 'By the living God I will dissolve the House.'[2]

Nor had he developed any greater respect for the law while in power. In November 1655, when George Cony, a former friend of his, refused to pay customs duty on some imported silk on the grounds that the duty had not been imposed by Parliament, Cromwell threw him in jail. When Cony's lawyer, the eminent Sir John Maynard, pleaded habeas corpus and the judges in the case invoked the provisions of Magna Carta against imprisonment without trial, Cromwell committed Maynard to the Tower and summoned the judges to tell them that 'their Magna Farta should not control his actions which were for the safety of the Commonwealth. Who made them judges? What authority had they to sit there but what he gave them?' This story, told in Clarendon's *History of the Rebellion*, rings true to me. Historians are prone to dismiss as Royalist propaganda the report by Roger Coke, grandson of the author of the Petition of Right, that Cromwell once called it 'the Petition of Shite'. But I can believe that one, too.

When Oliver first elbows his way into both the Short and the Long Parliament, he is turning 40, a plain man in a plain cloth suit with a speck or two of blood on his collar band, 'his countenance swollen and reddish, his voice sharp and untunable'. He was noticed only for the violence of his speech, reproved by the House for his language and several of his hotter rants against the bishops excised from the record. But these must have been the very qualities that drew a remarkable prophecy from John Hampden, who happened also to be his first cousin: 'That slovenly fellow which you see before us; I say that sloven, if we should come to have a breach with the King (which God forbid), in such case will be one of the greatest men in England.'[3]

Remarkably we have two doctors' reports on Cromwell at around the age of 30. His own family physician Dr Simcott reports that he would sometimes lie in his bed 'all melancholy' and would send for Simcott at midnight to share his hallucinations with him, including the fancy that one day 'he should be the greatest man in the kingdom.' Oliver also consulted the most fashionable doctor in London, the Huguenot émigré Sir Theodore de Mayerne, who found Monsieur Cromwell to be 'extremely melancholy'. Mayerne had been court physician to Cardinal Richelieu and was now the same to Charles I. Consulting Harley Street's finest does not seem to be the action of a plain russet-coated captain. More alarming were the fits of convulsive, often causeless laughter to which he was subject, most memorably after his famous victory at Dunbar, at which he had butchered probably about twice as many Scots as Cumberland was to kill at Culloden, though not as many Irish men as he himself had butchered at Drogheda and Wexford. According to Aubrey, when he saw the Scots' lines break, 'Oliver was carried on as with a divine impulse. He did laugh so excessively as if he had been drunk, and his eyes sparkled with spirits . . . The same fit of laughter seized him just before the battle of Naseby.'[4]

In his rumbustious biography God's Englishman, Christopher Hill diagnoses Cromwell, quite plausibly, as a manic depressive. When evaluating his performance in government, the Marxist Hill is more plain-spoken than some liberal historians, who tend to be mealy-mouthed when faced with such uncouth conduct, or sigh, as Austin Woolrych does of the Cony case, that 'one cannot make revolutions without breaking a few constitutional eggs.'[5] Hill freely acknowledges that in all Cromwell's disputes with his Parliaments, there 'was one fundamental problem: the problem of the electorate'.[6] After 1647, the Revolution had gone steaming on far beyond what the average MP or voter could approve. Hill draws the parallels which milder historians shrink from: 'This was a real problem, a problem which recurred in later revolutions. Rousseau thought that men might have to be forced to be free; the Jacobin dictatorship, and the Bolshevik dictatorship of the proletariat, justified themselves as covering the period in which the sovereign people were being educated up to their new responsibilities.'[7] I'm not sure how much irony there is in that, certainly less than in Brecht's celebrated wisecrack, 'Would it not be simpler if the government dissolved the people and elected another?'

In overthrowing the verdict of the voters, not just the survival of the Revolution was at stake. There was a more personal anxiety, expressed by the regicide John Lambert, with his usual candour when justifying the 1656 purge of unbiddable MPs: 'If a Parliament should be chosen according to the general spirit and temper of the nation, and if there should not be a check on such election, there may creep into this house [men] who may come to sit as our judges for all we have done in this Parliament, or at any other time or place.' If they lost control of events, they would be on the receiving end of some pretty rough justice from their old enemies. Which is indeed what happened at the Restoration, when one or two of Lambert's comrades were hung, drawn and quartered, and he himself was banged up in island fortresses for the last 20 years of his life where, according to some accounts, he went mad.

Cromwell and his officers purged or dissolved Parliament half a dozen times, in order to avoid a hostile outcome: in 1648, 1653 (in effect, twice in that year), 1654, 1655, 1656 and 1658. This record is not unique. To forestall royalist majorities, Napoleon broke up no fewer than three national assemblies in the coups of Vendémiaire, Fructidor and Brumaire. Lenin had to use force repeatedly, first to smash the Constituent Assembly, then to prevent it from reassembling elsewhere. But there is something uniquely repellent about Cromwell's claim in each case that he was merely fulfilling God's design, or that he had no foreknowledge of what the army was up to.

What is absolutely clear is that Cromwell had no respect at all for the decisions of the voters. It's not even as if the electorate was so unrepresentative. By the time of the Long Parliament, because of inflation, so many forty-shilling freeholders were entitled to vote that they made up about one-third of the adult male population – a proportion probably not surpassed until the late nineteenth century.

Cromwell's contemporaries were seldom disarmed by his protestations that his instructions came directly from God. On the contrary, many of his leading collaborators such as Edmund Ludlow thought that, when he ratted on them, he was driven by his own personal ambition. In the mid-seventeenth century, after all, they were rather better acquainted with religious humbugs than we are. I don't mean that Cromwell was a full-time humbug, only that he was no slouch at eliding his latest tactical decision with the will of the Almighty.

In particular, his contemporaries did not swallow his frequent protestations that the more embarrassing incidents in his career were really nothing to do with him and that he was unaware of the naughty intentions of other, more worldly folk. John Morrill in the new *Dictionary of National Biography* has drawn up a far from exhaustive list of occasions on which historians are more inclined to take Cromwell's word for it than many of his contemporaries were. Did he really not deliberately delay his return to London until after Colonel Thomas Pride's mass purge? Did he really not know that Cornet Joyce was going to kidnap the King from Holdenby House when Joyce had been to see Cromwell a couple of days earlier? Did he really not know that the Nominated Assembly, alias Barebone's Parliament, was going to dissolve itself and offer him the Protectorate? Paul Lay, in his history of the Protectorate, finds this one particularly hard to swallow, quoting Blair Worden's remark that Cromwell was 'practised at not knowing'. Did he really have no hand in engineering the proposal to upgrade him to King? We have, after all, the evidence of his walk in St James's Park with Bulstrode Whitelocke the preceding November, during which he raised, in an apparently offhand way, the question, 'What if a man should take it upon him to be King?' and Whitelocke replied tartly that, if a King were needed, Charles II would be a better choice. Cromwell was miffed, according to Whitelocke, and never such friends again.

In the succeeding century too, the philosopher David Hume spoke for the majority view when he denounced Cromwell as not only 'the most frantic enthusiast' but also the 'most dangerous of hypocrites, who was enabled after multiplied deceits to cover, under a tempest of passion, all his crooked schemes and profound artifices'.[8] Even after the French Revolution, the memory of his violent actions was still green. During Napoleon's coup of the 19 Brumaire, 1799, when he smashed up the Assembly of Deputies meeting at the palace of St-Cloud, some of the indignant members shouted, 'A Bas Cromwell!'[9]

Nothing would have seemed less likely than that another hundred years later, by the tercentenary in 1899 of Cromwell's birth, he should have been reborn as the most heroic figure in the whole history of Parliament, and that this splendid statue should have been erected to his memory and on the most hallowed site imaginable. It's only a few paces, after all, from the spot where his severed head had been stuck on a pole above Westminster Hall at the Restoration, after his remains had been dug up from his grave in the Abbey and brought out to be spat upon by the public.

How did this extraordinary *bouleversement* come about?

The Hero Worshipper

There is a simple, sufficient answer: Thomas Carlyle. Throughout the second half of the nineteenth century, Carlyle's edition of *Oliver Cromwell's Letters and Speeches*, first published in three volumes in 1845, stood on every respectable bookshelf, especially those of Carlyle's fellow Nonconformists, then more numerous than at any time before or since. Never out of print for a century, more like a weird, extravagant biography than a mere collection of Cromwell's works, these amazing volumes repackaged the Protector for posterity. Never had his words been so admiringly collected, embroidered and eulogized. Carlyle's 'Elucidations', his sulphurous, whimsical, hectoring interpolations, are as copious as the collected texts.

What Carlyle had in mind was a gigantic project that went beyond building up Cromwell as the greatest of England's national heroes. He wanted also to revive the cult of heroes in general. *On Heroes, Hero Worship and the Heroic in History* was published four years earlier, and Carlyle starts right in on page 1: 'as I take it, Universal History, the history of what man has accomplished in the world, is at bottom the History of the Great Men who have worked here.' Society is founded, and rightly founded on hero worship. And society is on the way to dismal decadence if it forgets how to worship its great men and obey their commands. 'No sadder proof can be given by a man of his own littleness than disbelief in great men.'[1]

Thomas Carlyle, dreaming of heroes.

In fact, all any country needs is a Great Man: 'Find in any country the Ablest Man that exists there; raise him to the supreme place, and loyally reverence him; you have a perfect government for that country; no ballot box, parliamentary eloquence, voting, constitution-building or other machinery whatsoever can improve it a whit. It is in the perfect state; an ideal country.'[2]

And in Cromwell the English had possessed such a man, but the little people let him down. With Cromwell's death, we witnessed 'the last glimpse of the Godlike vanishing from this England'.[3] For a brief moment in our history, it had been possible that the law of Christ's Gospel could now establish itself in the world.[4] Cromwell was the only man who had in his heart any such purpose. But the unheroic ordinary folk betrayed him.

General de Gaulle had very much the same view of himself. On the day Georges Pompidou was elected his successor as President, he told friends that France had chosen the path of mediocrity: 'The French of today have not yet become a great enough people, in their majority, to be able to sustain the affirmation of France that I have practised in their name for thirty years.'[5]

After his first visit to the battlefield of Naseby, Carlyle wrote, 'I pray daily for a new Oliver.'[6] For Carlyle, Napoleon was 'our last Great Man'. But even he 'does by no means seem to me as great a man as Cromwell . . . I find in him no such *sincerity* as in Cromwell, only a far inferior sort.'[7] After all Bonaparte's victories, 'the fatal charlatan-element got the upper hand.'[8] With Cromwell there was no such falling-off.

Carlyle admits that the envious detractors of 'Oliver', as he likes to call his hero in a rough, comradely fashion, had denounced him as a fierce, coarse, treacherous Tartuffe during his long and noble struggle for constitutional liberty.[9] But in reality, Carlyle insists, there was never a gentler, less puffed-up, more thoroughly *sincere* man. Any historian who dares to venture the contrary gets a full blast of Carlyle's incomparable abuse. Such pretended scholars are worthless Dryasdusts, pygmies incapable of appreciating the wonderful life force of Cromwell in full flow, whether he is kicking out the Rump or mowing down the Scots at Dunbar or massacring the Irish, 'barbarous wretches' – Cromwell's words, but they might just as well be Carlyle's. After the Parliamentary victory at Marston Moor, Cromwell famously wrote that 'God made them as stubble to our swords.' For Carlyle too, Cromwell was God's combine harvester.

These are amazing books, bullying, bemusing, tempestuous, yet also sometimes pawky and whimsical. They bowled their readers over by the thousand and left their brains washed, rinsed and tumble-dried. Cromwell carried into the twentieth century a reputation that had been utterly transformed. Gone was the prating, brutal humbug. In the old *Dictionary of National Biography*, Sir Charles Firth, foremost of Cromwellian scholars, now concluded that

> A study of Cromwell's letters and speeches leads irresistibly to the conclusion that he was honest and conscientious throughout . . . as a ruler he avowedly subordinated 'the civil liberty and interest of the nation' 'to the more peculiar interest of God'.[10]
>
> Save as a means to that end, he cared little for constitutional forms.

Which is a polite way of saying that he was ready to smash up anything that obstructed his angry will. Among historians, at any rate, this new image has stuck. A hundred years later, John Morrill, although rather more quizzical than Firth, at the end of his entry in the new

DNB describes Cromwell as 'a man of towering integrity. He was to himself and his God most true, if at great cost to himself and others.'

That was the first great trick that Carlyle turned. It was, I think, the one he cared most about, to convince the public of Cromwell's profound sincerity, his complete genuineness. But Carlyle also had a huge hand in refashioning Cromwell as the father of our parliamentary liberties. This is, as we have seen, an extremely dodgy claim. As Blair Worden remarks in *Roundhead Reputations*, 'a man whose troops four times used force on the House of Commons does not seem an obvious candidate for commemoration by the Mother of Parliaments.'[11] Yet when Westminster was being rebuilt after the terrible fire of 1834, almost immediately there was a public campaign, mostly in local newspapers and starting in 1845 around the time Carlyle published his extraordinary volumes, for there to be a statue to him put up in the new Palace as well as those to England's kings and queens. There was fierce resistance too, but great enthusiasm for the project among Nonconformists of all sorts. They did, after all, owe their religious liberty to him; Anglicans and Catholics had less cause to revere his memory. Carlyle admired Cromwell precisely because he did not believe in religious liberty for all. He detested 'the babble of toleration'. On the whole, Carlyle believed, as Cromwell did, that men are placed on this earth not to 'tolerate falsehoods' but to 'extinguish them'.[12] And Cromwell's intolerance was part of what Carlyle adored about his hero. On visiting Ely Cathedral, he recalled the occasion on which, 'in a voice still audible to this Editor, Cromwell commanded the Dean to "leave off your fooling and come down, Sir", when the Dean refused to stop holding his choir service'.[13]

By the time the tercentenary of Cromwell's birth loomed, the Prime Minister, Lord Rosebery, felt emboldened in June 1895 to ask the House of Commons to vote money for a Cromwell statue. His motive was not only admiration for a Great Man (he was a hero-worshipper too, Napoleon being top of his pops), but also to shore up his shaky administration with Nonconformist support. But he had forgotten about the Irish Nationalists, on whose support the government depended. There was an uproar in the House, as speaker after speaker recalled the massacres of Drogheda and Wexford. The motion had to be withdrawn in humiliating circumstances. Rosebery, who had himself conceded, in a masterpiece of understatement, that Cromwell was 'not a great Parliamentarian in the strict sense', paid anonymously for the statue out of his own pocket (or rather that of his Rothschild wife's). Even so, the uproar continued; petitions against the statue attracted thousands of signatures across the land. For fear of public disturbance, when Thornycroft's statue was finally unveiled after two postponements, it was at 7.30 a.m. on 14 November before a tiny huddle of spectators. There was what was described as a 'National Meeting' that evening in the Queen's Hall, addressed at length by Rosebery, who referred coyly to the anonymous donor who had paid for the statue, and quoted the most recent influential restorer of Cromwell's reputation, the historian S. R. Gardiner: 'It is time for us to regard him as he really was, with all his physical and moral audacity, with all his tenderness and spiritual yearnings – in the world of action what Shakespeare was in the world of thought; the greatest because the most typical Englishman of all time.'[14] Rosebery concluded by declaring: 'I will go so far as to say that, great and powerful and opulent as we are, we could find employment for a few Cromwells now.'

Rosebery cared nothing for the Roundheads; what he admired was a Great Man who got things done. He was a fan of the National Efficiency Movement, dreamed up largely by Sidney Webb, which included in its programme a healthy dose of eugenics to get rid of the superfluous and unfit who were holding up Progress. Rosebery disliked conventional politics, and once advocated a Cabinet made up entirely of businessmen, 'in which no member of an existing or former Government should be included'. What Britain needed, he said at the time of the tercentenary, was 'a dictator, a tyrant, a man of large mind or iron will who would see what had to be done and do it'.[15]

This is Carlyle's less understood achievement: to have promoted England's Caesar as indispensable to progress. For Carlyle, it's not simply that Cromwell was a wonderful man, whose courage, passion and tenacity brought parliamentary government and religious liberty several crucial stages forward. The truth, as Carlyle tells it, is that only a Great Man could have engineered this progress. Our English Caesar was the necessary man. Mere popular movements and parliamentary prating could never have done it.

Now if you look at the facts, this seems a rather farcical claim. The Restoration was, as Blair Worden points out, a restoration of Parliament before it was a restoration of the monarchy. Getting rid of the Protectorate was the essential step forward. It is certainly possible to sympathize with the view of historians such as Woolrych and Barry Coward that the Protectorate really didn't do too badly:[16] 'Taken as a body, the Cromwellian ordinances give little support to the stereotype of puritan repression, and convey an impression of sensible, unbiased effort to apply practical correctives to perceived ills . . . During Cromwell's rule as Protector, especially after 1655, things had been getting broadly better.' The postal service was improved, the tax system reformed a little, London's hackney carriages were regulated, if only to stop their feuding with the watermen. Energetic efforts were made to protect Britain's fishing waters against the Dutch. After nine years of civil war, stability at last.

The trouble is that you could say some rather similar things about the 1630s, what was once called 'the Eleven Years' Tyranny'. Charles I showed an almost Thatcher-like diligence in inventing a postal service, introducing building regulations and measures against smoke pollution, improving the system of poor relief and, yes, defending British fishermen against the encroaching Dutch. The regime was particularly active in protecting consumers against fraudulent monopolies and patents, one highlight being the public testing of new and old brands of soap by two laundresses. What might have been the highlight of Charles's modernization was the anti-plague programme proposed by Sir Theodore de Mayerne in March 1631: a perpetual Office of Health with an ongoing income stream, big new plague hospitals to be called Charles Godshouses, fierce quarantine restrictions, including the closure of all taverns and theatres, a ban on outdoor sports, plus fumigation of everything. All of which sounds familiar. In 1631, alas, nothing happened, because there was no Parliament to raise the money to pay for it. Otherwise Britain might have had its NHS nearly 400 years ago.[17]

In his gorgeously contrarian *The Personal Rule of Charles I*, Kevin Sharpe argued that Clarendon had a point in claiming of the 1630s that 'the like peace and universal tranquillity for ten years was never enjoyed by any nation.'[18] Young men preferred to spend their time in the alehouse or dancing round the maypole rather than training for the militia. Charles found it uphill work to raise any sort of army for his lunatic war against the Scots, let alone find the money to pay for it. And when the First Civil War broke out − that 'war without an enemy'− how reluctant most men were to join it. In many counties, the active neutrals who wanted to keep the conflict out of their patch far outnumbered the locally stationed troops. In Wiltshire, for example, the so-called 'Clubmen', because cudgels were all most of them had to fight with, claimed 20,000 followers.[19]

What a transformation, though, when we turn to the Protectorate. In the 1630s, the country had been the only major nation without a standing army. Now England had 50,000–70,000 men under arms, depending on whether she was fighting the Scots and the Irish at the same time. Not all of them up to the standards of Cromwell's Ironsides, perhaps, but trained and armed, and for the first time wearing uniforms. A country that had enjoyed deliciously low taxes in the absence of Parliament, and whose navy had staggered by on the increasingly contested ship money, now had steepling taxes and a navy to excite dreams of global domination.

As for religious liberty, Nonconformists, like Roman Catholics, found themselves just as much out in the cold at the Restoration as they had been under the Stuart tyranny. Both had to wait for the slow Parliamentary advances of the eighteenth and nineteenth centuries, centuries mocked by Carlyle, to have their rights to worship and eventually to vote enshrined in law. Cromwell was selectively friendly to the liberties of those sects which more or less echoed his own views, but he left little permanent mark on the religious life of England. The modest achievements of the Protectorate no more justify his military dictatorship than Charles I's achievements justify his brutish suspension of Parliament. Cromwell's most memorable experiment in governance, the rule of the Major-Generals in 1655, was a hideous flop.

But all this is really beside the point. What matters is that Carlyle and Rosebery and Gardiner between them had turned the trick. Despite the mutterings of diehard Royalists, Cromwell had been successfully cemented into the English pantheon. His military dictatorship had become an integral – and valued – part of our island story. We too had had our Caesar. And we shall see in the after-history of other Caesars – Napoleon is the ripest example – time and propaganda sandpaper the rough edges, and the brutal and ruthless methods by which they seized power explained away as unavoidable necessities. But it is the seizing of power that inflicts such serious damage on the constitutional arrangements, damage which may take years to repair.

Augustus and Auguste — and Adolf

Thomas Carlyle was not the only hero-worshipper on the loose in the 1840s. Nor were Cromwell and Napoleon the only available heroes to be worshipped. The 'Hungry Forties' were beset by crop failures, industrial unrest and political agitation, which in 1848 broke out into full-scale revolution across Europe. The ferocity with which these revolutions were suppressed only made the respectable classes yearn for a Strong Man who would restore and maintain order. By contrast, parliamentary reform seemed pettifogging and painfully slow and ineffective.

Carlyle himself admired, and in 1843 published a short book in praise of, the dictator of Paraguay, Dr José Francia (1766–1840). For 26 years, Francia, the forerunner of many such Strong Men who were to rule the freshly independent South American republics, was the Supreme and Perpetual Dictator of his little country. He humiliated the Church, outlawed all opposition and established a secret police, with an underground prison known as 'the Chamber of Truth'. He had his opponents hanged or bayoneted outside his study window and their corpses left to rot there, so he could be sure they were dead. Carlyle says approvingly that Dr Francia's so-called 'reign of terror' was merely 'a reign of rigour'.[1] Another admirer of Francia's, François-Auguste Romieu (1800–55), reports that the Paraguayan dictator kept in his cupboard the ropes for the malefactors who were to be garrotted or hanged, which he had himself cut to the proper length. An even more notorious South American dictator of the period, General Juan Manuel de Rosas of Argentina, carefully laid out on his daughter's piano the severed ears of those whom he had tortured. Rosas's reputation has undergone a Cromwell-type spring-clean at the hands of recent rulers of Argentina, such as the Kirchners. Romieu praises both Francia and Rosas for the promptness of their actions: 'They didn't follow this bizarre custom of our liberal Europe, which insists that force must be patient when confronted with outrage, so as to be overwhelmed at the moment of revolution; what they said got done; the action followed the word, and this is the reason for their success.'[2]

Romieu was almost as weird and multifaceted a character as Carlyle. He spent his early career as Prefect of the Dordogne, then of the Haute-Marne and of Indre-et-Loire. In these posts, he was a dedicated conserver of local antiquities, restoring almost single-handedly the beautiful abbey of Cadouin in the Dordogne. He was also a noted joker and wit. His friend Alexandre Dumas records in his memoirs several of his choicest gags. Romieu was a noted gastronome too, co-editing with Balzac's dodgy friend Horace-Napoléon Raisson *Le Code Gourmand*. And he wrote a popular novel about a Breton cabin boy. All this might suggest a jovial, free-and-easy type. But his travels round *La France profonde* had given him an intense loathing of his own times. In politics, he was the sternest of authoritarians and reactionaries.

When the 1848 revolution broke out in France, Romieu attached himself like a limpet to Napoleon's nephew, Louis-Napoleon, who had already attempted two *coups d'état* against the monarchy. After his hero had been elected President by an overwhelming margin, Romieu collaborated with Dumas on a new weekly, *Le Napoléon*, and then published in 1850 an extraordinary little book, *L'Ère des Césars*, which delivers exactly what the title promises.

The nation has gone to the dogs, Romieu tells us: 'The barbarians within have swamped us, and the moral order has been destroyed by the abuses of liberalism.'[3] The idea of progress is an absurdity, parliamentary elections are farces, majority voting is a fraud; there is no other answer but force. 'I know no worse tyranny than that of the vote, because . . . it deceitfully allows those whom it oppresses an apparent right to contradict and to reverse it.'[4]

> After three centuries, what is the result? The installing of senseless chatter [*bavardage*] at the head of state business; the great affairs of peoples delivered over to undignified debates, where the temporary absence of one man out of three or four hundred is enough to set the world aflame, as a consequence of the votes which are

passed; the passions of fifteen minutes instead of long considered plans… constant uncertainty in the progress of the nation, which is endlessly submitted to the hazards of a poll.[5]

Romieu looks back instead with reverence and longing to the great Napoleon:

When the strong hand of the modern Caesar came to put France right and to set in motion the eternal machinery of any human society — faith, justice, authority — it seemed that the world was going to forget the dreams of the *Encyclopédistes* and move on to different modes of the human spirit. There, if only for a moment, was Glory: with an eagle and a flag, the conqueror swept through the capitals of Europe, leaving behind, radiant and proud, the wounded and dying men who were falling in the names of these emblems. What a fine and noble thing it all was![6]

There succeeded the dismal, plodding age of parliamentary elections and juries, and the tyranny of the majority vote. But the old imperial longing still slumbered in the souls of the masses. It had survived all the experiments in the rule of law, all the ingenious constitutional formulas, still keeping green the memories of the Emperor's farewell at Fontainebleau and the long agony of St Helena.[7] It was impossible to deny that the real French people, not the sort you met in salons, still cherished this deep allegiance. How else could you explain Louis-Napoleon's landslide victory in the presidential election of 10 December 1848? 'When France had to choose a leader, the magic name of Napoleon resounded like an immense clamour, and the proscribed man who bore it was elevated to the throne.'[8] 'For there comes a moment in the history of peoples, when the inevitable outcome is "CESARISME"'[9] — Romieu's caps, and he is fully entitled to them, since Dauzat's *Dictionnaire Etymologique* tells us that this is the very first use of the word in French. *Césarisme* comes because it has to come. And it is futile, then or now, to weep over the loss of the old Republic.[10] For 'European society finds itself placed in conditions almost like those which characterize the epoch in which the Caesars appeared.'[11] And according to Romieu, Louis-Napoleon was the right man to spearhead this new Era of the Caesars, for he was not a bumptious mountebank, as his enemies claimed, but rather of 'a calm and meditative temperament, which had been formed by study and misfortune. He did not throw himself after the illusions of the masses. His courage had shown itself in the ordeals he had endured; his prudence had made itself manifest in these last days.'[12]

Still, Louis-Napoleon had a lot to live down. He appeared to have an unshakable confidence in his own destiny: 'I believe that from time to time, men are created whom I call volunteers of providence, in whose hands are placed the destiny of their countries. I believe I am one of those men.'[13] But his previous attempts to seize power had been discouraging, to put it mildly. The first coup against King Louis-Philippe, on 29 October 1836, when he was only 28, involved suborning a colonel in Strasbourg. Louis then arrived in uniform and, with the support of the colonel's regiment, seized the Prefecture, planning to march on Paris in imitation of his uncle's Hundred Days. Unfortunately, the general in charge of the local garrison rallied a loyal regiment. The mutineers surrendered and Louis fled back to Switzerland, and eventually to a fashionable exile in London. His second failed coup was an even greater fiasco. From his London exile in the summer of 1840, he bought weapons and uniforms and got together a scratch force of 50 exiled veterans, hired a small steamer, the *Edinburgh Castle*, and, after a queasy crossing, came ashore at Boulogne, where he was immediately stopped by customs officers, and after a skirmish with the local garrison arrested, put on trial and jailed for life. Six years later, he escaped from prison disguised as a workman carrying timber and managed to make his way back to England, where he resumed his place in high society.

How could this arrogant poseur hope to make it third time lucky? Yet only two years after his escape, the 1848 Revolution broke out across Europe and, in the turmoil that followed its brutal suppression in France by General Cavaignac, several members of the Bonaparte family were elected to the Assembly, and in the first ever presidential election in France in December that year, Louis-Napoleon won by a street, securing 74 per cent of the vote. Against all the odds, the hopeless loser of Boulogne beach had sailed into port.

His success may have taken bourgeois intellectuals by surprise, but it is not such a mystery. He owed his victory partly to the magic of the Bonaparte name – reverence for the Emperor's memory had been growing all through the Hungry Forties – and partly to the hope he offered to the people who had been left behind by the new capitalism of François Guizot, whose slogan '*Enrichessez-vous*' was the most blatant appeal to greed until Peter Mandelson's encouragement to the 'filthy rich'. Louis's pamphlet, 'L'extinction du paupérisme', made a huge impression when it came out in 1844. In this appeal, he follows the pattern of popular Caesarism, discernible from Julius Caesar to Donald Trump. The Caesar bypasses the elites, appealing directly to the worst off.

Romieu chooses to compare the present plight of France with that of strife-torn Rome before the Emperor Augustus restored stability and prosperity. 'If calm, grandeur, repose are the conditions for human happiness, no era in the world has offered, in this sense, a more complete spectacle than the time of Augustus.'[14] Besides, he was such an admirable man: 'This Augustus, Master of the Empire, lived in a little house, and his wife sewed her own gowns. He went about Rome on foot, by himself, hailing the passers-by, wearing an old grey felt cap, according to what Suetonius tells us.' And the golden age continued after his death. Romieu quotes Chateaubriand: 'Eighty years of happiness, interrupted only by the reign of Domitian, began with the elevation of Vespasian. We think of this period as that where the human race has been happiest.'[15] This a thought borrowed from Gibbon: 'If a man were called to fix the period in the history of the world during which the condition of the human race was most happy and prosperous, he would, without hesitation, name that which elapsed from the death of Domitian to the accession of Commodus.'[16] Though of course Gibbon's mission was to discover exactly why this splendid state of affairs came to an end — not least through the destruction of those free representative institutions which Romieu is so keen to see the back of.

Romieu is just as enthusiastic about the Praetorian Guard which kept Augustus and his successors in power:

> they were paid double the other troops, and had a camp entrenched on the Quirinal and Viminal Hills. Placed as a perpetual threat both against the people and against the Senate, the Guard secured both the tranquillity of the streets and of the Senate's deliberations. Caesar could sit happily in the Temple of Fortune, allowing to all appearances a very free discussion around him, and see himself contradicted on small things, without fear of opposition on the big ones.[17]

Now, all this might seem like a rather rosy picture of life under the Roman Empire, but there is one big thing that Romieu gets absolutely right. He tells us[18] that he is writing in July 1850 and that he is

sure that there's a storm brewing. 'Let's be ready for the eruption of
1852.'[19] At the end of Louis-Napoleon's four-year term, under the new
Constitution he will not be eligible for re-election. As a result, Romieu
declares that in 'this fatal year 1852' the fear of anarchy will return,
'and there may be one of those struggles that the world hasn't seen
since the Huns'.[20] And he is confident of the outcome. 'You will see the
proletarian mass arise, disdainful of the enacted laws, regarding them
as wretched pieces of paper. They will march to the poll, whatever
prefects and policemen may say, and place their forbidden votes,
which they will hold to be valid despite any regulation; and the next
day they will say to France: this is the voice of the people: obey!'[21]

In other words, the People will insist on having Louis-Napoleon as
their ruler, whatever the law says. Call it a *coup d'état* if you don't like it,
but it's going to happen. And it does.

The coup was a swift and nasty business, as these things have to be
if they are to succeed. No doubt Louis had learned much from his two
earlier botched efforts. But this time he had the priceless advantage
as President of already controlling the machinery of government and
the army. On the night of 1 December 1851, 30,000 troops moved
on to the streets of Paris, occupied the key buildings and dissolved
the national assembly. The coup was christened 'Operation Rubicon',
leaving no doubt about Louis's intentions. It was as dramatic and brutal
a suppression as anything done by his uncle, with the exception that
Louis was not present in person. We have a first-hand account from
the great Alexis de Tocqueville, who described the affair in a letter
to the London *Times* a few days later (11 December 1851). He was
one of the deputies who turned up at the Assembly on the morning
of 2 December, having heard that several of their colleagues had
already been arrested. They found the doors of the Palais Bourbon
locked and guarded by the Chasseurs de Vincennes, a rough regiment
recently returned from service in Algeria. The soldiers barred the
way and beat up several of them at the point of the bayonet. The
deputies then retired from the Palais Bourbon to the local *mairie*,
where they were again surrounded by troops. Undeterred, almost
300 of them, accompanied by their shorthand writer, who kept a
full record, now passed a decree declaring Louis-Napoleon's actions
illegal and depriving him of all authority. They opened the windows
of the *mairie* and read the decrees out to the people below, especially
the one declaring the deposition and impeachment of the President.
The soldiers then barged in and collared the deputies, and led them

two by two through the mud of Paris like a bunch of criminals, and banged them up in the Quai d'Orsay barracks for a couple of days. According to Tocqueville, this bunch of ex-ambassadors, dukes, merchants, writers and orators had a whale of a time there, shouting jokes and anecdotes to each other as they lay on the floor or on the soldiers' palliasses, though it was wet and cold and Tocqueville asked to be sent his greatcoat and galoshes.[22]

French troops on the streets of Paris during the 1851 coup.

Four weeks later Tocqueville, still smarting from his incarceration, told his friend the economist Nassau Senior, 'This is a new phase in our history. Every previous revolution has been made by a political party. This is the first time that the Army has seized France, bound and gagged her and laid her at the feet of its ruler.' Senior objected that it all sounded rather like the coups of Napoleon Bonaparte. No, said Tocqueville, the Directory did at least represent the people of France, whereas Louis-Napoleon didn't. We may be inclined to side with Senior. At all events, it was a brutal suppression of a properly elected Assembly.[23]

The High Court of Justice stood firm against the coup too. Tocqueville reports that, on hearing of the dissolution, the five judges swiftly gathered together and declared their intention to investigate the actions of the President under Article 68 of the Constitution. They fixed proceedings for the following day,

December 3, but their meeting was broken up by the police and the *chasseurs*, and so Louis had successfully silenced the courts as well as the parliament.

The eviction of the judges from the French High Court of Justice,
3 December 1851.

Out in the country, riots broke out in more than 30 cities, but the resistance was quickly crushed, and 300–400 opponents killed. Over the next few weeks, 26,000 people were arrested, thousands later being transported to the colonies for years. On 20 December, Louis held a plebiscite which approved the coup by a margin of ten to one. A further plebiscite the following December approved by an improbably large majority his wish to become Emperor, and he went on to rule as Napoleon III for another 18 years, 22 in all, a longer run than his sainted uncle's and undone only by foolish foreign adventures, just as Napoleon I's was, and forcing him into exile (in Chislehurst, Kent) where he died, again like his uncle. It was an absolutist regime which, especially in its early years, suppressed opposition, hounded opponents, and maintained a secret police. But it was also a modernizing regime, which drove through the *grands boulevards* of Paris, built the largest opera house in the world and a nationwide network of railways, as well as improving agriculture, introducing secondary education for girls and allowing a form of trade unions. As a reward for his loyal support, the Emperor immediately, in 1852, appointed Auguste Romieu as Director of the Beaux-Arts and then Inspector-General of the Libraries of the Crown. Alas, poor Auguste did not have long to applaud the achievements of the regime or enjoy the sweets of these great offices, dying in 1855. But he had made his point. Caesarism was alive and seemed to be doing rather well.

By contrast, Parliaments were in disrepute across much of Continental Europe. To their critics, they often seemed impotent talking shops, notorious for their *bavardage* and their disorder. In Vienna, any dignity of parliament had collapsed in the face of the vituperative rhetoric of the nationalist fanatics, producing frequent chaos. A bill in 1909, aiming to put the Czech language on an equal footing with German in Bohemia, had to be abandoned when a cacophony of rattles, bells, children's trumpets and banging desk lids rendered debate impossible, leading to fisticuffs and rival groups singing their own national anthems.[24]

Was parliamentarianism perhaps only a transitional stage to something different, something more stable, loftier, more in accord with man's destiny? Oswald Spengler argued as much in the second volume of his worldwide bestseller, *The Decline of the West* (1922). The old conventions were fast decaying: 'the *essence of parliamentarianism has already been evaporated* [Spengler's italics] . . . there is no way back to the old parliamentarianism from the domination of Lloyd George and the Napoleonism of the French militarists.'[25] 'With this enters the age of gigantic conflicts, in which we find ourselves today. It is the transition from Napoleonism to Caesarism, a general phase of evolution, which occupies at least two centuries and can be shown to exist in all cultures.'[26]

More unnervingly, Spengler tells us: 'Now dawns the time when the form-filled powers of the blood, which the rationalism of the Megalopolis has suppressed, reawaken in the depths . . . Caesarism *grows* on the soil of democracy, but its roots thread deeply into the underground of blood tradition.'[27] The coming of Caesarism is a historical necessity. It's in our blood.

One man who would have relished Spengler's words if he had read them (he was not one for reading long and demanding books, certainly not all the way through) was Adolf Hitler. While Spengler was being acclaimed for his cloudy prophecies in Munich, 40 miles away banged up in Landsberg Prison for his part in the Beer Hall Putsch of November 1923, Hitler was beginning to dictate the first volume of his life and times, first to his chauffeur-factotum, Emil Maurice, then to his secretary, the ever faithful Rudolf Hess. Spengler had his own shot in helping a Caesar to power, in the shape of General Hans von Seeckt, who was also courted by Hitler, but whose coup efforts in 1924 came to nothing. Later, Spengler met Hitler himself, but thought little of him, describing him as a dreamer and a numbskull; 'What Germany needs is a real hero, not a heroic tenor.' Spengler's last book, *The Hour of Decision* (1934), criticized the Nazis for their racism and warned of a coming world war. The Nazis banned it. Spengler typifies the sort of intellectual who approves of Caesarism in theory, but recoils from it in practice.

But in *Mein Kampf*, Hitler emphatically endorses Spengler's low view of Parliamentarianism, in his case provoked by the spectacle of the Vienna Reichsrat:

> How soon was I to grow indignant when I saw the lamentable comedy that unfolded beneath my eyes . . . The intellectual content of what these men said was on a really depressing level, in so far as you could understand their babbling at all; for several of the gentlemen did not speak German, but their native Slavic languages or rather dialects . . . A wild, gesticulating mass screaming all at once in every different key, presided over by a good-natured old uncle who was striving in the sweat of his brow to revive the dignity of the House by violently ringing his bell and alternating gentle reproofs with grave admonition.[28]

Hitler went back a few weeks later, and the place was three-quarters empty, with the few MPs present yawning or asleep. 'A year of this tranquil observation' (hard to believe that Hitler had the patience to sit through the Reichsrat debates for anything like this long, but then many facts in *Mein Kampf* are alternative facts), and he no longer thought that the misfortune of the Austrian Parliament was that there was no German majority in it: 'its ruination lay in the whole nature and essence of the institution as such.'[29] 'By rejecting the authority of the individual and replacing it by the numbers of some momentary mob, the parliamentary principle of majority rule sins against the basic aristocratic principle of Nature.'[30] 'There is no principle which, objectively considered, is as false as that of Parliamentarianism.'[31]

Adolf and Auguste, and Oswald too, are as one. It was not Caesars that were antiquated and outmoded, but parliaments.

4

The Comforting Illusion

This of course was not how most intellectuals in the salons of Paris saw the course of events. When they first used the word 'Caesarism', it was to mock the pretensions of Napoleon's nephew. They had derided his first two botched coups, and were horrified by this betrayal of the Republic of which he had been elected the President. This third time lucky provoked two classic instant polemics, Victor Hugo's *Napoléon le Petit* and Karl Marx's *The Eighteenth Brumaire of Louis Bonaparte*, both published in 1852. Marx begins his book with the famous wisecrack that, when Hegel remarked that all great world-historical facts and personages appear on the stage twice, 'he forgot to add: the first time as tragedy, the second time as farce.' Victor Hugo was so disgusted that he left France to live in the Channel Islands. He cannot have imagined that his exile was to last twenty years.

The pretensions of Napoleon III seemed absurd. Yet by the time Marx came to write the introduction to his book's second edition in 1869, he was clearly anxious that the idea of Caesarism might be catching on: 'I hope that my work will contribute towards eliminating the school-taught phrase now current, particularly in Germany, of so-called Caesarism [*Cäsarismus*]', which he saw as a thoroughly superficial analogy. The material conditions of the class struggle in the ancient world were so different that 'the political figures produced by them can likewise have no more in common with one another than the Archbishop of Canterbury with the High Priest Samuel.'

History, according to Marx, was an affair of masses and classes. So-called great men were merely the puppets of the process, not its masters. They might provide a spectacle for a time, but they were the surfers, not the tide. Such, broadly, speaking, was the underlying assumption among many historians, even those who did not begin to think of themselves as Marxists. The pygmies who set themselves up as little Caesars in the modern era were throwbacks, ultimately as futile as they were ridiculous.

This certitude that Caesarism was a hopeless retro enterprise rested on the widespread belief that the March of History was not to be interrupted. This belief was not described as what we now call 'historicist' until Karl Popper popularized the term in the 1940s, in his masterworks *The Poverty of Historicism* (first published in 1957, but delivered as a paper several times before the war) and *The Open Society* (1945): 'I mean by "historicism" an approach to the social sciences which assumes that *historical prediction* is their principal aim, and which assumes that this aim is attainable by discovering the "rhythms" or the "patterns", the "laws" or the "trends" that underlie the evolution of history.'[1] According to this assumption, there are certain laws of historical development which dictate the transition from one period to the next, and they are as inflexible as the laws of physics. Popper is the first to describe this mindset, and with icy contempt, and, as a result of his stinging attack, historicism has never quite recovered its self-confidence.

But the thing itself had been popular with intellectuals well before the French Revolution. The Marquis de Condorcet, in his *Sketch of a Historical Tableau of the Progress of the Human Spirit*, sets out a series of stages through which human society has passed and will continue to pass towards a state of universal happiness. For 'Man's moral goodness is as infinitely perfectible as his other faculties and nature links, in an indissoluble chain, truth, happiness and virtue.' We have merely to master the rules of nature; 'then will the march of every science be as infallible as that of mathematics and the propositions acquire, as far as nature will admit, geometrical demonstrations and certainty.' In the next century, John Stuart Mill, slightly less cocksure, talks of finding 'laws of succession' which are sufficiently uniform to be compared with a mathematical sequence, and expresses his belief that 'the general *tendency* is, and will continue to be, saving occasional and temporary exceptions, one of improvement – *a tendency towards a happier and better state.*' He calls this 'a theorem of the science'.[2] Far more brutally, Marx too claims scientific status for his theory of history. The class conflict and violent revolution which are eventually to lead to socialism in his schema constitute, he asserts, a strictly scientific process. In the Soviet Union, socialism was often to be described as 'scientific socialism'. But even Marx's historicism pales beside that of the philosopher from whom he originally learnt it. The ripest and most bizarre outbreak of historicism took place in Eastern Europe, and of all places in Prussia. In 1818, King Frederick William III summoned Georg Wilhelm Friedrich Hegel to Berlin to be his court philosopher, after he had purged his government of the reforming liberals. What Hegel became was the number one apologist for the Prussian monarchy as the acme of earthly perfection. He was the most high-flown spin doctor in history. And nobody before or since has deployed history to such extravagant ends.

Hegel begins by making the vast claim that 'The German spirit is the Spirit of the New World. Its aim is the realization of absolute Truth as the unlimited self-determination of Freedom.' And nowhere was that German spirit more gloriously fulfilled than in the absolute monarchy of Prussia, which could not conceivably be improved, certainly not by one of those deplorable new liberal constitutions which were all the rage in Europe.

This was a breathtaking claim. Germany, after all, did not exist as a single nation but only as a scattering of German-speaking societies – some of them gathered into princely states, both large and small, but others mingled with other nationalities in regions which did not begin to think of themselves as part of an embryonic Germany, even a Germany of the mind. And if the German spirit was to be concentrated anywhere, it was especially impudent to claim Prussia as its heartland. Only a few years earlier, at the Congress of Vienna, Prussia was still registered as 'a Slav Kingdom'. Certainly the population was predominantly of Slavic origin. Only a year before his death in 1831, Hegel himself spoke of Brandenburg and Mecklenburg as being peopled by 'Germanised Slavs'. For Slavs were, after all, the original inhabitants of these bleak sandy Eastern forests, only in the later Middle Ages to be interspersed with German immigrants in the so-called *Ostsiedlung*.

The claim that Prussia represented true Germanness was based on one thing only: Prussia's recent victory over Napoleon. For Hegel, success in battle was the ultimate decisive test of a true nation. Might was always right, 'for the History of the World is the World's court of justice'. War also preserved a nation's ethical health. In fact, 'war protects the people from the corruption which an everlasting peace would bring upon it.' In peace, people come to stagnate. 'Let insecurity finally come in the form of Hussars with glistening sabres, and show its serious activity!' The Prussian historian Heinrich von Treitschke, a huge influence on the formation of the Nazi mindset, put it even more strongly: 'The concept of the State implies the concept of war, for the essence of the State is Power. The State is the People organized in Sovereign Power.'

Quite a few power worshippers have made a similar linkage. Napoleon, Churchill, de Gaulle and Enoch Powell all explicitly believed that war was a healthy and necessary ingredient in the life and progress of any self-respecting nation state, and that it was in any case an inevitable and regular occurrence between nations.

In his scorching dissection of Hegel in *The Open Society*, Karl Popper lists what he regards as the six leading ideas that Hegel bequeathed to his numerous followers, both outside and, more fatally, inside the German-speaking world. I won't try to improve on his crisp encapsulation:

a) Nationalism, in the form of the historicist idea that the state is the incarnation of the spirit (or now, of the Blood) of the state-creating nation (or race); one chosen nation (now, the chosen race) is destined for world domination.

b) The state as the natural enemy of all other states must assert its existence in war.

c) The state is exempt from any kind of moral obligation; history, that is, historical success, is the sole judge; collective utility is the sole principle of personal conduct; propagandist lying and distortion of the truth is permissible.

d) The 'ethical' idea of war (total and collectivist), particularly of young nations against older ones; war, fate and fame as most desirable goods.

e) The creative role of the Great Man, the world-historical personality, the man of deep knowledge and great passion (now, the principle of leadership).

f) The ideal of the heroic life ('live dangerously') and of the 'heroic man' as opposed to the petty bourgeois and his life of shallow mediocrity.[3]

Now, Hegel did not invent these ideas. You can find quite a few of them in Machiavelli's *The Prince*, especially the idea of success through war as the only measure of the nation and, for the individual, the ideal of virtù, a non-Christian manliness which despises humility, modesty and remorse. But Hegel dressed them up in the cloudy wrappings of German Idealism and presented them as the essential vade-mecum for the modern age.

The intoxicating influence that Hegel exerted may seem mysterious to us today, but it was intense and enduring, most obviously on those who actually studied under him in Berlin, famously the young Karl Marx. In later life, Marx tried to shrug off the influence. He claimed that Hegel had crucially got things the wrong way round: whereas Hegel had declared that thought (*Geist*) determined the material world, Marx preached that material circumstances determined our mindsets. Hegel's cloudy dialectic 'must be turned right side up again, if you would discover the rational kernel within the mystical shell'.

Yet Marx continued to follow the main thrust of the Hegelian style and to mimic the colour of his rhetoric. History with a capital H was a global totality; it unfolded according to a single inevitable pattern; and it was driving on towards the full realization of human freedom. That drive could be sustained and brought to fruition only through intense and sustained struggle. Violence was the motor and midwife of human destiny. For Hegel, the war was between nations, for Marx, between classes. But for both, the conflict was necessary and glorious, the only true way forward.

It is a comforting illusion, this idea that history has a predestined and unalterable pattern and momentum and is leading to an end of which you profoundly approve.

To be 'on the right side of History' is a pleasant position to be in. How nice to know that we are going to a Better Place and without the inconvenience of having to die first. But as an overarching theory it remains at best unproven and at worst an illusion, certainly in the forms proposed by Hegel and Marx. That is what the experiences of the twentieth century tell us with a dreadful emphasis. The Prussian Empire disappeared in 1918, chased off the stage of world history, after having launched the most terrible war imaginable. Communism, or the hard Marxist–Leninist version of it, imploded in 1989, having brought misery and death to countless millions over the preceding 70 years.

Yet historicism offers such an alluring take on the world that, seemingly undaunted, the idea then immediately resurfaced, though in a far milder form. Francis Fukuyama, a 36-year-old scholar working at the US State Department and formerly a think-tanker with the Rand Corporation, wrote a paper with the mind-blowing title 'The End of History' for the summer 1989 edition of *The National Interest*, coming out only a couple of months before the Berlin Wall came down. With what appeared at the time like startling prescience, Fukuyama predicted that

> What we may be witnessing is not just the end of the Cold War, or the passing of a particular period of postwar history, but the end of history as such: that is, the end point of mankind's ideological evolution and the universalization of Western liberal democracy as the final form of human government.

Following Alexandre Kojève, the brilliant postwar exponent of Hegel, Fukuyama declared that the cloudy Prussian sage had been essentially right after all. Napoleon's defeat of the old Prussian monarchy at the Battle of Jena had assured the ultimate victory of the ideals of the French Revolution, liberty and equality. All that had happened since was that those ideals had spilled out all over the world as the result of two world wars and the attendant revolutions. Hegel, of course, was wrong to see the Prussian monarchy of his day as embodying those ideals, but he was right in seeing that the ideals had come to stay. Liberal democracy was to be the end point.

It's important, I think, to realize just how soaked in Hegelian ideas Fukuyama was then. It's not just that he points out how many of the strong and prosperous nation states today were liberal democracies. After all, quite a few major countries like Russia and China most definitely were not liberal democracies in 1989, and, he admits, unlikely to become so 'in the foreseeable future'. But at the forefront of his mind is the idea that history has an ineluctable pattern, and liberal democracy is where it finishes, although he hedges his bets by adding 'in the long run'.

Fukuyama's essay was an immediate worldwide hit, and he expanded it into a book, *The End of History and the Last Man*, which came out three years later. By then the Cold War was well and truly over, and Fukuyama's unabashed triumphalism was instantly appealing. He was only saying what a lot of people secretly thought but didn't quite dare to say out loud.

I am not sure, though, how many of his readers fully took in the strange conclusion to the essay. Fukuyama tells us that 'the end of history will be a very sad time.' He himself already feels 'a powerful nostalgia for the time when history existed'. He mourns 'the passing of the worldwide ideological struggle that called forth daring, courage, imagination and idealism'. Which of course was pretty much what Hegel felt too: conflict was the breath of life, to be fully human you had to take your sword out of its sheath. Even more bizarrely, Fukuyama forecasts that 'such nostalgia, in fact, will continue to fuel competition even in the post-historical world for some time to come.' So, we shall go on fighting the Cold War, though it's over.

Well, he was right there. We had in store the delights of Iraq (twice), Afghanistan, Syria, the Congo, Yemen, Bosnia and ultimately Ukraine. Great powers seemed to go on behaving very much as they always had, despite Fukuyama's assertion that 'the nineteenth-century model of great power behaviour has become a serious anachronism.' When we open our newspapers, the headlines seem to be recording History rather as we have always known it.

More disquieting, too, there has arisen in recent years a sort of nostalgia for the certainties of earlier nationalist regimes. This is nothing new. Throughout history, from the Roman Empire on, you can see posterity begin a weird softening-up process. The old Caesar may have died unloved and his body been defiled and butchered but, a few decades later, growing numbers of people begin to muse that the whole experience of his rule was not as bad as it was painted. From Julius Caesar, through Cromwell and Napoleon to Mussolini, historians and the popular memory collude to play up the positive side. His body is reburied in some national Valhalla. By 1840, Napoleon's body is back in France, in the Invalides waiting for his huge red mausoleum to be built. *Le Retour des Cendres* (in fact, his body not his ashes) is one of the most iconic moments in French history, attended by nearly a million people. The obsession with the Emperor's memory through the 1830s and 1840s and the campaign to bring his body back from St Helena softened the public up for the return of his nephew Louis-Napoleon and the eventual successful coup which ushered in the Third Empire.

The return of Napoleon's body – the *Dorade* docks in Paris,
14 December 1840.

Gradually the memory of the lost Caesar takes concrete shape. A forest of statues go up to him across the land. Think of the roads he built, the postal service, the railways, the swamps he drained, the countries he conquered. And the streets were so quiet then, and so tidy, there was no crime, you could leave your door on the latch, and above all there was so little wearisome argument about things, and the nation was respected then, both at home and overseas, even glorified. Caesars become popular above all by raising national morale rather than by improving living standards (most wages actually fell in Nazi Germany between 1933 and 1939). Isn't it possible, too, that the bad side has been exaggerated? The censorship, the detentions without trial, the deportations – well, they were not very nice, but they were probably regrettable necessities in the context of the times. And were the Gauls, or the Irish, or the Blacks, or the Jews, or the Mexicans or the Muslims really as badly treated as it said in the newspapers? Are those ghastly statistics reliable, could some of the harrowing photos have been faked? These softening-up manoeuvres may be a preliminary for a sort of 'tribute act', which trades on the better memories of the old days, while claiming that the new version is entirely cleaned up and remodelled. The neo-fascist movements in Italy and France today are prime examples of such tactics. They may be made more palatable by having women as their leaders – Marine Le Pen and Giorgia Meloni – suggesting that the new model may be less brutish than the old. The afterlife of Caesars is a seductive subject, and one fraught with peril for nations which are seduced by it.

The Restoration seldom enjoys the legitimacy it claims, however. The old constitutional structures have been so battered by the Caesar experience; they no longer enjoy the sanctity of unbroken tradition, however painstaking the efforts to put them back just as they were. The evil that men do lives after them; the good is oft interred with their bones. Even if this is not quite what Mark Antony meant, or what Shakespeare meant him to mean, it is true that the Caesarean rupture leaves a long trail in the public mind, both of shattered confidence and unquenched longings.

5

How It Starts

Suppose that we abandon the search for a single pattern of progress running through history. Let us try instead to look at the specific historic circumstances from which Caesars have emerged at different periods and in different countries.

Even taking only half-a-dozen examples, we cannot help noticing several things immediately: first, that the local causes of breakdown which enable a would-be Caesar, large or small, to step into the breach are strikingly varied. There are recurring phenomena, certainly, but there is not a single driving paradigm to them. Secondly, the causes are not tied to any particular stage of economic or social development. Marx famously argued that the revolution when it came would, and could only, break out in a developed industrial nation such as Germany, where class conditions were 'ripe' for the violent transformation to socialism that would inevitably follow. But in fact when the great revolution did come, it was in Russia, a relatively backward country which had begun to industrialize only in the previous two decades. Thirdly, the explosive conditions take an unpredictable length of time to brew up, ranging from months to years, even decades. The chain of events may start in the most unlikely places.

Let us anyway list a few of the more frequent fuses and detonators. The first of these is undoubtedly a prolonged and bitter civil war, one which leaves people longing for a strong and steady leader who looks as if he can restore calm and order and, with luck, prosperity too. This civil war may erupt along several different lines of division: between one sect or religion and another, or between the religious and the anti-clerical parties; between one tribe or sub-nation and another; between different regions of the country: between different economic and social classes; or between any combination of these divided parties.

Important too to note how long the agony may last before the Caesar spots his moment. In seventeenth-century England, the Civil War lasted, off and on, for seven years, to be followed by four unsettled years of the Commonwealth, before Cromwell seized absolute power as the Lord Protector. In ancient Rome, the civil wars had already lasted years before Julius Caesar crossed the Rubicon and precipitated the renewal of a civil war that raged across the Empire until Augustus finally restored stability. In Spain in the 1930s, the outright Civil War lasted three years, devastating large parts of the country and causing thousands of deaths before the victorious Franco gained effective power, to rule as the Caudillo for more than 30 years. Again, in running through the back history of Brexit, we cannot help seeing how deeply the issue of Europe had divided the Tory Party for decades, bringing an untimely end to the premierships of Thatcher, Cameron and May. It is so often forgotten what appalling difficulty Ted Heath had in passing the original European legislation in the first place, his majorities often down to single figures and squeaking through only with the aid of the Labour rebels led by Roy Jenkins.

In France, the revolutions of 1789 and 1848 created unbridgeable hatred between the royalists and the revolutionaries, and eventually led to the emergence of the two Napoleons, but only after prolonged and bruising civil discord. Historians of a Marxist or Whig flavour tend to see such revolutions as driven exclusively by materialist motives, generated by alarming social and economic change. They try to keep religion out of it, just as they underplay religious passions in their accounts of the English Civil War. This blindness becomes utterly absurd when we turn to examine present-day conflicts between Muslims and Hindus and between different sects of Muslims. The idea that religion would become insignificant in modern politics has been disproved time and again; belief in the inevitable obsolescence of religion is a subset of the comforting illusion.

But of course economic and social upheavals have their part to play too. The would-be Caesar has to draw to him the classes of the resentful, the expropriated, those who lost out. In the Brexit struggle, it was argued that the motive power was supplied by the 'Left-behinds', from the de-industrialized towns (not cities) of northern England, the so-called Red Wall of seats that went Tory for the first time since the war. This may only be a half-truth; the suburbs of the Midlands and the south (not the cities) also contributed hugely to the success of the Brexit cause in the referendum of June 2016. But the Left-behinds contributed something which the cause otherwise lacked, a moral focus of sorts, a justification which could claim to be more elevated than mere naked nationalism.

That's true too of the Trump movement. Millions of American blue-collar jobs had indeed been 'offshored' to China and South-East Asia, and the benefits mostly accrued to the educated elite, the people who had ready access to the knowledge economy. No *bon mot* of Trump's was more pungent than 'I love the poorly educated' – because nobody else seemed to. These upheavals too had been years in the making. The decline of the coal, steel and shipbuilding industries in the UK dates back decades. To what extent Thatcherism hastened the process continues to be a fiercely fought question. But the crucial point is that millions of people and whole communities were destined to lose their traditional vocations and their pride, and regional policy was a poor substitute. At the same time, politics and political parties have become hollowed out. The Conservative Party membership has shrunk from several millions in the late 1940s and 1950s to less than 200,000 today; this narrowed party is less and less representative of the millions who vote Conservative but more and more influential over the rhetoric and policy of Conservative MPs. Similarly, the trade unions have lost millions of members in industry and commerce and are increasingly concentrated in the public sector. The Labour Party, which was after all founded by the trade unions, now finds it notoriously difficult to connect with the people who used to be Labour through and through. The number of working-class Labour MPs is now vanishingly small. There is thus an unsettling void at the heart of British politics, in which large numbers of voters feel that there is nobody listening to them, nobody understanding their anxieties, nobody there for them.

We must be careful, though, not to accept the economic explanation as a complete and sufficient one. Outbreaks of nationalism surface in all sorts of places, often in comfortable suburban areas or small towns that have not been doing too badly, in southern England during the Brexit campaign, for example. Resentment boils up for various reasons: a feeling that your country or your class has lost its proper place in the world; that your race or religion isn't valued or is actively discriminated against; that you have simply lost status, for reasons you cannot quite put your finger on. The economic explanation, with its tinge of the old Marxism historicism, is certainly tempting, but it is also, in a curious way, a kind of comfort blanket for the Left, since it presupposes that there might be a simple economic solution. But the feelings of resentment are rather more tangled than that, and it is the skill of the demagogue to unravel them and knit them together again for his own purposes.

The art of the modern Caesar is to listen to those resentments, to give them a voice and to play them back to the audience with enhanced volume and passion. I say the modern Caesar, but Julius Caesar was just as adept at courting the resentful. To dismiss Trump and Johnson as a pair of buffoons half misses the point. What they do is enter into a conversation – crude, funny, mendacious – with people nobody has been talking to for years. To a large extent, the jokes *are* the conversation. Boris Johnson is campaigning every second we see him dangling on the high wire. We must never underestimate the amount of calculation and, undeniably, psychological insight that goes into what looks like mere knockabout improvisation.

At the same time, I want once more to squash any suggestion that there is anything inevitable about the processes that lead to the emergence of a Caesar, large or small. His success may be partly accidental, a quite unexpected result of forces he has had little or no part in generating. It may be simply the outcome of comprehensive political and social exhaustion: 'we have tried everything else; perhaps this fellow, however improbable, may help us out of this ghastly tangle.'

Let us take, by way of a sharp contrast to our previous examples, the emergence of one of the longest-ruling dictators of this or any other era, António de Oliveira Salazar, Prime Minister and effective ruler of Portugal from 1932 to 1968. No more unlikely Caesar could be imagined than this gaunt, pious, academic economist, no public man more averse to populist rhetoric or flashy gestures.

In the two decades before Salazar finally achieved power, Portugal endured every political disaster and upheaval you can think of. Throughout the later nineteenth century, the constitutional monarchy had been shaken by repeated Republican revolts, but the country had more or less held together, under the so-called *Rotativismo*, the alternation in power of bourgeois liberal and conservative parties who more or less agreed on the essentials. Then in January 1908, another revolt led to the assassination of King Carlos and the Crown Prince. Within two years, the new King, Manuel II, 'the Unfortunate', was toppled in the revolution of 1910, and after eight centuries the monarchy came to an end. The new Republican regime was fiercely anti-clerical and treated the Catholic Church with purposive brutality.

As a result, the country was torn apart by coup and counter-coup for the next 16 years; between 1910 and 1926, there were no fewer than 45 governments. The New Republic of Sidónio Pais appealed to monarchists and Catholics, but Sidónio Pais was assassinated in December 1918. The country continued in a desperate state after the First World War, tormented by regional violence and ground down by poverty, illiteracy and inflation. Finally, on 28 May 1926, there was a bloodless coup in Braga, which propelled a series of generals to power, culminating in the presidency of Óscar Carmona. By now, Portugal was effectively bankrupt, crushed by her huge public debt, so in April 1928, Carmona persuaded a reluctant Salazar to come out of Coimbra University and take on the Finance Ministry. Insisting on a free hand, over the next four years Salazar put the economy back on track by balancing the budget, reducing the national debt and so stabilizing the currency. In 1932, Carmona appointed him Prime Minister, which he remained until incapacitated by ill-health 36 years later, while Carmona took a back seat, remaining a non-playing President until his death.

Salazar, the unlikely warrior.

Salazar's *Estado Novo* was a one-party state, ruled by the bureaucracy and a highly militarized police. There was strict censorship, and the workers' syndicates were controlled by the employers. There were intermittent uprisings of old Republicans, but these were suppressed without much difficulty. Despite some later mild relaxations, Portugal was unmistakably a dictatorship throughout the Salazar years, but the majority of Portuguese preferred peace and order to liberty. The brutality of Salazar's secret police was certainly unpleasant, but overall the regime was less cruel than Franco's, and did not have the totalitarian pretensions of Lenin or Hitler.

The similarities between Salazar and other modern Caesars are interesting, but so are the differences. He came to power and restored order after a period of agonizing prolonged national turbulence, like Julius, Cromwell, Napoleon and the rest. But Salazar was not a military hero. He was an academic who had done no soldiering. Indeed, he had scarcely participated in politics. He was once elected to the National Assembly, but attended only a single day's session. He left the heavy lifting to the generals.

Nor did Salazar care for what he called 'the pagan Caesarism' of his fellow dictators. He abhorred the way they recognized no legal, religious or moral limits. Salazar was simply a conservative nationalist who thought that the Portuguese people had shown themselves incapable of parliamentary government. Historians still argue whether such a regime is properly called 'fascist', but clearly Salazar does fit into the spectrum of Caesars – towards the milder end, rather grimmer than Napoleon III, less awful than Mussolini. When it came to the crunch, he was prepared to inflict as much pain as was needed to repress opposition whenever it raised its head. No compunction, no compassion. And that is the ultimate criterion.

Perhaps the Portuguese example has a little more to teach us. Under the *Rotativismo* of the second half of the nineteenth century, by conventional standards Portugal made quite decent progress, better in some respects than Spain's performance, as Stanley G. Payne makes clear in his *History of Spain and Portugal*. The political parties kept changing their names – Septembrists, Regenerators, Progressives, Historicals – but whichever lot was in power, railroads, roads and telegraphs went on being built, tariffs lowered, peasant agriculture expanded considerably.

Yet there was unmistakably a feeling in the air of glory departed. More than a million Portuguese emigrated, the great days of Henry

the Navigator and the Portuguese venturers who mastered the globe –
Vasco da Gama, Christopher Columbus, Ferdinand Magellan, Tristan
da Cunha – were long gone. The concept of *saudade* – yearning,
nostalgia – was all the rage, and so was the new melancholy song
of love and loss, the *fado* (fate). The politics of the present seemed
so tawdry and pedestrian, the politicians unworthy to represent the
true greatness of Portugal. For such a proud people, *Rotativismo* was in
reality a demeaning treadmill.

You can find similar disillusioned yearnings in other pre-Caesarist
countries – in the France of the 1780s and the 1840s, for instance,
in the Russia of the 1870s and 1880s, in the USA today. In Britain,
a long time before Brexit became a practical political programme,
there were murmurings that 'I don't recognize my country any more'
– murmurings given air time so effectively by Enoch Powell and
Nigel Farage. When the revolt against the present actually breaks out,
it purports to demand 'a new kind of politics', but what many people
want is something beyond mere politics. They want a new kind of
state in which there will be no more grubby jostling for power, a
Estado Novo as Salazar called it. But to attain that realm of harmony
and grandeur, to recapture something of the (often misremembered)
Golden Age, only a Caesar will do.

PART II

THE MAKING OF CAESARS

6

The Invention of Charisma

Modern Caesarism has remained a strangely neglected subject. Scholars have found it difficult to think hard about these absurd posturing creatures, or to devote much attention to their techniques and pretensions. As on so many things, it was the great sociologist Max Weber who encouraged us to pause and think again. In 1917, when the whole world seemed to lie in ruins, he wrote a series of articles for the *Frankfurter Zeitung*, later collected into an essay with the misleadingly dull title of 'Parliament and Government in a Reconstructed Germany'. Here, pretty much for the first time, Weber takes Caesarism seriously. Who, after all, was the best example of a modern Caesar? For Germany, indeed for Europe as a whole, clearly it was Bismarck. How brilliantly the old Junker had reduced Parliament to a rubber stamp, what devastating use he had made of emergency legislation and popular appeals. His demagoguery, his expansion of German power to consolidate his own – all this might be deplorable, but it had worked. By embarrassing contrast, Kaiser Wilhelm II was an infantile imitation, another *Napoléon le Petit*.

You might think from this first section of the essay that Weber is going to tell us what a harmful thing this modern Caesarism is and how we must rebuild Parliament and the rule of law as bulwarks against its perils. So he does, but then he starts off on a new and more disquieting tack.

Isn't it possible, he muses, that this sort of demagoguery is actually inherent in modern democratic suffrage, just as it was in Periclean Athens? Apart from *demagogos*, ancient Greek had a dozen other words to describe 'people-flattery' of one sort or another. There was *demegoria*, popular oratory, claptrap; *demizo*, to affect popularity, cheat the people; *demoeides*, vulgar, low; *demokolax*, mob flatterer; *demokopia*, love of mob popularity; *demopithikos*, charlatan; *demoteros*, common, vulgar; *democharistes*, mob courtier. You sense from this linguistic abundance what an acute ear the ancient Greeks had for popular appeal that was *manufactured*. Why should that temptation have disappeared from modern societies? Surely every mass democracy had a tendency to Caesarism?

> Every kind of direct popular election of the supreme ruler and, beyond that, every kind of political power that rests on the confidence of the masses and not of Parliament . . . lies on the road to these 'pure' forms of caesarist acclamation. In particular, this is true of the position of the President of the United States, whose superiority over parliament derives from his (formally) democratic nomination and election.[1]

When travelling the United States in the election year of 1904, Max Weber had seen Teddy Roosevelt at work and was much impressed by his campaigning style.

The miracle ingredient by which the *demagogos* acquires and retains power is what Weber calls 'charisma'. It is Weber who first borrows from the Epistles of St Paul (notably Rom. 6.23; 1 Cor. 12.4) the Greek word for 'the gift of God's Grace', and gives it a new, entirely secular twist – or so we are told. But even Weber's own use of the term retains a Heaven-sent aura. The Man who has the Big C is 'meant to be'. He comes to fulfil the destiny of the nation, he is the Man on the White Horse in the Book of Revelation. When Hegel caught sight of Napoleon riding through Jena the day before the great battle, he wrote that he had just seen 'this World-Soul riding out of town'. That's charisma.

And it's the charismatic who announces himself, none more splendiferously than Napoleon in his proclamation after he took control of Cairo just before Christmas 1798:

> Is there a man so blind as not to see that destiny itself guides all my operations? Is there anyone so faithless as to doubt that everything in this vast universe is bound to the empire of destiny . . . If I choose, I could call each of you to account for the most hidden feelings of his heart, for I know everything, even what you have told no one. But the day shall come when all men shall see beyond all doubt that I am guided by orders from above and that all human efforts avail naught against me.[2]

Curiously, then, Weber, this infinitely thoughtful and sceptical observer of human affairs, had come to agree with the mountebank Napoleon III (and indeed his uncle too) that 'the nature of democracy is to personify itself in a man.'[3] By the time Weber was being consulted about the role and position of the German president during the making of the Weimar Constitution in 1918/19, he proposed the direct election of the president. Charismatic leadership by a single man was essential to cement the people's loyalty and persuade them to accept the dull impersonal weight of modern bureaucracy, which was both universal and inescapable. Yes, there must also be vigorous political parties and accountability to parliament. But a dollop of charisma was indispensable. This might be described as the Weber Wobble, and an apparent exception to the general thesis for which he is celebrated: that the modern world is characterized by a turning away from magical ways of thinking, the once-for-all *Entzauberung*. He recognized the necessity of charisma, but he remained uneasy and suspicious of the phenomenon. He died a year later, in 1920, of the Spanish flu during the great pandemic, aged only 56. If he had lived a couple of years longer, to witness Mussolini's March on Rome, he would have been more uneasy still.

In *Men on Horseback*, David A. Bell, Professor in the Era of North Atlantic Revolutions at Princeton, takes Weber's conjecture a stage further. Democracies, he points out, are particularly suspicious of charismatic leaders. 'Yet, paradoxically, the longing for such leaders acquired new importance, and a distinct new shape, during the very same period that witnessed the first stirrings of modern democracy: the eighteenth and early nineteenth centuries.'[4] It was during that moment of extraordinary intellectual ferment and then in the great revolutions that washed across much of the Western world between 1775 and 1820 that the powerful forms of political charisma we are familiar with today took shape. The coming of democracy transformed the relationship between the people and their leaders, and the personal magnetism of the leader electrified that relationship. Far from representing a backsliding towards older forms of government, the new charismatic leader, adored by the masses and personifying the new nation, was intrinsic to modernity.

In fact, one might argue, it is only in our own time rather than Weber's that we can see most vividly just how it all works. The leader's rallies, his broadcasts, his photo opportunities, his tweets – these do not simply decorate the serious business of governing, they are part and parcel of the business. The clowning, the apparently inconsequential rambling, the irreverent nicknames for his opponents – all these devices are designed to convince the viewers that they are part of an ongoing intimate conversation, and it is from this conversation that the leader derives his authority. In the past and perhaps in the present too, charismatic leaders have often threatened constitutional orders, but sometimes they were crucial to the initial creation of those orders, not only by engineering the rupture with the *ancien régime* but also by bonding the public to this chilly, depersonalized new world.

For the effective leader in a democracy, such as Clinton or Blair, charisma is a useful add-on which helps him get his message across and retain power. But the would-be Caesar sees the possession of this precious quality as something more, as a licence to *go beyond*, to break the rules, not just because, he claims, the rules are harmful to the people, but because breaking the rules shows that he has the charisma; he is beyond good and evil, and beyond a lot of other boring stuff too. As Weber says elsewhere, 'In order to do justice to their mission, the holders of charisma, the master as well as his disciples and followers, must stand outside the ties of this world, outside of routine occupations, as well as outside the routine obligations of family life.' Charisma is both revolutionary and unstable: 'it can only tolerate, with an attitude of complete emotional indifference, irregular, unsystematic, acquisitive acts.'[5] The charismatic can often be identified by the absence of certain normal human pulses. After a fractious meeting with Winston Churchill in 1914, Henry James said to Violet Asquith that it had been a very interesting experience to meet that young man: 'It has brought home to me – very forcibly, very vividly – the limitations by which men of genius obtain their ascendancy over mankind.'[6] The charismatic is, to a greater or lesser degree, not so much hollowed out as stripped for action, not impeded by encrusted loyalties or inherited ideologies, but with a marvellously unclouded eye for the main chance. He is dangerously free, which is part of his allure.

What we must understand at the outset, though, is that a huge effort of self-invention is likely to be involved in the generation of the Caesar's charisma. Julius Caesar himself, Suetonius tells us, was 'of imposing stature – white-skinned, slim-limbed, though rather too full in the face, and with dark, lively eyes' and, according to Cicero, a brilliant natural orator.[7] He took good care of himself, having his hair stylishly cut and his body hair regularly depilated; he wore his purple-banded senator's toga belted in an unusual casual fashion.

But most modern Caesars have not been so physically impressive or appealing. They have often been decidedly on the short side, 5 foot 2 inches to 5 foot 6 – Napoleon, Lenin, Mussolini, Hitler, Franco, Stalin, Churchill, Putin. At the other end of the scale, Charles de Gaulle, a rare exception, was so ungainly and sloping-shouldered that he was variously compared to a camel or a giraffe. Nor have their faces been much to look at. Churchill himself quipped that every new-born baby looked like him. Simón Bolívar, the great liberator of South America, was described at the height of his powers by a visiting British soldier in unflattering terms: 'He is short and meagre; his hair is now grey and his mustachios quite white. His eyes are large and very light, and the general effect of his countenance is unprepossessing. His voice is harsh and disagreeable, and his manners are cold and forbidding in the extreme.'[8] Napoleon, on the verge of greatness, was described by his friend the Duchess d'Abrantès:

At that period in his life Napoleon was ugly . . . His features, which were almost all angular and sharp, have become rounder [since then], because they have been cloaked in flesh, of which there was an almost total absence. His hair, so singular for us today . . . was very simple then, but his complexion was so yellow at that time, and he looked after himself so little, that his badly combed, badly powdered hair gave him an unpleasant appearance.[9]

A sergeant in the Army of Italy could scarcely believe he was their new commander-in-chief. 'His appearance, his dress, his behavior did not appeal to us. Here is how he seemed to me then: small, skinny, very pale, with big black eyes in sunken cheeks, long hair falling from his temples to his shoulders, forming, as they were called, "spaniel's ears".'[10]

Nor was Napoleon any more attractive to listen to. He spoke French badly all his life, and with a heavy Corsican accent he couldn't shake off. His nephew Louis-Napoleon had been exiled in Switzerland and partly educated in Germany, and all his life spoke French with a slight German accent. Joseph Stalin didn't start learning Russian until he was eight, and though he became fluent in the language, he never entirely lost his Georgian accent – which he sometimes played up when he wanted to sound folksy, just as Harold Wilson did with his native Yorkshire. Churchill had lifelong trouble with his lisp, despite having gone to a speech therapist as a young man. His strangely portentous, and often thrilling, manner of speaking was partly due to his determined efforts to control his s's. We have already heard about

Cromwell's 'sharp and untunable' voice, not to mention the warts on his swollen and reddish countenance.

Yet it is that very sharpness, that rough edge, that catches the attention, as it caught the attention of, say, Adolf Hitler's audiences: the sensation that this harsh unappealing voice is telling you some uncomfortable truth you need to hear. The word often applied to Napoleon on his road to power, as it was to the young Hitler, was 'farouche' – a sullen, awkward, unbiddable quality; the word derives ultimately from the late Latin, *forasticus*, 'out of doors', 'strange' – rather as we might describe someone as 'a space cadet' or even 'out to lunch', not quite all there. Napoleon's friend Madame Bourrienne said that he would sit silent in the theatre while the rest of the audience was roaring with laughter, and then break out into wild laughter at some tragic scene. We think of Cromwell's hysterical mirth during the slaughter at Naseby and Dunbar. Or indeed of the ghoul in the Charles Addams cartoon cackling at a weepie when the rest of the audience is sobbing.

Yet when the charismatic switches on, then suddenly he is all there. You are immediately aware of a terrible blinding clarity of vision, an unblinking cynicism and an intense concentration on the matter in hand. Here is Napoleon, for example, after conquering half of Italy in the name of republican liberty, talking to a French diplomat in the summer of 1797 in the gardens of Mombello:

> What I have done so far is nothing. I am only at the beginning of the career I must pursue. Do you think it is to enhance the position of the lawyers of the Directory, the Carnots, the Barras, that I have been winning victories in Italy? And do you think it is in order to establish a republic? What nonsense! A republic of thirty million people! With our manners and our vices! It is an impossibility! It is a dream with which the French are in love, but it will pass like so many others. They want glory, they want their vanity to be satisfied, but liberty? They don't understand it at all . . . The nation needs a glorious leader and not theories of government, phrases and speeches by ideologues which Frenchmen don't understand.

And who was to be this glorious leader? 'I do not wish to leave Italy until I can go and play in France a role similar to that I am playing here, and the time has not yet come: the pear is not yet ripe.'[11]

The path to power was already clear. The rest was merely a question of timing.

The Timing

By great good fortune, there has survived a detailed account of the timing of the most famous coup in history. Suetonius and Plutarch both give us an hour-by-hour report of the run-up to Julius Caesar's crossing of the Rubicon. These accounts are almost certainly based on a record, kept at the time but now lost, by Asinius Pollio, who was at Caesar's side throughout. Asinius Pollio was a remarkable character: general, poet, playwright, patron of Virgil, builder of the first purpose-built library in Rome. He seems a pretty reliable eyewitness. Though a supporter of Caesar's, it is he who does not hesitate to point out how slapdash and untruthful much of Caesar's account of the Gallic wars really was.

Julius has been campaigning in Gaul, all the time keeping in close touch with his supporters in Rome, who can keep him posted about what his bitter rival Pompey is up to. After crossing the Alps into Cisalpine Gaul – today's Northern Italy – he learns that civil authority has collapsed in Rome, because of the unappeasable conflict between Pompey's supporters and his own. The tribunes have been driven by Pompey's army from the Senate, which is in total uproar, and they have had to flee the city on mule carts disguised as slaves.

Camped at Ravenna, Caesar has with him no more than 300 horsemen and 9,000 legionaries. The rest of his vast army he has left beyond the Alps to look after Further Gaul:

> Caesar saw, however, that the beginning of his enterprise did not require a large force at present, but must take advantage of the golden moment [*kairos*, that is, the critical moment or the right time – a key concept for Greek historians and statesmen] by

showing amazing boldness and speed, since he could strike terror into his enemies by an unexpected blow more easily than he could overwhelm them by an attack in full force.[1]

As Tom Holland points out in *Rubicon*, as well as *kairos*, the Romans also had a Latin word for such a moment.

Discrimen, they called it − an instant of perilous and excruciating tension, when the achievements of an entire lifetime might hang in the balance . . . In addition to 'crisis point', *discrimen* had a further meaning: 'dividing line'. By crossing it, Caesar did indeed engulf the world in war, but he also helped to bring about the ruin of Rome's ancient freedoms, and the establishment, upon their wreckage, of a monarchy − events of primal significance for the history of the West.[2]

Caesar is adopting classic coup technique. Surprise is key: unwieldy numbers may only get in the way and give the opposition enough time to mass their own forces. But surprise may have to be manufactured. It requires deliberate stage management. So Caesar orders an advance party of his centurions to make a quiet occupation of the nearby town of Ariminum (Rimini today), just over the border inside Roman territory. Swords only, no heavy weapons, no bloodshed, no commotion.

The rest of the day Caesar spends in innocent diversion, to disarm the suspicions of any Pompey spy who may be watching:

He himself spent the day in public, attending and watching the exercises of gladiators, but a little before evening he bathed and dressed and went into the banqueting hall. Here he held brief converse with those who had been invited to supper, and just as it was getting dark, he went away, after addressing courteously most of the guests and bidding them await his return.[3]

Then he sends off his chosen friends by different routes, while he himself drives off in the dark, hiring some mules from a nearby bakery and harnessing them to a carriage. He drives off first in one direction, then down another lane towards Ariminum. Here comes the first inevitable hitch. Caesar's lights go out and he loses his way for hours. It's not until dawn that he finds a guide who takes him on foot by narrow bypaths towards the muddy little stream which divides Gaul from Rome. Here he meets up with his small platoon – and pauses, agitated by the magnitude of the fearful step he is about to take. If he crosses the Rubicon, he will be breaking the ancient rule of the Republic that no general may bring his army within the borders of Rome without express permission from the Senate, which he certainly won't get:

> He communed with himself in silence a long time as his resolution wavered back and forth, and his purpose then suffered change after change. For a long time too, he discussed his perplexities with his friends who were present, among whom was Asinius Pollio, estimating the great evils for all mankind which would follow the passage of the river and the wide fame which they would leave to posterity.[4]

This fit of brooding too sets a pattern which is to become classic. The pangs of conscience, the awareness of the weight of history upon his shoulders, the verdict of posterity – all this is the archetypal narcissism of the pre-coup soliloquy. It is an integral part of the performance that Caesar should share his qualms with his closest comrades. By doing so, he advertises the greatness of his mission, in particular his need to trespass beyond conventional morality, in this case literally trespass into forbidden territory.

In one respect at least, Caesar is absolutely correct. The Crossing of the Rubicon is to become just about the most famous phrase in the political lexicon, trotted out to describe decisive moments in any enterprise, large or small, heroic or bathetic.

In another respect, Caesar's ruminations are also correct. Great evils do indeed follow the Crossing. For decades, the Republic has been plagued by ghastly civil wars between rival generals. Now those civil wars are about to be renewed across the Empire, more bloody and destructive than ever. This is so easy to predict that you wonder whether any of Caesar's audience beside the muddy stream, Asinius Pollio perhaps, felt like piping up: 'You are so right, sir, about the terrible consequences that are likely to follow if we make the crossing, so why don't we have a rethink and go back to Ravenna for a nice breakfast?'

Perhaps there were such doubters present (there often are on such occasions), and it is to forestall them that Caesar here abruptly and decisively changes gear:

Finally, with a sort of passion, as if abandoning calculation and casting himself upon the future, and uttering the phrase with which men usually prelude their plunge into desperate and daring fortunes, 'Let the die be cast' [in the version of Suetonius, 'The die is cast' – *alea jacta est*. In fact, Caesar would have spoken in Greek, the line being lifted from the Athenian playwright Menander], he hastened to cross the river, and going at full speed now for the rest of the time, he dashed into Ariminum and took possession of it.[5]

The reader, though, may pause to reflect that the whole hesitation-and-remorse can only have been a piece of play-acting, in view of the careful plans of deception Caesar had been carrying out for the previous 24 hours. He never had the slightest intention of turning back. He wished only to let the world know that he was fully, magnificently conscious of the gravity of his venture.

In Rome, there is complete panic as soon as the news reaches the city – no doubt hurried along by Caesar's own couriers. Pompey and the consuls flee the city, along with most of the Senate and thousands of the citizens, including many of Caesar's own former supporters who are terrified of the carnage they see coming. Within 60 days, Caesar is master of all Italy with scarcely any bloodshed. That's a coup for you. Then he begins to exercise his much advertised clemency, starts distributing money and food and so lures friend and foe alike back, before going off to deal with Pompey.

There is no shortage of observers at the time who are well aware that Caesar has been willing to plunge the whole Mediterranean world into further misery for the sake of his own glory. Cicero, who has been tirelessly and vainly seeking to engineer a compromise between the two generals, wrote in a letter of January 49,

This insane miserable fellow has never had the least inkling of the good! Yet he claims that he is doing everything for the sake of his honour! But where does honour reside if not in honourable conduct? And can it be honourable to hold on to an army without the approval of the Senate or to occupy towns inhabited by our citizens in order to gain easier access to the city of our fathers? Indeed, how can it be permissible to start a civil war for the sake of one's own honour?[6]

One of the ways in which posterity condescends to the ancient Greeks and Romans is to assume that they were incapable of the humanitarian impulses that come naturally to us. Look how the Senate meekly acceded to Julius Caesar's *supplicatio* for a Triumph as news of his mass slaughter of the Gauls filtered through to Rome. Even Caesar's critics, we are told, were licking their lips at the prospect of thousands more muscular blonde Gauls coming onto the slave market. The Romans adored victories, worshipped strength and had no time for compassion. Well, not all Romans. Summing up Caesar's campaigns, Pliny the Elder remarked in his monumental *Natural History*:

> I would not myself count it to his glory that in addition to conquering his fellow citizens, he killed in his battles 1,192,000 human beings, a prodigious even if unavoidable wrong inflicted on the human race, as he himself confessed it to be by not publishing the casualties of the civil wars.[7]

The extraordinary precision of Pliny's enormous figure for the dead is in one sense ridiculous, based as it must be on totting up the unreliable figures that Caesar himself gives in his *Gallic Wars*, but it is an admirable early attempt to do what historians of holocausts have attempted ever since, to calculate the exact toll of campaigns of mass murder. What Pliny points out is that, for Julius, barbarian deaths didn't really count; by contrast, he did not think of boasting how many of his fellow citizens he had killed. But for Pliny, both sets of casualties were 'humani generis iniuriam'. So much for the idea that Romans had no concept of common humanity. In Latin, after all, humanitas has the same double meaning as 'humanity' in English, of 'humankind' and 'kindness'.

That implacable moralist Cato the Younger opposed the Senate granting Caesar a triumph after the massacre of the Usipetes and the Tencteri. Rather than voting sacrifices and celebrations in his honour, Cato said, they should be handing him over to the Gauls as a punishment for abusing a truce to murder so many of them. Caesar responded with a furious letter. Unmoved, Cato launched a further attack in the Senate, declaring that 'if you are in your right mind, it is not the sons of the Britons and the Celts whom you must fear, but Caesar himself.'[8] As Luciano Canfora asserts in what he calls 'The Black Book of the Gallic Campaign', 'Gaul, the Celtic world, was thus, through violence and genocide, brought into the realm of Roman "civilization" . . . Caesar's conquest of Gaul brought the autonomous development of Celtic civilization to an abrupt end.'[9]

As for Cicero, he had said many flattering things about Caesar, especially during the dictatorship, but after his death he summed up Caesar's ferocious and interminable wars: '*res bello gesserat, quamvis rei publicae calamitosas, at tamen magnas.*' Great wars they were, you had to admit that, but for the republic they were calamitous.[10] And ten times as calamitous for the Gauls. Some modern scholars have calculated that, as a proportion of the population of Gaul, the losses were equal to, or even surpassed, those of the Germans and the Russians in the Second World War – and all done without the benefit of modern technology but with swords and bows and arrows.

Yet ever since there have been hero-worshipping historians ready to excuse Caesar's elephantine ego on the grounds of his indispensable greatness. For example, Jacob Burckhardt: 'Great men are necessary for our life, in order that the movement of world history can free itself sporadically, by fits and starts, from obsolete ways of living and inconsequential talk.'[11] All I wish to point out here is that most Caesars are pretty well aware of what they are doing and of the possible cataclysmic consequences. Their immoralism is of the sort applauded by Nietzsche – that true greatness transcends and is indifferent to the snivelling concerns of little people.

Gaius Julius Caesar (Vatican Museum).

As soon as Caesar was proclaimed dictator, he lost no time in packing the Senate with his supporters and appointing most of the magistrates himself. The elaborate systems of selection and election, built up over centuries of the Roman Republic, were unceremoniously dumped. Their memory survives only in the odd etymological inheritance: 'ambition' from *ambitio*, the going around of candidates in search of votes; and 'candidate' itself, from *candidus* or 'white', from the white gowns worn by those seeking office. To assert his new-won authority, Caesar stormed into the Senate, but found only a thin house. Most of the already soured and disillusioned senators had stayed away, and so were spared the catalogue that their new master poured out of all the indignities and affronts he had suffered.

In order to scrape together funds to prosecute his civil war against Pompey, which was to inflict such misery on the Roman people, Caesar then demanded the right to break open the Treasury, or *Aerarium*, in the Temple of Saturn in the Forum, which contained the city's emergency funds. A plucky young Tribune of the Plebs, Lucius Caecilius Metellus, had the guts to use his veto to block this. Caesar flew into a rage. 'In future everything will be decided by me,' he shouted. He ordered troops into the Forum, which meant crossing the hallowed boundary of the city (where, according to law, his military command ended) – a second Rubicon crossing, so to speak.[12]

Finding no keys to unlock the chamber under the altar (the fleeing consuls had taken them), Caesar sent for a locksmith. Still Metellus barred his way, citing the laws which forbade any such seizure of state funds. Caesar gave him a blast, a foretaste of the rhetoric of Caesars to come down the ages: 'Arms and laws do not share the same season. If you don't like what is going on, get out of the way, since war has no use for free speech. When the war is over, there will be time for your harangues.' He then threatened to kill Metellus if he did not stop interfering: 'And you must be well aware, young man, that it is more unpleasant for me to threaten this than actually to do it.' Plutarch tells us that Metellus went off in a fright, as many another Metellus has done since. Caesar had his gold and his war, and the Senate never interfered with his wishes again, at least not until the Ides of March five years later.

The use of troops to violate sacred space, the brutal language of menace, unabashed abuse of the law: how forcibly it all reminds us of the first irruptions of later Caesars – Cromwell, Napoleon and Hitler, to name but a few. Julius Caesar breaking open the *Aerarium* to fund his war is in the same tradition as Donald Trump declaring a national emergency and grabbing billions of dollars voted by the Congress for other purposes to fund his Mexican Wall. It is interesting, though, that this vivid incident has not lingered in the memory of posterity, as Caesar's murder has. The truth is that, as so often, history has been kinder to Caesar than his contemporaries were. That is partly because, like Winston Churchill, he wrote much of the history himself.

Cassius Dio wrote, when recounting the plundering of the *Aerarium* in his *Roman History*, that, here as in his other projects, Caesar

> carried them out in the name of democracy [*onomati isonomias* – the word *demokratia* was still pejorative], but with the substance of despotism. Both Caesar and Pompey called their opponents enemies of the country and declared that they themselves were fighting for the public interest, whereas each alike was really ruining those interests and advancing merely his own private ends.[13]

Caesar himself in his book on the Civil War says nothing of seizing the funds, remarking only that

> Lucius Metellus, one of the tribunes, was suborned by Caesar's enemies to . . . embarrass everything else which Caesar should propose. Caesar, having discovered his intention, after spending several days to no purpose left the city in order that he might not lose any more time, and went to Transalpine Gaul without effecting what he had intended.[14]

No mention of the fact that he had got away with 15,000 gold bars, 30,000 silver bars and 30 million sestertii, plus the contents of the special fund set aside over the centuries against a repeat of the invasion by the Gauls in 390 BC. Caesar told Metellus that, now that he had settled the Gauls' hash, the fund was no longer needed. The ripest cover-up imaginable, made all the riper by Caesar's habit of writing about himself in the third person.

We have in our own time a recent example of a narcissistic soliloquy not unlike Caesar's, if on a Lilliputian scale. The day before he decided to come out in favour of Brexit and lead the campaign which was eventually to propel him to the Tory leadership and on to No. 10, Boris Johnson composed two alternative drafts for his weekly column in the *Daily Telegraph*: one advocating that the UK remain in the EU; the other advocating departure. Johnson later tried to laugh these off as merely exercises in testing the strength of the alternative arguments. But of course they were paths for him to choose between: whether to splash out into the muddy waters, or to sit quietly on the bank and watch the flow of the river.

He spent much of that weekend discussing what he should do with his sister Rachel and her husband Ivo Dawnay (both, as it happened, staunch Remainers). When I bumped into the Dawnays the following day at a party, they stressed how long and intense the discussion had been, and how tortured Johnson was by the decision he had to make. When he stood on the steps of his Islington home that Sunday, 21 February 2016, he announced his decision 'with a huge amount of heartache'.

His critics instantly riposted that his heart was aching only for himself. Had he plunged into the right stream? His alternative articles were all about the benefits or damage for Britain's trade and foreign policy. But what would his decision mean for his own political prospects: glory or the wilderness? Whether his actions would topple two Prime Ministers, smash the old Tory Party, inflict severe damage on Britain's overseas trade, leave Northern Ireland in the lurch and the rest of the EU bitter and distraught did not really concern him much.

His personal calculation was quite simple. By placing himself at the head of the Brexit campaign as Mayor of London (he had no rivals in Parliament worth speaking of), he was lining up with what was now the majority in the Conservative Party, both in the Commons and in the country. For many members of this sadly shrunken body, Brexit was the central issue of modern British politics. For the UK to continue inside the EU would be, in the words of their ultimate guru Enoch Powell, 'a living death'. Even if the Remainers won a narrow victory, Johnson would have spoken up for the heart and soul of the party at a time when they really needed a spokesman who mattered. He would earn their undying trust, as he had seldom earned trust anywhere else in his previous political career. Well, not quite undying, perhaps. By the spring of 2022, some of the hardline Brexiteers were beginning to have their serious doubts about the moral character of their champion.

But at the time of the coup – and it was a coup – Johnson's political arithmetic was impeccable. Win or lose the referendum, he had become a Personage. He had seized the 'golden moment', the *kairos*. He had struck the unexpected blow.

The term 'coup' in this political sense seems to occur first as far back as 1646 in a description of Cardinal Richelieu's *coups d'état*. But the word itself has a much more ancient lineage: from the Latin *colaphus* and the Doric Greek *kolaphos*, meaning cuff or buffet, and both deriving ultimately from the Greek *kondulos*, knuckle, and *kondulizo*, strike with the fist. Which brings us back to the bare bones of what we are talking about.

Not long after the war, the journalist and TV interviewer Malcolm Muggeridge went to interview Charles de Gaulle at his home at Colombey-les-deux-Églises. The General was in his wilderness years –or *'le désert'* as he called it – having stalked out of office in January 1946 because he could not bear to work under the thumb of an elected parliament. So what was he doing now? Muggeridge asked. *'J'attends'*, the General replied. Caesars usually have to do a good deal of waiting, and de Gaulle was to have to wait longer than most.

He had refused to give a proper public explanation for his resignation. Nothing, he told his intimates, was more effective than silence. 'One's acts have to be picturesque . . . What is picturesque is not forgotten. I take my mystery away with me.'[15] Thus the cryptic manner of his resignation was intended both as a demonstration of his greatness and as a preparation for returning to power on the terms he wanted. In private, he was quite candid about his reasons. He told Jules Moch, the Socialist Interior Minister, that he was convinced 'that it is – he articulated each syllable – im-poss-ible to gov-ern with the par-ties . . . I do not feel I am made for this kind of fight. I do not want to be attacked, criticized, contested every day by men whose only claim is to have had themselves elected in some small corner of France.'[16]

Acclamation, not election, was his preferred route to power: the crowd-bath, *le bain de foule*, not the ballot box. Even after he had been voted into power,

> he spoke or wrote of his 'election' in inverted commas. He reluctantly consented to the creation of a Gaullist party, the Rassemblement du Peuple Français, only to serve as an obstructionist force, not because he wanted it to take power in a parliamentary regime. He made his egomania plain in 1952: 'I admit that I do not believe in the value of any government that I would not have the honour of presiding over.'[17]

Even in the *désert*, he was never really idle. The image (which he helped to promote) of him sitting quietly at Colombey listening to the rain pouring down and the clack of Yvonne's knitting needles was largely baloney. There was always a stream of significant visitors to update him and to plot with. Like some ageing rock star, he was constantly touring the country, speaking night after night at vast rallies in *la France profonde*. In 1950, before the municipal elections, he visited 70 *départements* and was on the road for 53 days.

His determination to bring down the Fourth Republic was as patient as it was unrelenting. He had plenty of false starts. As early as October 1947, after the RPF had got 40 per cent of the vote, he was exulting that 'it is the death of the regime.' Once the final results were known, 'I will grab the microphone to declare that on arriving in Paris I have taken note of the disintegration of the existing political authorities ... and that in the absence of any government I will temporarily head the government to accomplish the necessary task of national salvation.'[18] But President Vincent Auriol held firm, and so did the system. De Gaulle sensed, again wrongly, another opportunity in 1952.[19] And a third one, in 1954, after the fall of Dien Bien Phu and the French humiliation in Indochina. He announced that on VE Day, 8 May, he would pay his respects to the Unknown Soldier at the Arc de Triomphe, expecting a huge demo that would sweep away the tottering regime and sweep him back to power. In fact, when he arrived at 4 p.m., there was only a modest turnout, rather smaller than had greeted the President of the Republic earlier in the day, and after shaking a few hands, he slunk off into what looked like definitive obscurity.

The *bain de foule* – General de Gaulle lays a wreath at the Arc de Triomphe to celebrate the German capitulation, 8 May 1945.

But then came the Algeria crisis and, after vigorous plotting by de Gaulle, both in Paris and Algiers, to convince the army that only a strong regime with himself at the helm could make *Algérie française* a reality, insurrection began to spread. Committees of Public Safety began to be formed in several provincial capitals, and eventually after some ungainly manoeuvres he made it to the Elysée. So, third or fourth time lucky, depending how you are counting.

Several things need to be noted: first, the original genesis of the coup in colonial France far from the metropole – reminiscent of many another coup, from Julius Caesar to Napoleon I and Francisco Franco. It is always easier to generate a critical mass of rebellion far away from the watchful eyes of your rivals. Next, it is important not to be led astray by the self-justifications of the Caesar's propaganda machine. The Fourth Republic had a perfectly respectable economic record and produced several notable Prime Ministers; it presided over an important part of France's postwar recovery from 1949 to 1979, *les trente glorieuses*. One is reminded here of the efforts of Cromwellians to big up the record of the Protectorate at the expense of the not wholly useless domestic record of Charles I. Above all, we must take note of the ruthless readiness of de Gaulle to twist the truth. The biggest lie he told on this occasion was that 'I had nothing to do with the insurrection of Algiers. I knew nothing of what was being prepared . . . I did not raise a little finger to encourage the movement.'[20]

The Art of Noble Lying

But then de Gaulle's regard for truth had never been conspicuous. Recall the famous words of his speech at the Hotel de Ville on 25 August 1944: 'Paris liberated! Liberated by itself, liberated by its people with the help of the armies of France, with the help and assistance of the whole of France, of that France which fights, of the only France, of the true France, of eternal France.'[1] Not a mention of the Allies, not a mention of the *Résistants*, many of whom were present to savour this historic moment. De Gaulle's claim, as Churchill had pointed out to Roosevelt just after D-Day with pardonable exaggeration, 'is remarkable, as he has not a single soldier in the great battle now developing' (in fact, a number of French commandos had landed with the British and Leclerc's armoured division did join the Normandy campaign). Nothing must be allowed to interfere with the legend that France had liberated herself and, no less important, that de Gaulle had no need to proclaim himself President, because 'The Republic has never ceased to exist . . . Vichy was always, and remains, null and void. I am President of the Republic. Why should I proclaim it?'[2]

He had such intense contempt for the French people that he felt no duty to tell them the truth. At the beginning of 1968, the year that was to see *les évènements* that were to hasten his fall, he confided to his loyal lieutenant Foccart:

In reality, we are on the stage of a theatre where I have been keeping up the illusion since 1940. I am trying to give France the appearance of a solid, firm, confident and expanding country, while it is a worn-out [*avachie*] nation, which thinks only of its own comfort, which doesn't want any problems, which does not want to fight, which wants to upset no one, neither the Americans, nor the English. The whole thing is a perpetual illusion. I am on the stage of a theatre, and I pretend to believe in it.[3]

After it was all over and he was back in Colombey, he confided to André Malraux, 'The French no longer have any national ambition . . . I amused them with flags.'[4]

As we have seen, Napoleon I in the gardens of Mombello had expressed a similar contempt for the French people. And like de Gaulle, he was tireless in promoting his own image and quite unscrupulous in his methods. He was quick to realize that his bulletins from the battlefield offered a matchless opportunity to sell himself as the invincible saviour of France. Presentation was key to Napoleon's long-lasting success. The stream of bulletins and orders of the day that he issued formed a running narrative, unquenchably bullish and boastful, shamelessly exaggerating the enemy's losses and minimizing his own. These bulletins are intrinsic to the Napoleonic legend and frequently republished by editors who seem blithely indifferent to their mendacity. By contrast, Philip Dwyer kicks off his superb three-volume biography of Napoleon (2007, 2013, 2018), which jostles with Adam Zamoyski's for current supremacy, by exposing a particularly ripe example: the Bridge at Arcola, Napoleon's iconic victory in his second Italian campaign. According to the legend, Napoleon seized the flag from the standard-bearer and stormed the narrow bridge under a hail of Austrian bullets. The scene was immortalized, not only in the Bulletin, but also in countless engravings and paintings, notably Antoine-Jean Gros's *Bonaparte at the Bridge of Arcola*. In reality, Bonaparte started across the bridge with the flag, but his troops refused to follow him and the French forces were driven back from the river by Austrian fire. In the chaos of the retreat, he was shoved into a ditch up to his neck in water and nearly drowned. Two other generals had to be sent to take Arcola from the rear. Nobody crossed the bridge. In private, French commanders denounced the cowardice of their men and praised the fighting spirit of the Austrians.

Napoleon not quite at the Bridge of Arcola.

I cannot resist tossing in here David's even more iconic painting of Napoleon crossing the Alps on a prancing white charger, perhaps the most familiar of all images of the great man in action. In reality, the track over the Great St Bernard Pass was so steep and icy that Napoleon and his men had to trudge up the pass on humble mules and slide down the other side on their bottoms.

Napoleon crossing the Alps, as seen by Jacques-Louis David.

The untruthfulness of the Bulletins became so notorious that the expression, 'to lie like a bulletin' crept into popular parlance. On St Helena, Napoleon's hagiographer, Emmanuel de Las Cases, asked him about the Bulletins (you could ask him anything, he was curiously approachable):

> The Emperor declared them to be very correct . . . If they had acquired an ill reputation in our armies – if it was a common saying, *as false as a bulletin*, it was personal rivalships, party spirit, that had established it; it was the wounded self-love of those whom it had been forgotten to mention in them, and who had, or fancied they had, a right to a place there; and still more than all, our ridiculous national defect of having no greater enemies to our successes and our glory, than ourselves.[5]

In other words, the slurs on the bulletins were fake news, put about by losers who wanted to talk their country down.

Almost more outrageous than the Bulletins is the Proclamation that Napoleon himself composed and had plastered on the walls of Paris the next day after he had seized power on the 19 Brumaire:

> I went to the Council of Five Hundred, alone, unarmed, head uncovered . . . Daggers were immediately raised against their liberator [i.e. me]; twenty assassins threw themselves on me and aimed at my chest. The grenadiers of the Legislative Corps, whom I had left at the entrance to the hall, ran to put themselves between me and the assassins. One of the brave grenadiers was struck and had his clothes torn by a dagger. They carried me out.[6]

This version of events inspired a number of pamphlets in the following weeks and months, not to mention a number of melodramatic engravings, such as Charles-Melchior Descourtis's *Séance du corps legislatif a l'Orangerie de St Cloud, apparition de Bonaparte et journée libératrice du 19 brumaire.*

Almost every word of it is false. In reality, Napoleon burst into the Council accompanied by a dozen armed men, against all the rules. He was jostled by indignant deputies, shouting 'Down with the Dictator!', 'Down with Cromwell!' and so on. Bonaparte was seized by the scruff of the neck, and almost fainted. He didn't manage to utter a word. The only casualty was a grenadier who cut his arm on the bayonet of one of his comrades. There were no daggers, no assassins.[7]

There are few greater pleasures than listening to Napoleon on St Helena, reminiscing for hours on end, with Las Cases taking down every word. For example, he can't stop talking about the execution of the young Duke of Enghien, a Bourbon prince and so a threat to Boney, although a distant one, whose kidnapping and execution in 1804 shocked respectable Europe. Either Talleyrand or Fouché famously said, 'It was worse than a crime, it was a blunder.' Napoleon kept on telling Las Cases that he would do the same again if he had to, while insisting that he hadn't really wanted him executed, and that it was Talleyrand who had come in one day when he was having coffee and bounced him into it, and in any case 'I didn't know exactly who the Duke of Enghien was – the Revolution happened when I was very young, I never went to Court and I didn't know where he was living.' If he had known that he was at Baden just over the German border, in fact, he wouldn't have allowed it and the Duke's life would have been saved, and by the way it was a myth that Josephine had pleaded for his life and he had refused.[8] In short, every excuse except 'the dog ate my homework.'

Napoleon had an illustrious predecessor in the art of embroidering his bulletins – with the big difference that he was never found out. For two millennia, Julius Caesar's *De Bello Gallico* has been taught by schoolmasters as a model of military history: limpid, economical – and true. Only in the latter half of the twentieth century did it dawn on scholars that Julius Caesar might have made a lot of it up – that he was 'an artful war reporter', in T. P. Wiseman's phrase. Yet even at the time, Gaius Asinius Pollio, who served alongside Caesar and crossed the Rubicon with him, said, according to Suetonius, that Caesar's memoirs 'were put together somewhat carelessly and without strict regard for truth; since in many cases Caesar was too ready to believe the accounts which others gave of their actions, and gave a perverted account of his own, either designedly or perhaps through defect of memory.' Modern scholars consider that some of the figures that Caesar gives for the casualties and for the size of the opposing armies are grotesquely improbable. At one point, the Nervii are described as having been wiped out, before they resurface in numbers to be wiped out again.

As we have already seen, while unashamed to give the full horrific casualty figures for the Gauls, ready even to magnify the statistics for his own glory, Julius Caesar shrinks from giving us the figures for the thousands of Roman citizens wiped out during the civil wars, for which he himself was primarily responsible.

The impulse to embroider is not confined to Caesars in the West. The seventh-century Tang Emperor, Taizong, was very concerned for his reputation in posterity and often pressed his official diary keeper, the historian Chu Suiliang, to change the Court Record, the basis of future official histories, to enhance his reputation. Chu Suiliang did what he could to limit the changes and dared to point out that the Emperor's reputation would suffer if these attempts became public. One fact impossible to suppress was that to become Emperor, Taizong had ambushed and murdered his two elder brothers at the gate of the palace, a not infrequent occurrence in the dynasties of imperial China.[9] Five centuries earlier, when the general recommended by the great court historian Sima Qian was defeated in battle, the Emperor Wu had Sima Qian castrated.[10] Even the desk job was no safe haven from an Emperor's wrath.

There are many other early examples of media manipulation. The defeat of the Spanish Armada is something of a spin doctor's masterclass. For continental historians, the skirmishes off Plymouth Hoe and Gravelines are barely worth mentioning: it was the appalling weather that scattered the galleons to the Hebrides. But at least the details are on the record, whereas the humiliating failure of Drake's Counter-Armada the following year was so brilliantly suppressed by Queen Elizabeth that for the next three centuries no Englishman was aware of it. Then there's Cromwell's attempt to suppress the ghastly fate of his expedition to capture Hispaniola – to the extent of keeping the ships bearing the bad news in quarantine and then pretending that the consolation prize of Jamaica had been their real goal all along. The most comforting of all illusions about history is that the truth will out.

The most heinous form of the Big Lie is not the misrepresenting of a battle's outcome but the provoking of a war by staging a bogus *casus belli* which puts the blame on the other party. Since the sixteenth century, this has been known as 'a false flag operation', and it has not been confined to Caesars. Constitutional monarchies and republics too have flown false flags to justify their wars of choice.

A ripe early example is recorded in Stockholm in 1788. The head tailor at the Royal Swedish Opera received an order to make up a number of Russian military uniforms. These were then worn by Swedish troops when staging an attack on Puumala, an outpost on the Russian border on 27 June. This apparent incursion on Swedish soil enraged the Swedish Parliament, which until then had been denying King Gustav III the necessary permission to launch an offensive war against Russia. The Russo–Swedish War followed and dribbled on until 1790. Gustav gained little from it and was assassinated a couple of years later, oddly enough at the Stockholm Opera House.

But the most evil and calamitous 'false flag operation' was the one that started the Second World War, Operation Himmler or Operation Canned Goods. Hitler had ordered an elaborate SS exercise combining 21 separate incidents on the Russo–Polish border on the night of 31 August 1939. The most notorious of these was at Gleiwitz, where a small group of German agents dressed in Polish uniforms seized the radio station, broadcast an inflammatory anti-German message, then skedaddled, leaving behind several corpses, also in Polish uniforms. More of these mis-dressed corpses, prisoners from Dachau and other concentration camps freshly killed by lethal injection, known as 'canned goods' or Konserven, were strewn at customs posts and other sensitive spots. The next day, 1 September, Hitler told the Reichstag that his patience was exhausted and declared war on Poland. As so often with false flag ops, this deceitful prelim convinced scarcely anyone outside Germany, but then the German public was the principal target audience.

To take a more recent, equally flagrant example: in the run-up to the Russian invasion of Ukraine of 24 February 2022, the Russian state media issued a slew of fabricated reports about Ukrainian forces attacking Russian targets. These disinformation videos were of such poor quality (they often carried the wrong dates) that nobody outside Russia believed them for a moment. But it's the thought that counts. Inside Russia, this was the beginning of a drip-drip narrative which, by the time the invasion had reached its first brutal peak with the destruction of Mariupol, had convinced the great majority of Russian viewers.

Western democracies cannot congratulate themselves on being too high-minded to stoop to such vile fabrications. For example, in April 1953, the CIA was tasked to undermine the government of Iran as a prelude to overthrowing the Prime Minister, Mohammad Mosaddegh. This operation, codenamed TPAJAX, involved carrying out false flag attacks on mosques, which were to be blamed on the local communists who supported the government. Other subversive tricks continued until the democratically elected regime was toppled. The CIA files have since been comprehensively shredded.

The Suez conspiracy offers a more complex example. In the autumn of 1956, the British and French governments colluded with Israel to recover the Suez Canal after Egypt's President Nasser had nationalized it. The plan, agreed in the secret Treaty of Sèvres, was that Israeli troops should invade Egypt; then French and British forces would 'intervene' to separate the two combatants, forcing them to withdraw and allow Britain and France to regain control of the Canal. They would be stopping the war, rather than starting it.

The dismal fate of the whole scurvy enterprise need not concern us here. But it is worth noting that the defenders of it were unapologetic. Selwyn Lloyd, the British Foreign Secretary at Sèvres, continued to assert that 'I have no sense of guilt about the events of 1956. Whatever was done then, was done in what was genuinely believed to be the national interest . . . I have always thought collusion a red herring – I did not mislead the House of Commons – I certainly did not tell them the whole story.'[11] What was wrong with the operation was not the collusion but that it was 'bedeviled by lack of a clear political aim'.[12] The unanswered question, Lloyd thought, was, 'supposing we had reoccupied Egypt, what would we have done with it?'[13] Which of course was the question that bedevilled the Allies years later when they did reoccupy Iraq on an equally flaky pretext.

Worldly commentators at the time also brushed aside the deceit. The historian Robert Blake in an essay on Eden's premiership remarked that 'No one of sense will regard such falsehoods in a particularly serious light. The motive was the honourable one of avoiding further trouble in the Middle East.'[14] But how, precisely, would a successful invasion have assisted that project? The Big Lie so often seems more like a dodge for avoiding serious onward calculation, designed not only to deceive the public but also to lull the liars themselves into a false sense of having solved the problem.

Maintaining such views so stoutly did their proponents no visible harm. Selwyn Lloyd went on to become a highly respected Speaker of the House of Commons, and Robert Blake remained the doyen of Oxford historians and also became a Conservative peer. I cannot resist recalling here that Blake was for a time my politics tutor at Christ Church, Oxford, and also that I served Selwyn Lloyd as his assistant for six months when he was out of office and carrying out an enquiry into the organization of the Tory Party. Both men seemed to me kindly and decent, a little old-fashioned, perhaps, even a touch strait-laced.

Tony Blair and his in-house Svengali, Alastair Campbell, were equally unapologetic for the untruth about the non-existent Weapons of Mass Destruction which provided the pretext for the second Iraq War. This was plainly a perversion of the known facts about Iraq's armoury. There was a yawning gap between Blair's claim to the House of Commons on 24 September 2002 that the intelligence on Saddam's WMD was 'extensive, detailed and authoritative' and the Joint Intelligence Committee's assessment that the evidence available was 'sporadic and patchy' and 'remains limited'.[15] Nor can Blair's statement be excused as an inadvertent misspeak made in good faith. Evidence of clear intent to mislead inexorably trickled out. There was the memo of 14 March 2002 from Sir David Manning, Blair's foreign policy adviser, reporting to Blair on his conversation with US Secretary of State Condoleezza Rice: 'I said that you would not budge in your support for regime change but you had to manage a press, a Parliament and a public opinion that was very different from anything in the States.'[16] There later surfaced in *The Sunday Times* of 1 May 2005 the report dated 23 July 2002 of the conversations that 'C', alias Sir Richard Dearlove, head of MI6, Britain's intelligence service, had had with his counterparts in Washington, which contained the killer quote: 'the intelligence and facts were being fixed around the policy.' All this betokened not a careless overstatement but a deliberate untruth. And on top of that, an untruth which failed to foresee its own consequences.

So there are plenty of examples of leaders in democracies being prepared to lie to save their skins. Are Caesars any worse? There are, I think, two significant differences. In Caesarist regimes, the lying is systematic, proactive and unabashed, not simply an isolated set of untruths to get the leader out of a tight spot. Secondly, the Caesar denies his opponents any means to challenge his version of events. At least in a democracy there are consequences when and if the lie is exposed. The policy will be challenged in Parliament and the newspapers, chewed over by select committees and for years afterwards by inquiries like the Chilcot Report. Democracies have long memories. The Caesar and his public live for and in the moment. In a constitutional state, power exists to be challenged; in an unconstitutional state based on personal rule, it exists to be worshipped. The Suez lie turned out to be a disastrous blow to Britain's reputation: it was the end of imperial pretensions, and it precipitated the immediate end of Prime Minister Anthony Eden's career. Tony Blair's reputation was similarly trashed by the Iraq war and has never recovered. Democracies may tell lies, but they do not dare tell them with the brutal insouciance of Caesars.

The idea of the 'Noble Lie' – the untruth that is justified in the interests of the State – has an ancient parentage, and the arguments in its favour have seeped into the mindsets of political leaders ever since. It is a shocking discovery that the man who has been acclaimed for centuries as the Father of Philosophy should turn out also to be the Father of Lies. In his *Republic*, Plato introduces his Myth of Blood and Soil with the candid admission that it is in fact a fraud. Well, then, says his Socrates, 'could we perhaps fabricate one of those very handy lies which we indeed mentioned just recently? With the help of one noble lie [*pseude gennaios*] we may, if we are lucky, persuade even the rulers themselves – but at any rate the rest of the city.'[17] Karl Popper points out in *The Open Society* that it won't do to pretend that Plato was merely talking about 'a bold invention' – to quote Francis Cornford's formulation – or 'a necessary myth', as it is sometimes presented by other charitable commentators. The word Plato uses is *pseude*, lie, not *muthos*, myth. Nor is it the case that the Greeks in general were soft on lying. On the contrary, Liddell and Scott's *A Greek–English Lexicon* lists about 200 compounds of *pseude* to fit every kind of deplorable falsehood – even more than it has for the varieties of demagoguery. I am disappointed only not to find there my own coinage of *pseudagora*, or 'fake marketplace', to describe the new press centre at No. 10 Downing Street. Plato's praise of the high-flown lie in *The Republic* is a deliberately shocking flight of fancy, designed to emphasize the artificial, fragile nature of a good society, and the need for its Guardians to deceive the common people, and as many as possible of the upper echelons as well, in order to keep the show on the road.

It is an intriguing possibility that even Plato in the fifth century BC was not quite the first thinker to praise lying as a necessary technique of the successful ruler. Plato had an uncle (or possibly a cousin) called Critias whom he mentions several times and of whom he was clearly fond. Critias was a well-known poet and playwright and a friend of the real-life Socrates. He was also a leading political figure in Athens. And when Sparta defeated the city in the bloody and prolonged Peloponnesian War, with Spartan backing he seized power along with a band of oligarchs who became known as the Thirty Tyrants. Their reign in 404 BC was as brief as it was brutal. It lasted only eight months, but is said to have caused the deaths of 5 per cent of the city's population. Another cousin of Plato's, Charmides, was also a prominent member of the junta. But it was Critias whose conspicuous cruelty has led him to be described as 'the first Robespierre'. He was killed during a successful counter-revolution by the democrats in the city. Critias and the Thirty were apparently commemorated by a bizarre anti-democratic monument showing the figure of Oligarchy setting fire to the figure of Democracy with the inscription: 'This is a memorial to those noble men who restrained the hubris of the Athenian demos for a short time.'

Only a few bits and pieces of Critias's wide-ranging work have survived. One fragment, attributed to Critias by the later Sceptic philosopher Sextus Empiricus, has also been said to be part of a lost tragedy about Sisyphus written by Euripides. But whoever wrote it, the surviving lines give us a full-blooded account from the fifth century BC of how men were ruthlessly conned into believing their founding myths of nation and religion. Originally, we are told, in the state of nature men lived lives of bestial anarchy – much as Hobbes was to describe the state of nature two millennia later. But Critias's story of the transition to civilized society bears little relation to the account of a peaceful agreement to set up a government – the 'social contract' made famous by John Locke and Jean-Jacques Rousseau. No, Critias tells us that it was all done by fraud and force (the way the Thirty Tyrants wanted to do it). Men were first bounced and diddled into civilization by a resourceful liar:

> Then came, it seems, that wise and cunning man
> The first inventor of the fear of gods . . .
> He framed a tale, a most alluring doctrine,
> Concealing truth by veils of lying lore.
> He told of the abode of awful gods,
> Up in revolving vaults, whence thunder roars
> And lightning's fearful flashes blind the eye . . .
> He thus encircled men by bonds of fear;
> Surrounding them by gods in fair abodes
> He charmed them by his spells, and daunted them –
> And lawlessness turned into law and order.[18]

So, Critias (or Euripides) concludes, that's how religion got invented:

And thus first did some man, as I deem, persuade
Men to suppose the race of gods exists.

Note that this is not just an argument in favour of atheism. It's a claim that religion was deliberately manufactured by lying rulers to persuade the common people to obey their laws. The 'noble lie' is not just a convenient fiction to get the Rulers out of a hole (though it may be that too), it is the basis of effective government. However much later commentators may try to soften and dilute the doctrine of Plato and Critias/Euripides, it remains the most cynical account of human political development you can imagine.

Machiavelli tells us pretty much the same story. In his *Discourses on Livy*, he says that 'it will be evident to anyone who carefully examines Roman history how useful religion was in controlling the armies, in giving courage to the plebeians, in keeping men good and in shaming the wicked.' In praising Numa, the successor to Romulus, he tells us that those times were very religious and the men with whom Numa had to work very ignorant, so he could imprint their minds with whatever he fancied.[19] But in Machiavelli's own day, even the sophisticated people of Florence were easily persuaded that Fra Savonarola, the ascetic friar whose thunderous oratory bewitched them, spoke with God (in a letter, Machiavelli describes Savonarola's teaching quite simply as 'lies'). In other words, religion is vital as a means of social control, but no grown-up person can be expected to believe all this stuff. Deceit is, in any case, an essential part of the successful ruler's armoury:

> a sensible leader cannot and must not keep his word if by doing so he puts himself at risk, and if the reasons that made him give his word in the first place are no longer valid. If all men were good, this would be bad advice, but since they are a sad lot and won't be keeping their promises to you, you hardly need to keep yours to them. Anyway, a ruler will never be short of reasons to explain away a broken promise.[20]

Machiavelli gives as a ripe example Pope Alexander VI, who 'never did anything but con people. That was all he ever thought about. And he always found people he could con . . . no one ever kept his promises less; yet his deceptions always worked, because he knew this side of human nature so well.'[21] Essentially, the argument is that the prudent

Prince must be 'a great feigner and dissembler' if he is to survive. He must break promises when he needs to, because other men are equally dishonest.

Niccolò Machiavelli's works were considered shocking the moment they began to circulate. Both his major works were placed on the Index of Prohibited Books by Paul IV in 1559. By then, there were 15 editions of *The Prince* and 19 of the *Discourses on Livy* in circulation. In England, the Machiavel became a stock figure on the Elizabethan and Jacobean stage. In Marlowe's *The Jew of Malta*, Machiavel delivers the prologue, denouncing religion as 'a childish toy' and declaring that 'there is no sin but ignorance'. The adjective 'Machiavellian' is first found in 1568, and then abundantly in the works of Greene, Chapman et al., with the same meaning it has today: deceitful, manipulative, ruthless, operating in the belief that the end justifies the means, the end being to secure and hold power over others at all costs.

Yet very soon, among intellectuals at least, Machiavelli begins to develop a quite different reputation, as the father of modern political science, perhaps the first, even the only man to see the world as it really is and then to tell it like it is, without fear of popes or princes. Quite early on, he is identified as a key figure in the transition from the medieval to the modern, from the religio-moral to the results-based secular approach on which we pride ourselves today. J. G. A. Pocock discerns 'a Machiavellian moment' in his seminal work of that title. On this reading, it is Machiavelli who injects the civic humanism of the Renaissance into the English and American thinkers of the seventeenth and eighteenth centuries.

This is a breathtaking double reputation for one man to possess. No less breathtaking, I think, is the ease with which the new Niccolò shrugs off Old Nick. Harvey Mansfield sets out to calm any lingering qualms at the outset of his massive treatise, *Machiavelli's Virtue*: 'in our situation the danger that we might regenerate the uncomprehending moral indignation of the early anti-Machiavellians is minimal. We moderns are all too cool, and we need a spark to sustain our interest in a question that used to stir serious passions.'

But there is a third group of readers, whose passions certainly have been stirred. The Big Beasts of the modern era, almost to a man, have lapped up *The Prince*. As well as Thomas Cromwell and Henry VIII, Charles V, the Holy Roman Emperor, was an early fan. Louis XIV called it 'my favourite nightcap'. Hitler had a copy by his bedside. Mussolini called it 'the statesman's supreme guide' and wrote a new introduction. During the Hitler–Mussolini honeymoon, high-ranking Nazi officials scurried to get up to speed with the book. Metternich said that Napoleon had told him Machiavelli was the only author worth reading, although the story that a copy of *The Prince* annotated in the Emperor's hand was found in his carriage after Waterloo seems to be a Jesuit fabrication. Stalin certainly did annotate his copy.

It would be charitable to imagine that this third group of high-profile Machiavelli buffs were drawn by his subtle and rigorous analysis of the ten available books of Livy. It seems more probable that what made them salivate was the raw red meat: 'If you always want to play the good man in a world where most people are not good, you'll end up badly. Hence, if a ruler wants to survive, he'll have to learn to stop being good'; 'It's much safer to be feared than loved'; 'A ruler, then, must never stop thinking about war and preparing for war'; 'There is nothing more important than appearing to be religious.' And so on, and irresistibly on. How punchy, how deliciously shocking these bite-sized chunks are – just right for leaders whose attention span is notoriously short.

What strikes us forcefully both in his letters home and in his later re-castings in *The Prince* and *The Discourses* is Machiavelli's apparent lack of moral horror, or even physical recoil at what he sees in the world around him. His adulation of Cesare Borgia is not in the least dented when Borgia gathers his wayward *condottieri* together under false pretences at Sinigaglia and has them strangled, then goes on to behead his own Governor-General for the Romagna, Ramiro de Lorqua, placing his bloody head on display in the piazza at Cesena: 'Having given this summary of everything Cesare Borgia did, I can't find anything to criticize; on the contrary, I mean to propose him as a model for anyone who comes to power through fortunate circumstances or with the help of another ruler's armed forces.' The only black mark Machiavelli can think of is that Cesare was then had for a sucker by the equally vicious Pope Julius after he succeeded Cesare's appalling father in the Vatican.

Being a diplomat not a soldier, Niccolò had no experience of military command until he became Secretary of the Dieci and took charge of launching yet another attack to recapture Pisa. He cheerfully gave orders to ravage and lay waste with fire and sword, to demolish warehouses, burn down houses and, if necessary, kill the inhabitants. Three years later, he set off again with his half-trained yokels on a similar mission, burning crops and blocking Pisa's access to the sea until children were starving and the Pisans were living on rats. When neighbouring Lucca caved in, the Pisans were done for. If the siege had lasted longer, there is no reason to think that Machiavelli would have conducted its final stages with any more mercy than would Cesare Borgia. He clung to the argument that he had put back in 1499 in his *Discorso sopra le cose di Pisa* that the city could never be taken by love, only by brute force.

Thus Machiavelli had the opportunity to put into practice what he preached, and he did so with a vengeance, I think is the right phrase, although his friendlier commentators have not always drawn attention to his exploits in the real world. For Machiavelli, lying and brutality go together as the twin tools essential to the long-term survival of any ruler.

Friedrich Nietzsche had no such opportunity to leave his mark on practical politics. But he too heartily approves of leaders who deceive their subjects. For Nietzsche, in fact, lying takes on an extra dimension. It is not only an indispensable expedient to hang on to power, but also one of the ways the Great Man demonstrates his indifference to conventional morality, and hence his superiority. Unabashed mendacity is one more sign of his greatness: 'he must be forced to fight his way up with ingenuity and disingenuousness; his will to live must swell into an unconditional will to power and to supremacy.'[22] Nietzsche repeatedly emphasizes the need for total unscrupulousness. 'The great man senses that he has power over a people and that his concurrence with a people or a millennium is only temporary; he has an enlarged sense of himself . . . This forces him to adopt new means of communication; all great men are *ingenious* in devising such means.'[23]

This sense that telling the truth is for little people pops up among the modern American neocons, as it did in the belief of Leo Strauss, the favourite philosopher of American conservatives, 'that not all truths are always harmless': the popularization of some truths 'might import unease, turmoil and the release of popular passions hitherto held in check by tradition and religion'. There were, according to Irving Kristol, the founder of neoconservatism, 'different kinds of truth for different kinds of people', some suitable only for highly educated adults. Which was only to repeat the view of Senator Buzz Windrip, the would-be American dictator in Sinclair Lewis's dystopian novel, *It Can't Happen Here* (1935), that 'it is not fair to ordinary folks – it just confuses them – to make them try to swallow all the true facts that would be suitable to a higher class of people.'[24]

At the time, Buzz Windrip was widely compared to the unscrupulous Louisiana populist Huey Long, erstwhile Governor of Louisiana, who was assassinated in 1935 just before the publication of It Can't Happen Here when he was about to run for President on a populist ticket. But Huey Long was instantly forgotten when Donald Trump burst upon the national political scene in 2015–16. Immediately writers on both sides of the Atlantic agreed that, as Jacob Weisberg wrote, 'one can't read Lewis's novel today without flashes of Trumpian recognition.'[25] Trump was scarcely less candid about his technique than the fictional Buzz. What the Donald gave the people was, he said himself, 'truthful hyperbole which plays to people's fantasies'. It was only 'an innocent form of exaggeration'.[26] 'Hyperbole' must be about the longest word Trump has ever used in public. His discourse is otherwise at all times artfully monosyllabic.

The hostile media did not see this 'hyperbole' as innocent at all. Trump's whole campaigning style seemed to them part of a wider 'assault on truth' which was damaging politics all over the world. There are at least six books now in print with 'Assault on Truth' in their titles.

Clocking up Trump's lies has become something of a cottage industry for fact-checkers. The Washington Post's team recorded no fewer than 30,573 untruths uttered by Donald Trump during his presidency – averaging about 21 erroneous claims per day.[27] According to them, the rate of mendacity speeded up during his term, as though he were possessed by an increasing urge to lie. Some of the lies were trivial, of course, some were frivolous, some weaselly half-truths, but a hefty proportion were outright and serious. As an example of the trivial: Trump claimed that he was once named Man of the Year in Michigan. He never was. There was and is no such award. Yet in Michigan this lie was repeated at rally after rally. As was the most serious example, repeated ad nauseam: that he won the 2020 election – 'We won big' – and that the election was stolen from him by systematic and widespread voter fraud.

Nor has he ceased to fib since being thrown out of office, rehashing all the old disproved claims of voter fraud and the victory that was stolen from him. At a rally in Michigan in April 2022, he insisted: 'We did win. And you know, if we didn't, I'd be the first person to stand up and say we didn't.' In fact, 'I ran twice, I won twice, and we did much better the second time than the first. Now we may have to do it again.'[28] He also claimed to have won the state of Michigan, which he lost by 150,000 votes (repeated investigations have failed to find any evidence of fraud in the state), and of course he claimed yet again to have been named Michigan's Man of the Year.

Peter Oborne points out how long Trump has been at this game. In his detailed study of Trump's tweets, he quotes with deadly effect the messages that Trump issued between 11.29 and 11.39 p.m. on 6 November 2012, the night of Obama's re-election:

> We can't let this happen. We should march on Washington and stop this travesty. Our nation is totally divided! . . . Let's fight like hell and stop this great and disgusting injustice! The world is laughing at us . . . More votes equals a loss . . . revolution! . . . He lost the popular vote by a lot and won the election. We should have a revolution in this country![29]

These last two tweets were later deleted. But the damage was done. Eight years before he provoked that catastrophic march to the Capitol, he was already promoting the same lies and the same system-smashing – what Boris Johnson was to dismiss as 'all the toings and froings and all the kerfuffle'. The Trump-led campaign to overturn the Democrats' majority continues today with an even intenser ferocity. Republicans in 43 states have introduced 250 Bills to stiffen requirements for voter ID, restrict voting hours and postal voting and limit the number of drop-off boxes, despite the absence of any significant evidence of voter fraud in November 2020.[30] Yet all the polling evidence suggests that a large proportion of Republican voters, perhaps as many as half, continue to believe even Trump's most implausible claims.

Boris Johnson was first sacked for lying at the age of 23 when he fabricated a quote from his godfather, the Oxford scholar Colin Lucas. The editor of *The Times* gave him a second chance, but then Johnson wrote another equally unfounded story on the subject, and he had to go. He was sacked again when he was simultaneously editor of the *Spectator*, MP for Henley and a Tory shadow minister – having falsely assured the proprietor of the *Spectator* and the *Telegraph*, Conrad Black, that he wouldn't ever become an MP while editing the magazine. This time, he denied tabloid allegations that he was having an affair with a colleague, describing them as 'balderdash' and 'an inverted pyramid of piffle'. This was the first of many illicit affairs, and the Tory leader, Michael Howard, sacked him for lying about it. When Johnson left *The Times*, he crossed over to the *Telegraph*, where he became Brussels correspondent, and sent back a stream of confections and exaggerations about the EU's future plans: that the EU was about to ban prawn cocktail crisps; that there were plans to blow up the Berlaymont, the headquarters of the European Commission, and replace it with a skyscraper a kilometre high; that there were EU plans to standardize the size of coffins; that Brussels would be sending out inspectors to monitor how smelly farmyards were; that British sausages would be outlawed; that condom sizes were to be standardized because Italian men had smaller penises. None of these things ever happened. But their combined drift was to convince the British public that the EU was becoming a superstate that was out to destroy the British way of life and standardize everything. Conrad Black, himself no stranger to untruth (he was later jailed for fraud), paid generous tribute to his former editor as Johnson was about to enter Downing Street in July 2019 as 'such an effective correspondent for us in Brussels that he greatly influenced British opinion on this country's relations with Europe'.[31] Which is putting it rather mildly, but not untruthfully.

And when Johnson became, first the standard-bearer for the cause of Brexit, and then Tory leader and Prime Minister, he carried on where he left off. Oborne, formerly an admirer of Johnson and a supporter of Brexit, said, I think rather regretfully, that 'I have never encountered a senior British politician who lies and fabricates so shamelessly and so systematically as Boris Johnson.'[32] Reporters on the campaign trail lost count of the spanking new hospitals that were to be built which never materialized, the A&E departments to be kept open that then weren't, the thousands of extra policemen who never replaced the numbers lost after the Tory cuts, the non-existent 'baby boom after the Olympics'. In the Brexit campaign, the most eye-catching fib was the promise blazoned on the campaign bus that Britain would save £350 million a week by coming out of the EU; then there was Johnson's claim that Turkey was about to join the EU, followed by the denial that he had said any such thing. The worst lie, and the one still causing grievous problems, was the pledge that there would be no customs checks or controls between Great Britain and Northern Ireland, which became utterly implausible after Johnson struck his revised deal with the EU in October 2019.

The question is, how did a man so widely denounced as a habitual liar come out on top after the frenzy of the Brexit wars? We need to ask, not what made Boris run, but why did nobody stop him?

Boris Johnson and the Brexit Bus.

The Resistible Rise of Boris Johnson

In any crowd he stands out, and not just because of his tousled blond mop. There is a wilful apartness about this low-slung, chunky, slightly hunched figure. He wants to be in the thick of the crowd, you can see that, but he also wants to make you see that he is not part of it. His cold, grey-blue eyes stare straight ahead, not at the people around him, but rather, it seems, at some imagined, vaster crowd beyond. You can sense how precious his solitude is to him, as to other would-be Caesars, great and small. As de Gaulle once wrote, the leader 'dedicates himself to the solitude that is the sad fate of superior beings'. Sad, because 'That state of satisfaction, of inner peace, of calculated joy is incompatible with leadership.'[1]

Boris Johnson is so often described as a colourful character, not least by his inalienable fans. But when he was growing up, the colours were mostly dark ones. His family history was troubled and spasmodically violent. Johnson's great-grandfather, Ali Kemal, had become Interior Minister in Turkey after the fall of the Sultans in 1918. Forced to resign, he then waged a brave but vain campaign against the nationalism of Ataturk. In November 1922, he was kidnapped by his enemies and lynched. His corpse was hung from a tree. His son, Osman Ali, by his British–Swiss first wife, had the good fortune to be born out of harm's way in Bournemouth, in 1909. Osman Ali's mother died soon after his birth, and her own mother Margaret, née Johnson, adopted him and renamed him Wilfred Johnson, always known as Johnny.

While managing an estate in Egypt, Johnny met and married Irene Williams, a Lloyd's insurance heiress. During the Second World War, he volunteered as a pilot for RAF Coastal Command.

He crashed on a Devon hillside in front of his wife while dipping a wing in salute to her. Badly burnt and permanently lamed, Johnny bought a farm on Exmoor with his wife's money. This became a refuge for his son Stanley and the four children Stanley had with his wife Charlotte Fawcett. It remains a beloved bolt-hole for the family to this day.

This Exmoor idyll was clouded by Johnny's drinking and his regular infidelities and occasional violence. The pattern was repeated by Stanley, who, according to Charlotte, once broke her nose while he was hitting her.[2] Charlotte and Stanley eventually divorced, and she had a prolonged nervous breakdown, which meant that the children had more or less to bring themselves up. In later years, Charlotte said of her eldest son Boris, 'I have often thought that his being "world-king" was a wish to make himself unhurtable, invincible, somehow safe from the pains of your mother disappearing for eight months.'[3] Certainly Boris's serial adulteries and his ruthless competitive instinct were inherited if not copied from his father. Charlotte claimed that 'Boris's adultery is just like his father's. The motives were lack of love for their wives, boredom, selfishness and insecurity.'[4]

Both father and son won scholarships and prizes at their public schools and Oxford. But Boris's application was always more intense, more focused than his father's. An early training ground for his announced ambition to become world-king was his obsessive campaign to become president of the Oxford Union, which he achieved at the second attempt. Other driven characters have intrigued for this office, but none with quite the same concentration. Never good at making friends with other men, he gathered round him what he himself called 'a disciplined and deluded collection of stooges', promising them his help in campaigns for other Union posts. But of course he could not support them all, reflecting later that 'the terrible art of the candidate is to coddle the self-deception of the stooge,' an art he practised with increasing facility over the years. Already we can see, fully formed, his chilly, instrumental attitude to his colleagues (an attitude to be found in many aspiring politicians, but developed in Johnson to an extreme degree).

What was also already developed was his spiel, his patter, which he first worked up as a King's Scholar at Eton and which has never really altered: a hectic mélange of allusions to Wodehouse, Molesworth, Just William and the *Beano*, further enlivened by snatches of pop songs and dialogue from old junk movies, and given a top-dressing of quotations from Pericles and Homer. He also tosses in some of the cheesy intimacies of the stump preacher, addressing his audience, whether at party conferences or in his columns for the *Daily Telegraph*, as 'folks' or 'my friends' – which would have come across as fake and patronizing coming from anyone else, but from Boris merely confirms that what we are witnessing is a spiffing performance.

It all went down a storm at the Union. His contemporary, the journalist Toby Young, was bowled over, seeing in him 'something of Nietzsche's *Übermensch*. He had an electrifying, charismatic presence of a kind I'd only read about in books before.' His appearance and speaking style projected 'a state of advanced dishevelment and a sense of coiled strength, of an almost tangible will to power. He was the finished article.'[5]

It's important to catch our hero at this early wing-spreading stage, to grasp from the start how the persona was deliberately contrived as a political propellant, down to the careful rumpling of the hair just before coming on stage. The genius of it – I think the word is not too strong – was to package himself as a bumbling clown, someone whose motives could only be endearing ones and must therefore spring from a warm heart. We must feel sorry for his difficult childhood. His superb biographer Tom Bower, from whom I have gained much irreplaceable information, calls it 'untidy' – one can think of sharper, sadder adjectives. But we also have to take note of how quickly he weaponized his insecurities.

What kindly bystanders described as Boris's chaotic carry-on had in fact more purposeful objectives. The pursuit of sex and power came first; duties towards his colleagues and the institutions he was supposed to be serving barely figured in his priorities. This was first visible in adult life during his editorship of the *Spectator* (1999–2006). Or rather invisible, because he was out of the office so much of the time chasing women and parliamentary seats. So absent was he that he had to take the flak for a *Spectator* editorial (12 October 2004) blaming the Liverpool football fans for the Hillsborough disaster, although the leader was written by his deputy Simon Heffer and Johnson may not have even read it. All the same, Michael Howard, his party leader, forced him to go up to Liverpool and apologize, which he somehow managed to do and survive. A week later, his devoted girlfriend Petronella Wyatt endured a miscarriage (she had already reluctantly had an abortion). At least two later girlfriends did have children by him, making a total of around eight to date, although nobody is quite sure of the exact figure. The children of his much betrayed second wife Marina seem to have come off the worst. Not for the first or last time, 'the greased albino piglet', as one of his *Telegraph* colleagues had nicknamed him, survived these scrapes. His employer Conrad Black forgave his peccadillos with awed admiration: 'He's a very cunning operator. He is a fox disguised as a teddy bear. I don't know how he's kept it going for so long.'[6]

Johnson's election as MP for Henley in 2001 launched him on a parliamentary career which has now stretched over more than 20 years, but it was always a parliamentary career like no other. He showed little interest in the duties of a backbench MP. He did not volunteer for select committees, made few friends and few speeches and was seldom to be seen in the Chamber. In his first four years as an MP, he attended just over half the Commons votes, declining to 45 per cent in his second term. He was not much seen in the tea-room either. I do remember seeing him once or twice slouched in his seat under the gallery, appearing indifferent to the proceedings, rumpled and sulky-looking, rather like an offender who has been dragged along for an interview with his probation officer. The former Tory leader Iain Duncan Smith reflected that 'Boris did not enjoy Parliament. He was only interested in what would get him attention. Boris was always about Boris.'[7]

By contrast, he was an assiduous performer on television. Having first come to attention on *Have I Got News for You*, he was soon popping up everywhere: on *Question Time*, *Breakfast with Frost*, even *Top Gear* (he had somehow contrived to become Motoring Correspondent for *GQ* and loved whizzing about in the snazzy cars they provided). He was by now a national figure. Only at Westminster did his profile remain obscure and his bobbish gusto dampened.

Looking for where to go next, he became aware of the upcoming contest for Mayor of London. Ken Livingstone had slaughtered the Tory candidate in the previous two elections, to the extent that London was coming to be regarded as a Labour city. After initially hesitating, Johnson decided that it was worth a punt. With no better candidate in sight, David Cameron gave his consent, though with a certain nervous reluctance. If Boris could not pull London back, who could?

In contrast to his lackadaisical approach to the boring stuff at Westminster, Johnson threw himself into the campaign, concentrating his efforts on the Tory boroughs of outer London, which had been strangely neglected in previous campaigns. Commuters coming home to the end of the line – to Stanmore and Cockfosters, Richmond and Wimbledon – found Boris waiting for them with all his oomph and optimism. The Australian election guru, Lynton Crosby, had been pressed into service, and taught him how to concentrate on the core Tory issues, especially crime.

Johnson's victory against the odds was a brilliant one. For the next decade, he was to enjoy a deserved reputation as an election winner. And the Mayoralty offered him a perfect platform: prominence in the metropolis without overmuch responsibility. This agreeable situation was due to Margaret Thatcher's determination that Ken Livingstone should not be able to run rings round them again, as he had as leader of the Greater London Council. In her 1986 Act which abolished the GLC, the major functions were devolved to the individual boroughs, and the Labour Act of 1999 which invented the Mayor gave him real powers only over transport and the Metropolitan Police, Blair being as fearful of Livingstone as Thatcher had been.

So Johnson was left free to use his unique gifts to sell the city to the world, to weave extravagant schemes which never happened but kept people amused – the airport in the Thames Estuary (Boris Island), the Garden Bridge. One of his few memorable legacies, Boris bikes, had in fact first been mooted under Livingstone. His apotheosis as Mayor came during the London Olympics of 2012, which he boosted to the skies, literally so when he took to a zip wire in Victoria Park and got stuck halfway, waving two Union Jacks. It was an apparent debacle which endeared Boris to the whole nation. Crowds in Hyde Park and at the victory parade down the Mall roared his name. By contrast, George Osborne had been booed at the Olympic Stadium after his 'omnishambles' budget. The wonderful thing about being Mayor is that you weren't responsible for raising taxes.

In his early years as an MP, he was certainly not overtly hostile to the European project. He told the Commons in 2003: 'I am not by any means a Eurosceptic. In some ways, I am a bit of a fan of the European Union. If we did not have one, we would invent something like it.'[8] Preoccupied with his love affairs and then with being Mayor, he does not seem to have given much thought to the issue. But these were the years in which the Tory grassroots were drifting into an increasingly pronounced Euroscepticism, and UKIP was making alarming headway, under the ingenious leadership of Nigel Farage. By 2013, an opinion poll was reporting that 83 per cent of Tory party members wanted an EU referendum, and 70 per cent would vote Leave. Cameron had already promised in July that year that the next Conservative manifesto would include a commitment to hold a referendum. At a pub lunch with Johnson near Chequers just before the 2013 party conference, Cameron concluded that Johnson had no clear ideas on the subject, but in fact Boris was already drifting with the tide against the EU, and had proposed an In–Out referendum, in which he might vote to come out. At other times, he declared, as he did to Peter Ricketts, the British Ambassador in Paris, that 'I would vote to stay in the single market.'[9]

During the weekend of 17 February 2016, after visiting Cameron at No. 10, he sat down and wrote his two alternative versions for his *Daily Telegraph* column on Monday. Set side by side, he claimed, the case for Leave was 'blindingly obvious', and the Remain version 'stuck in my craw'. None of his Remainer friends, including his sister Rachel, could argue him off his decision. At teatime on Sunday, he went outside his front door to announce to the waiting scrum of reporters: 'I want a better deal for the people of this country, to save them money and to take back control. People are enraged by the inability of British politicians to control immigration.'[10]

He had crossed his Rubicon. It was still not clear in his mind exactly what Leave meant. But what was clear was that only by hitching himself to the Leave wagon train had he any hope of seizing the leadership. His fan base was all outside Parliament, among the people who were infatuated by the idea of kicking free of the Brussels bureaucracy. Inside Parliament, where there was an overwhelming preponderance of Remainers, he had few supporters. Even if the Remainers had won the referendum, he would have stationed himself as the sole leader of the true beating heart of the Conservative Party. It was, if not a no-brainer, a decision requiring only modest mental exertion.

During the months that followed, there was plenty of debate about what shape Brexit should take. Should the UK imitate Norway or Switzerland, remaining in some version of the single market and the customs union, but with no voice in either – a rule-taker, not a rule-maker? But wasn't that the worst of both worlds? Or should we go for a bare-bones trade deal, such as the EU was still negotiating with

Canada? Or would it be best to make a clean break and go for no deal at all? What was so congenial, though, was that Cameron had deliberately refused to plan for the consequences of a No vote, so the No voters were under no obligation to declare their hand either. The Vote Leave campaign followed the advice of its rapidly emerging guru, Dominic Cummings:

> Creating an exit plan that makes sense and which all reasonable people could unite around seems an almost insuperable task . . . There is much to be gained by swerving the whole issue . . . The sheer complexity of leaving would involve endless questions of detail that cannot be answered in such a place even were it to be 20,000 pages long, and the longer it is, the more errors are likely.[11]

And so they swerved.

Nothing could have suited Boris better. He was able to promise that Britain could continue to enjoy all the benefits of free trade with none of the ghastly Brussels bureaucracy and no steepling contributions to the European Budget, and above all no more immigrants taking British jobs. We would, in short, be able to have our cake and eat it. Never was Johnson's 'cakeism' more shamelessly and successfully deployed. The government's Project Fear gained little or no purchase. Since the debate on practical options never really happened, the field was left clear for a debate based on passion and loathing, and here Vote Leave held most of the high cards. Sovereignty was their ace of trumps. As a result, the greased albino slithered through to enjoy a triumph that was most conspicuously his.

But he had crossed only his first Rubicon. It was his vim and unscrupulous campaigning style that had delivered the goods. When David Cameron immediately stood down, was this now the moment for him to run for the leadership? He was all set to declare when Michael Gove, still his chief lieutenant as he had been throughout the Brexit campaign, emailed journalists to say that 'I have come, reluctantly, to the conclusion that Boris cannot provide the leadership or build the team for the task ahead.'[12] He had seen Boris at work over the past few days, not least at the Johnson family cricket match, and had concluded that he was too chaotic, too frivolous for the job (although Gove had had ample time to notice this during the months of the campaign). Instead, Gove proposed to complete the stab in the back by running for leader himself.

Immediately dozens of MPs switched over to Gove, having never really trusted Johnson. Besides, their constituency associations were said to be solid for Theresa May. By midday, Johnson had decided to pull out. Britain's new leader would need to unify the party and represent the country. 'But I must tell you, my friends . . . I have concluded that that person cannot be me.'[13] His more loyal supporters were shocked and angered by what they saw as bottling out. Yet there is a good case to be made that, in his own terms, he was right not to cross the second stream. He probably did not have enough support. Rather than split the party even further, and perhaps fail to reach the second round of the contest, he was able gracefully to accept Mrs May's offer of the Foreign Office, and build his profile in Parliament (he had, after all, not yet held any government office). From that distinguished eyrie, he could safely wait for her government to implode, as the European Reform Group flatly rejected every deal she put to Parliament, and Jeremy Corbyn equally flatly refused to collaborate with her (it was, after all, only with the Labour votes of Roy Jenkins and his pro-Europeans that Ted Heath had got Britain into the Common Market in the first place). After her rash decision to call a snap election in 2019, she found herself eight seats short of an overall majority.

As May slid towards a soft Brexit, Johnson hardened his line and made his opposition more vocal. This involved several further changes of position. When May accepted the Northern Ireland 'backstop', under which all Ireland would remain in alignment with the EU, perhaps indefinitely, Johnson first tweeted his congratulations,[14] then 24 hours later warned that Britain was on the way to becoming a vassal state of the EU.

On and on the battle raged, until on 5 July 2018 Theresa May unveiled her final offer to the EU, which amounted to a soft Brexit, with the UK staying in the single market and in alignment with the EU rule book, for the time being at least. Boris's reaction was rather more memorable than the contents of the 'Facilitated Customs Agreement', as it was called. 'It's a big turd which has emerged zombie-like from the coffin.' At the Chequers meeting the next day, he repeated that 'it's a big turd', and, looking round at May's Remain-heavy team, added, 'I see there are some excellent turd-polishers here.'[15]

This was another crux in the whole saga, not just because it precipitated the resignation of David Davis, the Brexit minister, and the next morning of a hesitant, rather shamefaced Johnson. His behaviour at the Chequers meeting had injected a new brutishness into the political debate. It was the equivalent of the rough language that Cromwell had deployed when dissolving the Rump. And Johnson carried on in that vein. When the Chequers plan was actually published in early November, he described it as 'an absolute stinker, leaving Britain a vassal state, a colony. This is not taking back control. It is a surrender of control.'[16]

Johnson's rough tactics were damnably successful. Theresa May did survive a confidence vote on 12 December; 117 out of 317 MPs voted against her. But she was fatally wounded. On 15 January 2019, the Withdrawal Agreement was defeated by a majority of 230, including 118 Tories, the biggest anti-government majority in history. In a second vote on 12 March, the Agreement was defeated by 149 votes. Then on 23 May, the Tories were almost wiped out by Nigel Farage's UKIP in the elections to the European Parliament. On 7 June, Mrs May resigned. On 23 July Boris Johnson scooted to an overwhelming victory over the Remainer Jeremy Hunt.

The new Prime Minister set about appointing a second-rate Cabinet composed almost exclusively of dedicated Brexiteers, and steamed on to fulfil his pledge to 'Get Brexit Done' – Cummings's peppy slogan. He had first to overcome the opposition of a Remainer-dominated Parliament, in which for the first time in the whole story Labour and Tory MPs combined to frustrate a no-deal Brexit. Hilary Benn's short Bill, known in its brief life as the Benn Act, made crashing out of the EU without a deal unlawful. Johnson responded, under Cummings' prompting, by approving a Prorogation of Parliament, during which he intended to put the screws on Brussels to offer a more favourable deal. This ingenious plan was eventually scuppered in the Supreme Court by the unanimous decision of Brenda Hale and her fellow justices to declare the Prorogation null and void.

The whole extraordinary affair exploded, as it was bound to do sooner or later, in another general election, which Johnson won hands down against Corbyn's enfeebled Labour Party, coming out with a comfortable majority of 80.

By an amazing sequence of coups, by turns daring, fluky and near-illegal, this improbable Prime Minister had become lord of all he surveyed, including hundreds of Tory MPs who had never liked him and still did not trust anything about him, except his unique ability to win elections.

Johnson's achievement looks all the more remarkable when you consider that he achieved it virtually on his own, without any corps of devoted supporters in Parliament (though plenty in the right-wing press). His only allies were allies of convenience, the successors to those hapless stooges who had helped him to the presidency of the Oxford Union. His true friends were 'out there', in the pubs and street markets and golf clubs and gathered round the TV screens. In this unrivalled popular appeal, he was unique among the British politicians of his age. As Edmund Burke said of the demagogue John Wilkes, whose campaign for liberty he supported: 'There has been no hero of the mob but Wilkes. He is not ours, and if he were, he is little to be trusted. He is a lively agreeable man, but of no prudence and no principles.'[17]

What sort of world-king would he turn out to be? For the emerging shape of his regime, we must first turn to the heart of it, to No. 10 Downing Street.

The Lectern

There was always something a little weird about the scene: the heavy lectern hurriedly dragged out into Downing Street from behind the iconic front door, as though the premises were suddenly out of action because of flood damage or bomb threat; then, on the other side of the road, the hacks and the pap pack awkwardly mustered and jostling for position. And the PM's statement itself, all too obviously scrabbled together at the last minute by some sleep-deprived spad, striving to match the historic significance of the occasion – an election lost or won, a leader toppled or triumphant – yet failing to conceal the struggle to hit the right note. How strange that the Queen's First Minister had nowhere else to speak to the nation from but a draughty pavement, competing with the noise of the birds and the rain and the traffic in Whitehall.

Not any more. Carved out of the old Privy Council Court Room in No. 9 Downing Street, where the judges used to meet to hear appeals from some convicted murderer in Barbados or the Cayman Islands, there is now a purpose-built *grande salle* for press conferences, knocked up for a mere £2.6 million by some friendly Russian contractors. It is not a pretty sight, resembling one of those crematorium chapels painted in bright colours to reassure you that death is nothing to be frightened of. The polished pilasters and the Union Jacks hanging limp either side of the podium suggest a newish nation-state searching for self-confidence – one of the lesser-known former Soviet-stans, perhaps. The lectern has DOWNING STREET gilded on it, as though we might otherwise forget where we are.

But the gimcrack fixtures and fittings should not delude us. This is deliberately designed to be a crucial new space in British politics: a place where day after day the Prime Minister can get his message across, unvarnished and unspun except by himself, mediated by nobody, with only footling interruptions from a tame Lobby. That process of disintermediation which swept over British banks 50 years ago has now well and truly arrived in British politics. The pandemic gave Boris Johnson and his ministers licence to address us directly almost daily, even when they had nothing very new or very true to tell us. Now it looks like becoming a permanent feature.

Under the old dispensation, familiar to us from the pages of Bagehot, Dicey and Jennings and surviving into the Crossman era and beyond, the Prime Minister spoke first and foremost to the House of Commons. By contrast, communications (not yet shortened to comms) to the media and via the media to the public were sparse and obsessively private. In the morning, the PM's Press Secretary briefed the parliamentary Lobby in No. 10 in a scruffy underground cavern. In the afternoons, we trooped up a winding stair to a pokey room at the top of the Palace of Westminster. There, on Thursdays, we were briefed by what were coyly termed 'Blue Leader' and 'Red Leader' – the Leader of the House and the Leader of the Opposition or vice versa – and coded signals and sly digs were doled out to the hungry journos. All on terms of the utmost secrecy. Now the Prime Minister speaks to the nation whenever it takes his or her fancy.

At the same time, the role of Parliament as the grand inquisitor of the nation has been slipping. By 1995, Jack Straw was lamenting that 'in the last six years, every serious newspaper has abandoned its straight reporting of Parliament.' Almost overnight, a tradition that dated back to the Victorian era of devoting a page or more every day to coverage of the most important speeches delivered in the House had simply vanished.[1] Much was hoped from the televising of the Commons (1989 onwards), but the networks chose to broadcast only juicy snippets, and fewer and fewer of those as time went by, leaving it to their own correspondents to gloss the goings-on. Only the sketch writers remained in the reporters' gallery to squeeze whatever fun might be had, a standing temptation to MPs to try to entertain rather than to argue or inform.

The stage was already set in Blair's time for what his Chief of Staff, Jonathan Powell, warned would be 'a change from a feudal system of barons to a more Napoleonic system'.[2] The staff at No. 10 had notoriously been no larger than the staff of a mayor in a middle-sized German town. Over the last decades, it has swelled to a cast of hundreds. When asked on a BBC Radio 4 programme to describe the experience of being Prime Minister, Boris Johnson openly exulted that 'it's a job that is brilliantly supported by a massive team of people who have all evolved over hundreds of years into what is a big department of state now . . . So this is an incredible institution that has evolved over time into this extraordinary centre of a G7 economy.'[3] The centralization of power in Downing Street was taken a stage further in May 2022 when the Cabinet Office was split; the units responsible for economic, domestic, national security and intelligence policy were now to report to Samantha Jones, the Permanent Secretary at No. 10, rather than to Simon Case, the Cabinet Secretary. This move was embroidered with much talk of 'streamlining', 'cohesion' and 'accountability'. In practice, the effect was to clench more power in the Prime Minister's fist.[4]

All this has been deliberately engineered, not simply in the supposed interests of better government, but in the interests of dominating 'the narrative' – that post-modernist vogue word which was unknown in British politics before Tony Blair. New Labour told the government press officers at the outset: 'We are going to take the initiative with the media, announcing stories in a cycle determined by us.'[5] Less well remembered, perhaps, is Alastair Campbell's creation of a 'Head of Story Development'. This extraordinary post of Official Fabulist was filled by one Paul Hamill, who was to play an inglorious role in the fabrication of the Dodgy Dossier of September 2002. Boris Johnson could be relied on to act as his own Head of Story Development.

We were not too careful what we half-wished for. We did not anticipate what the effects of the new free-flowing, direct, 24/7 style of communication might be on the quality of the output. Here if anywhere, Kingsley Amis might have been right: that more might mean worse. In retrospect, the stuffy old rules guaranteed a certain vigilance against inaccurate, overblown or deceitful statements. Corrections and withdrawals could be demanded and insisted on, by the Speaker or by a resolution of the House. Careers could be wrecked on a single breach of etiquette, on a casual 'misspeaking' (another devious neologism). Take, for example, three celebrated post-war resignations: Hugh Dalton in 1947 as Chancellor for casually letting slip a couple of Budget secrets to a reporter, John Profumo in 1963 as Secretary for War for lying about his affair with Christine Keeler, Amber Rudd as Home Secretary in 2018 during the Windrush scandal for claiming to be ignorant of the government's immigration targets, although the figures had been sent to her. In Dalton's case, it was at worst a bit of indiscreet showing off. In Profumo's case, the lie was outrageous, but more remarkable perhaps was the fact that he could be compelled to come to the House to make a statement about a girlfriend (let's not think about the demands on parliamentary time if such a compulsion still operated today). In Rudd's case, if she hadn't read the figures, she ought to have. But they all had to go.

As for policy-making, a concern for accuracy was supposed to go hand in hand with a thorough and detailed examination of the pros and cons, proper submission of papers and keeping of records, rather than an aide scribbling on his knees during coffee on the sofa. There might, after all, be something to be said for 'the hard grind'.

It is important to repeat that all these rules and conventions are not merely the encrusted flummery of the ages. They are the machinery by which ministers are held accountable to Parliament, and also by which ministers and members of parliament are constrained by certain rules of conduct. These rules are crucial to the honest dispatch of business, not simply because they are of long standing. Take the Ministerial Code: 'It is of paramount importance that Ministers give accurate and truthful information to Parliament, correcting any inadvertent error at the earliest opportunity. Ministers who knowingly mislead Parliament will be expected to offer their resignation to the Prime Minister.' That Ministerial Code was introduced in 1997 as a response to the sleaze of the dying Tory government. But it is really only an offshoot of Erskine May, the guide to Commons practice and procedure which was first published by Thomas Erskine May in 1844 and has been revised in umpteen editions while essentially remaining the same, demanding honesty, probity, truthfulness and conformity to the rules of the House.

Could Boris Johnson's government be expected to maintain the same respect for accuracy and truthfulness, or to show the same reverence for the rules and decisions of Parliament? It seemed unlikely, given his own past indifference to the truth, his dislike of Parliamentary life and his insistence on getting his own way. His chief adviser, Dominic Cummings, was even more dismissive of Parliamentary flummery. Any assault on Parliament could also be expected to have the support of the tabloid press, which ever since Northcliffe's day has been impatient of Parliamentary deliberation and delay. Right from the outset, Northcliffe had promised his readers that 'a page of Parliament and columns of speeches will NOT be found in the Daily Mail.'[6]

Johnson's first administration lost no time in setting a more abrasive tone. The 2019 Tory Manifesto begins by proclaiming that 'we have been paralysed by a broken Parliament that simply refuses to deliver

Brexit.' Once again the rough language immediately recalls the violence of Cromwell's lambasting of the Rump: 'You are no Parliament,' 'You have sat here too long for any good you have been doing.' Nothing could beat the headline in the *Daily Mail* of 4 November 2016: 'ENEMIES OF THE PEOPLE'. This headline was written in response to the judgment of the High Court that government could not simply use its prerogative powers to trigger Article 50 and leave the EU without consulting Parliament. The journalist who wrote the headline, James Slack, later became May's and then Johnson's press spokesman at No. 10. He must have found a cheery welcome there. Johnson himself frequently echoed his Home Secretary, Priti Patel, in her attacks on 'lefty lawyers' – a phase I cannot imagine any previous Prime Minister or Home Secretary deploying. What was clear was that the right-wing press now saw Parliament as the barrier to a full-blown nationalism.

Daily Mail front page, 4 November 2016.

Boris Johnson's defenders will argue that all these squabbles vanished into the dustbin of history with his thumping victory in the election of 2019. How can you argue with a Commons majority of 80?

The Five Acts

Johnson's personal ambition fitted in neatly with the ambitious programme upon which the Tory Right was already engaged, of which leaving the EU was only the first and most conspicuous project. They hoped also to undo the constitutional and administrative reforms of the Blair years. The overall goal is often described as a sort of national populism, of the kind practised by Trump, Orbán, Bolsonaro and Erdoğan. But the mechanisms by which this new style was to be delivered and entrenched are peculiar to Britain, although we see certain common features pop up in most such regimes.

The hard Right always loathed what I'll call the Blair reforms (although some of them pre- or post-date him, and he wasn't always their most enthusiastic proponent). The indictment has been drawn up most plangently by the late Roger Scruton and most pugnaciously by Professor David Starkey. It accuses 'the liberal elite' of foisting five abominations on the long-suffering British people, who asked for none of them and find each of them alien intrusions: membership of the European Union, mass immigration, devolution to Scotland and Wales, the introduction of human rights into English and Scottish law and the invention of the Supreme Court. Taken together, Starkey claims, these reforms have led to 'serious and perhaps irreversible damage to the fabric of the historic British constitution'.

The Johnson government began the long haul of mitigating, if not obliterating these unwelcome innovations: by leaving the EU and abolishing the free movement of people; by forbidding another referendum on Scottish independence and denying any further powers to the devolved assemblies (if possible, cutting down the pretensions of the Scottish Executive to be a full-blown government).

Less often noticed but crucial is the refusal to restore in full the old financial freedoms of local government; the new initiatives to revive the North are strictly London-led, as was George Osborne's Northern Powerhouse.

The principal features of the programme were set out, quite candidly, in the Conservative manifesto for the 2019 general election. This is a remarkable document. Although in parts it repeats the bromides common to all party manifestos, promising more schools and hospitals, lower taxes and more policemen on the beat, it is unique in its personal focus on the party leader. Boris Johnson appears in seven large pictures, variously wearing Remembrance Day poppy, hard hat and hi-vis jacket. No Cabinet colleague gets much of a look-in. Half a dozen horny-handed labourers are allowed in on the final page, holding up a home-made cardboard placard reading 'We love Boris.'

Apart from this wince-making cult of personality, the manifesto includes several reforms of the political system with the unabashed intent of strengthening the Tory hold on power. These reforms need to be listed severally and with care, as they add up to a systematic challenge to our system of parliamentary democracy as it has evolved over several centuries.

The intended net effect would be to restore the unqualified control of the majority in the House of Commons in all matters. It was to restore, in all its brutal simplicity, what Lord Hailsham in his Dimbleby lecture of 1976 famously called Britain's 'elective dictatorship'. (The phrase had first been used of Garibaldi.) Hailsham had used the phrase before in 1968 and 1969, thus always when Labour was in power; never, heaven forfend, when he himself was Lord Chancellor. He assumed, and most Conservatives would have agreed with him, that the dangers of an unbridled Commons majority applied only to a left-wing government. Only Labour governments proudly deployed their majority as the 'battering ram of social change', to use Dick Crossman's pretty phrase. Not any more. This Long March through the institutions is being conducted by the Right. Let us run through its marching orders.

- *Dissolving Parliament* The manifesto promises that 'we will get rid of the Fixed Term Parliaments Act – it has led to paralysis at a time the country needed decisive action.' And in March 2022 this pledge was amply fulfilled, when the Dissolution and Calling of Parliament Act came into force, repealing the 2011 Fixed-Term Parliaments Act. But the new Act purported to do rather more. Section 3 contained an 'ouster clause', which seeks to ensure 'the non-justiciability of the revived prerogative power'. In other words, no future Supreme Court would be able to strike down the Prime Minister's use of his power to dissolve. The old ambiguity about when and if the King could refuse a request to dissolve is now claimed to have been ended (although some legal experts continue to doubt how fully effective the new law is likely to prove). In future, the King is to dissolve 'on the advice' of his Prime Minister. He has no alternative. And the courts are to have no say in the matter. The House of Lords attempted to offer the House of Commons a get-out, by inserting a clause requiring a Commons vote before the dissolution could happen. The Tory majority in the Commons took the clause out again. In other words, the Commons was being offered a say, and what it said was 'no thanks', thus clarifying that the net effect of the Act is to diminish the power of Parliament for good and all.

In future, the Prime Minister of the day will have untrammelled power to dissolve Parliament whenever he fancies. Before 2011, he had, let us say, two-thirds of that power, but he was bound by some conventions of decent behaviour. Not any more.

• *Sacking MPs* Boris Johnson's first really striking act as Prime Minister was to expel 21 of his senior pro-European MPs from the parliamentary party on 3 September 2019. The purge included two ex-Chancellors, Philip Hammond and Kenneth Clarke, and seven former Cabinet ministers, many of them substantial figures, such as David Gauke, the former Justice Secretary, and Dominic Grieve, the former Attorney-General. Brexiteers regarded this as tit-for-tat after John Major's temporary expulsion of the Maastricht rebels in 1992. The difference is that Johnson's purge of the pro-Europeans became permanent for most of them at the subsequent general election. The manifesto made this brutally clear: 'With a new Parliament and a sensible majority government, we can get that deal through in days. It is oven-ready – and every single Conservative candidate at this election, all 635 of them, have [sic] pledged to vote for this deal as soon as

Parliament returns.' This brutal Stalinist uniformity has introduced a climate of fear unknown in the Conservative Party, and the loss of the 21 members has unmistakably weakened the Conservative Party's ability to represent the whole spread of Tory voters and to confront the future in a realistic spirit. Not simply was it difficult for the Conservative party to have a sensible debate about future relations with the EU, it was difficult to have a candid debate about anything. Johnson had already exiled most of his more talented MPs to the backbenches. For the rest of his brief time in office, even the second- and third-raters who succeeded them were quaking in their ministerial chairs.

• *Sacking civil servants* The centralization of power in Downing Street became apparent as soon as Johnson took office. The staff at No. 10 was hugely increased, and Dominic Cummings insisted on controlling the whole corps of special advisers in other departments. Most striking was his insistence, backed up by Johnson, that Sajid Javid as Chancellor should have his advisers chosen for him by No. 10. When Javid very properly refused to accept this indignity, he was removed and replaced by the more pliable Rishi Sunak.

No less remarkable was Johnson's removal, first of the Cabinet Secretary, Sir Mark Sedwill, and then a string of other permanent secretaries: Sir Philip Rutnam at the Home Office, Sir Jonathan Jones of the Government Legal Department, Sir Simon McDonald at the Foreign Office, Sir Richard Heaton at the Ministry of Justice and Melanie Dawes at the Ministry of Housing. No purge on this scale had happened before, certainly not in peacetime. In addition, Theresa May and Johnson had removed several of Britain's lead negotiators in the Brexit talks, regarding them as too soft on the EU. The latter was at least a defensible decision in the management of a specific mission, but getting rid of so many heads of government departments on an exasperated whim really alters the balance of power in Whitehall. Previously, and only very occasionally, if a Cabinet minister really found it impossible to work with his or her permanent secretary, the head of the civil service would find the perm. sec. in question another berth. But part of the essence of the British Civil Service was its independence as well as its impartiality; it existed to serve ministers, not to be hired and fired by them. Now it is clear that power over the Civil Service comes hot and strong from Downing Street. In these circumstances, the chances of young civil servants being ready to speak truth to power are sharply reduced. It also has to be pointed out that civil servants are responsible to Parliament and are frequently called to give evidence to select committees. If they are known to be merely puppets of their ministers, why bother calling them?

- *Taming the judges* Judicial review is a very good thing. I think any fair-minded person would applaud the power of British judges to strike down or reverse unjust or oppressive decisions by the authorities. Judicial review has always been with us, for 400 years at least, but it has expanded by leaps and bounds in recent decades. Mostly not because governments have passed a lot of new laws on the subject, but because government at all levels has become more complicated and there are more opportunities for incompetent or unkind decisions by central and local government and by other official bodies. And it is the powerless who get hurt most: the poor, victims of industrial injury, benefit claimants, refugees and other immigrants, prisoners, the unemployed or the unjustly dismissed. There has been a virtuous knock-on effect from this increase in judicial review: bureaucrats worry about 'the judge over your shoulder' and take more care about framing new laws and about administering them too.

Ministers used to grumble now and then when their decisions were overturned but, by and large, we were rather proud of this feature of the British system. That is, until the new Tory party became obsessed with illegal immigrants and refugees. 'Judicial overreach' was alleged to be allowing a flood of foreign undesirables to swamp our crowded island. Combined with abuse of the Human Rights Act, the law was undermining the British way of life. And so emerged the extraordinarily devious passage in the 2019 Manifesto, in which one perfectly reasonable sentence is followed, without any logical chain, by an unargued and illiberal pledge: 'The ability of our security services to defend us against terrorism and organized crime is critical.' Well, nobody is going to dispute that. But then: 'We will update the Human Rights

Act and administrative law to ensure that there is a proper balance between the rights of individuals, our vital national security and effective government.' So who says there isn't a proper balance now? And what proof is there that the Human Rights Act is to blame?

Similarly, moving on to judicial review: 'We will ensure that judicial review is available to protect the rights of individuals against an overbearing state' – oh, splendid, but – 'while ensuring that it is not abused to conduct politics by another means or to create needless delays'. But who is to decide whether the delays are needless, and what exactly does 'conduct politics by another means' imply?

Naturally, after the election, there had to be some sort of task force to work out what these cloudy threats might mean in practice. Lord Faulks, a QC and former Conservative Justice Minister, was appointed to head an Independent Review of Administrative Law. The Faulks Committee reported in July 2021 that, although there were one or two worrying cases, they couldn't see much wrong with the system. This wouldn't do. The Attorney-General deliberately misread the report and got going on the Judicial Review and Courts Act of 2022. As you might expect, while claiming to uphold the right of individuals to obtain remedy against unjust treatment, in practice the bill nibbles away at the individual's rights of appeal and access. And it provides an unsettling precedent for further limits, if hardliners come to think that this first bill hasn't gone far enough. I wrote this last sentence in the early months of 2022, shortly after the passage of the Act. On 8 August 2022, the *Guardian* reported that the Justice Secretary and Deputy Prime Minister, Dominic Raab, was indeed considering further slicing away at the right of judicial review, making it more difficult for claimants to sue the government and easier for the government to override the findings of the courts.

Even if Raab (or his successor) does not get his way, what is likely is that ministers, emboldened by this new protective cladding, will increasingly feel tempted to include 'Henry VIII clauses' in their Bills, giving themselves sweeping powers to interpret their Bill in any way they see fit. In the past, judicial review has provided a handy deterrent against this egregious style of lawmaking. If there was 'ministerial overreach', there was a good chance that the minister's decision might be overturned in the courts. So here's another way in which the Tory government is setting out to slash the trammels on its power.

• *Voter suppression* But of course in order to exercise power in this exuberant style, the Tories have to acquire power and hang on to it. The first priority is to win the upcoming general election, and prepare for the election after that. What is the best method of improving your chances? First, to adjust the boundaries of the constituencies to maximize the impact of your votes – so-called 'gerrymandering' – after Governor Elbridge Gerry in the nineteenth century, who fiddled the shape of the constituencies in the Boston area of the state of Massachusetts into an optimal pattern which resembled the outline of a salamander. Then, not only to encourage your voters to turn out by every possible means, but also to discourage the potential voters for the other side, either by preventing them from registering on the electoral roll or to make it difficult for them to cast their votes – so-called 'voter suppression'. Thirdly, most flagrantly, by stuffing the ballot boxes with votes by people who don't exist or have already voted or are not qualified to vote.

Modern Caesars unhesitatingly adopt all these tricks. In Hungary, for example, Viktor Orbán has secured a succession of thumping victories, sufficient to secure a super-majority of two-thirds, which enables him to change the constitution as he fancies. Hundreds, if not thousands, of illegitimate voters are regularly bussed over the border from Ukraine to vote for Orbán's Fidesz party. Within Hungary, improbably large numbers of voters are often registered at a single address. Postal votes of overseas Hungarians are systematically tampered with, to produce an incredible victory for Fidesz in this category of 96 per cent. Fidesz has also used its power to redraw the boundaries of constituencies, so that the opposition parties would have to win 300,000 more votes to win as many constituencies as Fidesz.[1]

In the United States, voter suppression is widespread and of long standing – sufficiently so to be referred to simply as VS. In recent years, more than 400 Bills have been introduced in 48 states to discourage voting by the worst off, either by requiring them to produce 'proof of citizenship', which the poor are unlikely to possess, or to introduce other stiff qualifications for registration, on the usually specious grounds of deterring voter fraud. Many such laws date back to the Jim Crow era, when legislators tried to deter black Americans from voting by imposing poll taxes. Today 36 states have ID requirements at the polls, and 21 million Black Americans are estimated to be disenfranchised. Recent Supreme Court judgments have undermined the access requirements of the 1965 Voting Rights Act, in *Shelby County v Holder* (2013) and more recently in *Brnovich v Democratic National Committee* (July 2021), where the right-wing majority on the court upheld the right of Arizona to reject certain ballots and to ban collection of early or absentee ballots. In a passionate dissenting judgment, Justice Elena Kagan declared:

> What is tragic here is that the Court has (yet again) rewritten – in order to weaken – a statute that stands as a monument to America's greatness and protects against its basest impulses. What is tragic is that the Court has damaged a statute designed to bring about the end of discrimination in voting.

In the wake of Trump's defeat in 2020, the Big Lie that the election was stolen has set Republican activists feverishly to work. By 24 March 2021, according to the Brennan Centre for Justice, legislators in 47 states had introduced 361 Bills with restrictive voting provisions.

In Brazil, Jair Bolsonaro has tried to change the voting system, adopting paper ballots after unfounded claims of fraud in the electronic system – but he was blocked by the lower house of Congress. In fact, hitherto Brazil's voting system has been remarkably snag-free and the elections notably fair. But Bolsonaro, faced with polls that showed him losing badly in the 2022 presidential election, decided to follow Trump's playbook and declare widespread fraud before the election even happened. In the event, Bolsonaro lost narrowly, sulked for a few days, then accepted the result, though with an ill grace. This was not quite the end of

Bolsonaro. Like Donald Trump, he retreated to Florida in a bitter rage. Then in a carbon copy of the Trump assault on the Capitol, on 8 January 2023, Bolsonaro's supporters in their thousands stormed the Presidential Palace in Brasilia, as well as the Parliament and the Supreme Court, and smashed them all up, in the vain hope that the indulgent military would come out in their support and overthrow the elected government of President Lula. Order was soon restored, but the damage to Brazilian democracy lingered.

British general elections, like Brazil's, have been remarkably free and fair for a long time – ever since voter personation and other dodges were finally eliminated in Northern Ireland. There has been no substantial evidence of fraud at any recent general election. Yet the Tories' 2019 election manifesto included this pledge: 'We will protect the integrity of our democracy by introducing voter identification to vote at polling stations, stopping postal vote harvesting and measures to prevent any foreign interference in elections.'

All this, now contained in the Elections Act, is an egregious solution to a non-existent problem. It can have one purpose only: to suppress the votes of the poorer and less organized voters who are less likely to possess photo ID. When voter ID was made mandatory in Northern Ireland in 2002, the number of voters on the new register dropped by 120,000 or 10 per cent. This suspicion is confirmed by a second pledge, to make it easier for British expats to vote in parliamentary elections, expats being plausibly thought far more likely to vote Tory, just as the worst off are more likely to vote Labour. Thus one set of voters whose fortunes do not depend on the actions of the UK is to be encouraged, while a far larger number of voters who do depend – often desperately – on what the British government does or does not do for them is to be discouraged. It is hard to imagine a more flagrant strategy to rig the result. It may be that as holding voter ID becomes more universal over the years, the adverse effect will diminish. But what is clear is that the motive behind the Elections Bill is to secure party advantage under the cloak of fairness.

At the same time, the Elections Act also introduces a new structure for the Electoral Commission, which has always been independent of government. In future, the Bill enables the government to set a strategic direction for the work of the Commission, which covers everything from the limits on campaign finance to the actual conduct of the polls. The Commission itself protested vigorously against the new arrangements (5 July 2021), that this overall government control was 'not consistent with the role that an independent Commission plays in a healthy democracy'. The Commission asserts, quite rightly, that 'this independence is fundamental to maintaining confidence in our electoral system.' The change is driven by Tory Brexiteers who are sore about being accused of having broken the law during the campaign for the 2016 referendum, an accusation of which they were eventually cleared. With government backing, the Tory Right may push the boundaries rather further next time.

To people who are not much interested in politics – which is most of us – these measures may sound relatively modest and technical. But once the government has power to reset the rules, it can progressively squeeze the shape and size of the electorate, make it easier to fiddle constituency boundaries and re-mould the rules of campaign finance. Johnson's Five Acts remain in force, and there are no plans to repeal any of them.

The Enemy at the Gates

The incoming Caesar loses no time in setting up an opposition between Us and Them. He mobilizes his supporters, by praising their unique patriotism and virtue and by promising to protect them and give their interests top priority. At the same time, and by lurid contrast, the Caesar will identify a pressing threat to their security and prosperity in the shape of the Other, the Enemy who is Within, or at the Gates, or both at the same time.

Sometimes the favours the Caesar dishes out to his supporters are straightforward material ones. Julius Caesar rewarded the veterans of his campaigns with large grants of land and money, but he also handed out a fair dollop of cash to the plebs of Rome to keep them happy. When the veterans complained that they should have received the lot, Caesar personally grabbed hold of one complainer and led him off to be executed. Two more complainers were ritually sacrificed by the priests on the Campus Martius. His clients had to be taught how to be grateful.[1] At the same time, he shored up his power, not only by reducing the power and activity of the Senate (the comitia was allowed to meet only with his permission, and not at all when he was away campaigning), but also by increasing the size of the Senate from 600 to 900, all the new arrivals owing their favour to him, many of them freedmen and Gauls, who were strangers to Rome. 'Here's a good deed! Don't show a new Senator the way to the Curia!' ran one graffito.[2]

Napoleon I owed a lot to the hard-faced men who had done well out of the Revolutionaries' forced confiscation of the abbeys and sale of the property of the aristos who had fled abroad. They would have been much reassured by the clause in his Coronation Oath which promised 'the irreversibility of the sale of the biens nationaux'.

The earlier Constitution of the Consulate had already been founded on 'the sacred rights of property, equality and liberty'. Goodbye to fraternity in the new bourgeois supremacy.

The same anxieties had to be appeased during England's Cromwellian Revolution. Oliver's great-grandfather, Morgan Williams from Glamorgan, who became an innkeeper in Putney, lucked out when he married Katherine Cromwell, the elder sister of Henry VIII's great minister. Morgan's son Richard changed his name to Cromwell some time before Thomas's fall from grace. Now and then, like others, Oliver would refer to himself as 'Cromwell alias Williams'. As a result of this match, the Cromwells acquired great estates on the site of a dissolved abbey and a dissolved convent outside Huntingdon. In this, they were like so many of Cromwell's associates among the Parliamentarians, notably Robert and Henry Rich, earls of Warwick and Holland, descendants of the iniquitous Sir Richard Rich. They were not simply ardent Puritans, they were also hard-faced men who had done well out of the Dissolution. The firebrand John Lambert too, the only one of them with the *cojones* to succeed Oliver, had inherited estates on the site of Bolton Priory. For all the bright moment of the Levellers, the Puritan leaders being who they were, this was never a revolution likely to end in substantial redistribution of property. As John Morrill hazards, 'It may indeed be that some of the obsessive anti-popery of the English landed groups in the 1620s and 1630s derived from a residual fear that their titles to land might become insecure if a popish or popishly-inclined king sought to unmake the Reformation.'[3] How they would have welcomed an explicit guarantee like the one Napoleon offered his supporters.

In our own time, Boris Johnson richly rewarded the Brexiteers he had staked his career on, who brought him to power and kept him there. All the best jobs in his government went to them, with dozens of seats in the House of Lords and the well-paid chairmanship of every kind of quango. At the same time, although Johnson personally had been on record as an enthusiast for openness and the benefits of immigration, he had to take on the rhetoric – and the programme too – of the Brexiteers, which was focused on the dangers of immigrants destroying the British way of life: hoovering up the best jobs, jumping the housing queue, hogging the social security budget, clogging up the NHS surgeries and hospital beds. Much of this rhetoric was absurd, seeing that employment remained surprisingly high throughout the recession, and that young British workers were reluctant to take on the backbreaking jobs picking fruit and veg customarily done by migrant workers, or the long hours and low pay in the hospitality sector. As for the NHS, you had only to look around you to see how many of the staff, from porters and nurses to senior consultants, were immigrants – and how many of them died during the first terrible outbreak of Covid-19. As soon as the new controls came into force shortages of key workers in all these sectors immediately became apparent. The rhetoric sounded especially graceless coming from senior Ministers who were themselves the descendants of recent immigrants. It is tempting to call them 'Drawbridge Tories', keen to bring down the portcullis as soon as they and their own families were safely inside 'this fortress built by Nature for herself / Against infection and the hand of war', to quote John of Gaunt.

The demonizing of immigrants as the Other became especially embarrassing when Russia invaded Ukraine in March 2022 and the rest of the EU suspended their visa requirements for Ukrainian refugees. Only the UK maintained its cumbersome system, while boasting about Britain's traditional openness to people fleeing injustice and repression. It was explained that the elaborate visa system had to be maintained to screen out sex traffickers or Russian spies, and not just the men either. 'I'm afraid it is naïve and misguided to think that only men can be covert operatives,' the Home Secretary, Priti Patel, told the Conservative Party conference in March 2022. 'There are those who would come to our country who would mean us harm and who plot to strike at our very way of life.' This ominous claim shows how Johnson and his claque were utterly subservient, even in the tragic circumstances of the war in Ukraine, to the hardliners who put them into power.

Immigrant panics are not exactly new in English history. The present system of controls was initiated by a series of Commonwealth Immigration Acts in the Sixties and Seventies, passed by both Tory and Labour governments (1962, 1968, 1971). Well before then there were the Aliens Acts of 1914 and 1919, targeted at German enemy aliens, and the trailblazing Act of 1905, directed, rather ineffectively, at the thousands of Jews fleeing the Czarist pogroms. Before that, there was the Aliens Act of 1793, targeted at refugees from the French Revolution.

Even Good Queen Bess was not immune from the virus. Although she employed Black musicians, she also issued proclamations against Black immigrants. In 1596, she wrote to various Lord Mayors telling them that there were 'of late divers blackamoores brought into this realm, of which kind of people there already here to manie', and ordered that these kinds of people should be 'cast forth of the land'. To assist the process, she cooked up a scheme with a German merchant called Casper van Senden to deport Blacks in exchange for English prisoners held by Spain and Portugal. Her proclamation of 1601 claimed that Blacks were 'fostered and relieved here to the great annoyance of the Queen's own liege people that want the relief, which those people consume' – in other words, that they were battening on the new social security system the Queen had just introduced. Unfortunately, the employers of the Blacks refused to let them go without proper compensation (shades of the abolition of the slave trade two centuries later), and van Senden failed to deport a single Black. At the time, there was also growing indignation against the hordes of skilled Huguenot refugees who had begun flooding in from France after the massacre of St Bartholomew. There is an interesting echo of this controversy in the play *Sir Thomas More*, by Shakespeare and others, although the immediate topic was the Mayday riots a century earlier, against the Lombard workmen who were said to be taking the jobs of decent Londoners. The case against intolerance to immigrants is put, once and for all, in a speech delivered by More, which is generally attributed to Shakespeare because it stands out for its brilliance:

Grant them removed, and grant that this your noise
Hath chid down all the majesty of England;
Imagine that you see the wretched strangers
Plodding to the ports and coasts for transportation,
And that you sit as kings in your desires,
Authority quite silent by your brawl,
And you in ruff of your opinions clothed;
What had you got? I'll tell you: you had taught
How insolence and strong hand should prevail,
How order should be quelled; and by this pattern
Not one of you should live an aged man,
For other ruffians, as their fancies wrought,
With self same hand, self reasons, and self rights,
Would shark on you, and men like ravenous fishes
Would feed on one another . . .

You too, More tells his audience, may be banished in your turn, and flee to countries that will treat you as strangers with barbarous contempt. You too may not find a safe abode on earth. This, he sums up, is 'the strangers' case, / And this your barbarous inhumanity'.

Thus none of the anxieties and complaints about immigrants 'swamping' the country are new, and neither are the proposed remedies. But none of the previous controversies has achieved quite the centrality that Boris Johnson gave the immigration question. At times, it seemed as if the whole Brexit argument and indeed the whole thrust of his government's policies were directed against illegal immigration. In his speech in Kent on 14 April 2022, boosting the new scheme to offshore refugees to Rwanda, he declared that 'the British people voted several times to control our borders, not to close them, but to control them.'

This deliberate foregrounding of the immigration issue is pungently reminiscent of Donald Trump's prime line of attack, carried out with his characteristic vulgar vim: for example, in his outburst to US Senators in January 2018: 'Why are we having all these people from shithole countries coming here?' – meaning among others Haiti, El Salvador and various African nations. This had consistently been his major theme. As he stood in Trump Tower in 2015 to announce his run for the White House, he denounced Mexicans attempting to enter the US as 'rapists and murders'. Hence 'the beautiful wall' which he planned to build along the border. Some of these remarks were glossed or diluted at the time or later, but never so much as to diminish their impact on Trump's fan base.

Nor of course are these inflammatory remarks lacking in practical follow-up. One of Trump's early actions as President was a commitment to end the Deferred Action for Childhood Arrivals Program to protect unaccompanied children at risk (the programme was immediately restored by Biden in January 2021). Immigrants from various Muslim-majority countries were also mostly forbidden entry to the US. And if the 'beautiful wall' was not actually completed, large sections of it were built at hideous expense and with little practical impact on rates of immigration, both legal and illegal.

In the UK, the Borders and Nationality Act became law at the end of April 2022 with the rest of Boris Johnson's Five Acts. Among a host of other provisions, it removes rights of family reunion from some categories of refugee. It's designed to deter desperate families from crossing the Channel in small boats. Instead, it proposes to submit them to 'offshore processing' in some third country (though it's not clear that this will be an effective deterrent). Several cash-strapped nations had already declined the privilege before Rwanda opened its arms. This small and dismally poor African country is still recovering from a hideous civil war and its human rights record is still widely criticized. The idea that such an unlucky place could provide the 'humane treatment' that Priti Patel promises is laughable. Not since English prisoners were jammed together out at sea in rotten hulks has a UK government displayed such a callous and dehumanizing attitude. Many of the agreement's provisions are deplorably vague and arbitrary – for example, all single male asylum seekers who crossed the Channel would be subject to detention and then deportation.[4] Critics of this bizarre scheme were divided between those who thought it unworkable and those who thought it cruel and inhumane; some people thought it both. In his Easter sermon, the Archbishop of Canterbury simply called it 'ungodly' – for which he was duly pilloried by Tory hardliners, who loved it.

Illegal migrants crossing the Channel from France to Britain
on 15 March 2022.

The notorious Clause 9 of the Act would allow the Home Secretary to strip individuals of their British nationality, in some cases without even notifying them. The UNHCR has declared that the Act breaches the UK's obligations under international law and under the Refugee Convention. Some of these provisions were softened or even removed under the constant pressure from the House of Lords. But the stain remains, and deliberately so. The hostility of this Conservative government to refugees is now purposefully baked into the public mind.

People can protest against all these measures, or can they? Steaming alongside in this same flotilla of illiberal legislation has been the enormous Police, Crime, Sentencing and Courts Act, all 300 pages of it. As such acts usually do (and have been doing ever since the mid-eighteenth century), it increases the maximum sentences for all sorts of serious crimes, stopping short of reintroducing capital punishment. These clauses are largely declaratory, designed to convince the public that the Tories are being tough on crime. The meat of the Bill is in the power it gives police forces to shut down and criminalize public demonstrations for being too noisy, including even a protest by a single individual. The police are of course to be their own judges of what is excessively noisy. Along with extending the powers of stop and search without any visible cause for suspicion, the Bill gives an ill-disposed police commander free rein to prevent people doing almost anything in the street of which he disapproves. We might note in passing that, in case the police find themselves short-handed when restoring order, Priti Patel also empowered special constables for the first time to carry tasers, light sabres by another name.[5] Shades of the Yeomanry sabres slashing and smashing at Peterloo! Nor will there be any shortage of storage space for the noisy offenders. The government boasts that it has embarked on the biggest prison-building programme for a century.

There were five of these Acts of Parliament receiving Royal Assent in the spring of 2022. They are all intended to increase government control in one sphere or another: over Parliament itself, over elections, over the courts, over immigrants and over public demonstrations. No legislative blitz like this has been seen in a century and more, not even when the notorious Sir William Joynson Hicks ('Jix') was Home Secretary. We have to go back to 1819 and the repressive panic after the Peterloo Massacre to find anything comparable, in the shape of the Six Acts cooked up by Lord Liverpool and his Home Secretary Henry Addington, by then Lord

Sidmouth. These Acts included restrictions on seditious meetings, on bail for defendants and on blasphemous and seditious libels (with a potential sentence of transportation), and new taxes on newspapers. Several of these acts were later diluted or repealed, but the collective impact of them has remained in our minds, as marking a low point in the history of British liberty. The Six Acts helped to provoke the Cato Street Conspiracy of 1820, the most violent plot against the British state after the Gunpowder Plot. Cato Street is one of the ripest examples of a coup that failed miserably (see 'The Dinner Party that Never Was', below). I cannot imagine that the Five Acts of 2022 will be remembered any more kindly. Let's be quite clear. A parliamentary Conservative Party which contained anything like the traditional broad spread of opinion would never have conceived, let alone assented to a single one of these ghastly laws.

One final flourish in this year-long campaign to reinforce the Prime Minister's power was the dilution of the Ministerial Code, which was all Johnson's own work and was personally signed off by him. Ministers who broke this code would no longer be expected to resign but, if they retained the PM's trust, would simply have to make a public apology or take a temporary salary cut. More flagrant still was Johnson's removal from his foreword to the code of the previous demand that ministers behave with 'integrity, objectivity, accountability, transparency, honesty and leadership in the public interest'.[6] In future, ministers may fail to fulfil any of these requirements with impunity, so long as they retain the PM's favour.

Big Caesars in the past have been no slouches in tightening their grip on power. After terrifying the wits out of the Establishment with a march on Rome by 30,000 Blackshirts, Benito Mussolini took office as Prime Minister on 28 October 1922 from the trembling hands of the King. In point of fact, he had not actually marched himself, preferring to descend as a sort of *deus ex machina* to rescue the nation from chaos (there is a nice parallel here with Trump not actually joining the March on the Capitol and watching the whole show on television). The next year, he passed the so-called Acerbo Law, which transformed Italy into a single national constituency and granted a two-thirds majority of the seats in Parliament to the party that received at least 25 per cent of the votes (his own) – what you might call a system of disproportional representation. Between 1925 and 1927, he transformed Italy into a one-party state. Then in 1928, he abolished the unpredictable inconvenience of parliamentary elections altogether, in favour of a plebiscite in which voters were presented with a single party list, which was then approved by 98.43 per cent. You can see why Attlee and Thatcher were so suspicious of referendums.

Adolf Hitler was even quicker off the mark, learning lessons perhaps from Mussolini's relative hesitancy and encouraged by his predecessor's unimpeded progress to one-man rule. After he had been sworn in as Chancellor in January 1933, the Nazi Party's share of the vote increased to 43.9 per cent in the March elections. Still without an overall majority, Hitler brought in the Enabling Act – its delicious official title was the *Gesetz zur Behebung der Not von Volk und Reich* (Law to Remedy the Distress of People and Realm). This was a euphemism of Olympian proportions for an act which gave Hitler's Cabinet the power for four years to enact laws without the consent of the Reichstag. Elections to the Reichstag were still held in 1936 and 1938, but voters were now presented with a single list of Nazis and fellow travellers ('Guests') – approved by over 96 per cent. Independent trade unions were in effect abolished as early as May 1933. In July 1933, the Pope signed a craven Concordat with Hitler, which kept the Church quiet. A network of Special Courts was set up in the same year, without rights of appeal or proper defence. In a plebiscite in July 1934, nearly 90 per cent of voters approved of Hitler becoming Führer. Job done. And of course the resident aliens, otherwise known as German Jews, were gradually stripped of their rights, their property and eventually their lives.

Little Caesars have to proceed more gingerly with their more limited ambitions, professing always to have the best interests of everyone at heart – voters, Parliament, the administration of justice, immigrants, even refugees – while at the same time semaphoring wildly to their supporters, 'Don't worry, you won't have to worry about these lefty do-gooders any more.' So-called 'virtue-signal' ʼg' by the Left has become a term of abuse. Its counterpart on ʦ'
Right is what the Australian political guru Lynton Crosby
'the dog whistle' – the signal to your fan base that their ˙
are being played, but played in too high a register tᴦ
nice-minded people. I've always thought this a ˙
whole point of these messages is that they havᴦ
loud and crude terms that even the thickᴦ
a virtuoso in this dark art, professing ʼ

decent policies, while at the same time talking about 'piccaninnies' and 'bum boys'.

But there should be no mistaking the strategic intent of his policies, as embodied in the Five Acts. The purpose is to narrow the possibilities of opposition and to remove as many impediments as possible to the exercise of power by the majority in the House of Commons. It is also to define first-class British citizenship more narrowly and to intensify border controls in every possible way.

Much cruder and more blatant is the campaign pitch adopted by Marine Le Pen in her 2022 presidential campaign. She claimed that her renamed party was offering a softer, more open approach than the Front National her father led. Yet her key proposal was to hold a referendum on 'citizenship, identity and immigration' that would enshrine discrimination in the constitution of France. There would be a 'national priority' for 'real' French citizens in employment, social benefits and public housing. This law would exclude non-nationals and dual nationals from any public sector jobs and restrict their access to welfare, and cancel automatic citizenship rights for children of non-nationals born in France. The same referendum would enshrine the primacy of French law over international treaties, to allow France 'to solve the problem of mass, uncontrolled immigration, so the French choose who comes, who stays, who leaves' – her words in the TV debate with Macron. This of course would undercut the freedom of movement inherent in EU membership and, if followed literally, would make it impossible for France to continue in the EU at all. This is the language of a modern Caesar, and you can pick up echoes of it in Viktor Orbán's Hungary, Jair Bolsonaro's Brazil or Vladimir Putin's Russia. But nowhere else today except the UK and the US has the fear of immigrants become the driving force behind a whole reorientation of domestic and international policy. In this department, Donald Trump and Boris Johnson – that remarkable mutual admiration society – have stood alone.

PART III

THE UNMAKING OF CAESARS

Most bets are losing bets. Most plays never make it to the stage. And most coups fail. The vast majority of would-be Caesars splutter briefly before being extinguished into exile if they are lucky, or hung, drawn and quartered if they aren't. Even if they make it to the podium, history offers no guarantee that they will manage to cling on for any significant length of time. Every Caesar sets out to cultivate 'the illusion of permanence' – once described as the aim of the British Raj in India, which did endure longer than most. The Third Reich in Germany was supposed to last for a thousand years; it lasted only 12. Even in his declining days, Boris Johnson was looking forward to ten years in power; he lasted barely another ten months. Just as there is no ineluctable process which certifies that any given liberal democracy will endure for ever, so the success and survival of Caesars are matters of rough contingency. There's nothing God-given about them, however much every Caesar may pretend to be Heaven's choice.

It is just as valuable to study why most Caesars fail as why a few succeed. By examining the factors that stop the majority in their tracks, we see more clearly how the weakness or absence of those factors lets through some candidates for power who, on the face of it, seem the most improbable chancers. In this section, we shall look at half a dozen of the most notorious failed coups in history: the Catiline Conspiracy, the Gunpowder Plot, the Cato Street Conspiracy, the Beer Hall Putsch, Mrs Gandhi's Emergency and Donald Trump's March on the Capitol. We shall also look, in some detail, at the toppling of Boris Johnson by his own MPs from a seemingly impregnable position. These are ripe and often bloody episodes that have lingered long in the memories of the nations which have suffered them. Their picturesque quality should not obscure the causes which contributed to their failure – in fact it highlights them. These causes can conveniently be grouped under five distinct headings, at least two or three of which usually combine to frustrate each abortive or short-lived coup. It goes without saying that a sixth cause is, quite simply, bad luck: the vital message which goes astray, the conspirator who oversleeps, the train that fails to arrive on time.

The first factor is **Force,** applied promptly and firmly enough to squash the plot as near its birth as possible. In practical terms, this means that there must be enough police and troops on the spot or near at hand, with commanders who will not hesitate to ͏ ͏ilize them and give them orders to wield their batons and fire ͏ ͏ This is a morally neutral observation. Nice-minded ͏ ͏that the force applied will be proportionate and not excessive or vengeful, not least because taking vengeance in such circumstances often rebounds, sooner or later, on the avengers. All I am saying is that there are circumstances — say, when the would-be Caesar has an army marching towards the gates of the city — in which counter-force, quickly, firmly and steadily applied, is the only way to stop the mischief.

But far more often the conspiracy against the status quo begins in a much smaller, more intimate forum, if not literally the Forum. Here the state's first requirement is for early and reliable **Intelligence.** Almost every regime known to history has deployed a secret service of some description to gather information about subversive movements and, with luck, nip trouble at its earliest budding. In reviewing the history of the British state, we cannot help noticing the remarkable penetration achieved by her spymasters, from the Elizabethan age to the present day. The failure of the intelligence services to detect that they themselves had been penetrated by Soviet agents during and after the Second World War is an embarrassing exception to the general rule. The use of *agents provocateurs* and the devising of ingenious set-ups to entice and ensnare the plotters have been frequently resorted to without hesitation or shame, and with the full approval — sometimes direct participation — of senior ministers of the Crown. But good intelligence, though vital, is not enough. The state has also to devise a narrative that establishes the moral turpitude of the plotters and justifies the legitimacy of its own counter-actions.

Here, **Eloquence** by the representatives of authority is a crucial, rather undervalued element in the process of restoring civil peace and the lawful order. All of them — parliamentarians, ministers, judges, generals, police chiefs — need not only to make vivid the threat to the established order which they are trying to foil but also convince the public of the legitimacy of that order. The importance of this has never been better shown than in Cicero's four famous speeches as Consul — two in the Senate, two out in the Forum — against Cat'²'
Conversely, the absence of articulated indignation from thᵣ democrats smoothed the seizure of power by Mussoliní
What an easy time of it they had, as they serially dᵛ machinery of democracy on their remorseless waᵛ one-party state. On a Lilliputian scale, we have
Five Acts, designed to dampen dissent and stᵣ slip through, not without public demonᵣ
little more than a whimper from the ·

Lawfulness. If the spokesmen for the status quo are to convince the public, they have to demonstrate that they are concerned to defend a legal order which is constitutionally grounded and is not simply a racket to protect the rich and powerful. They have to make clear that the would-be Caesar is intent on destroying rules and freedoms which have been carefully devised, often over the centuries, for the benefit of all citizens, not just the plutocrats. This public revaluation of the law as the foundation of civilized society is crucial, not only in the immediate campaign to discredit the Caesar as a callous destroyer, but also in the aftermath to rebuild public trust and re-establish the civil peace.

Finally comes **Diligence.** The revaluation of the law has to be demonstrated, not only in high-flown speeches but also in practical action. During and after the coup, officials at all levels have to show that they are carrying out their duties with honesty and diligence. As we shall see, Cicero's insistence on strangling, almost by his own hand, the five coup leaders in Rome, without affording them the due right of appeal, permanently besmirched his reputation. Conversely, the insistence in November and December 2020 of the returning officers in the close-fought US states that Joe Biden had been elected quite legitimately undermined Donald Trump's claim to have won (although millions of besotted Trumpers went on believing otherwise). The more meticulously officials carry out their duties, the quicker the attempt will fade into an evil memory rather than a still present danger.

There is no sharper, or more tragic contrast to be made than the comparison between the conduct of two modern European monarchs when faced with an extreme political challenge. When Mussolini's Blackshirts marched on Rome in 1922, the Prime Minister, Luigi Facta, wanted to declare a state of siege, but to his surprise the King, Vittorio Emanuele III, overruled him and, on the following day, appointed Mussolini as his Prime Minister, thus ushering in a brutal regime that was to last more than two decades and end with the Duce strung upside down by partisans at a petrol station. Yet in the general election the year before, the Fascist Party had secured only 50 out of 500-plus seats. There had been fewer than 30,000 men on Mussolini's March. Although his *squadristi* had been kicking up trouble all over the country, it should still have been possible to ˉare martial law and crush the uprising. Untold evil followed from ˙ ˉaving in, for which the word 'abject' is too mild.

By contrast, in Spain nearly 60 years later, it was the decisive action of King Juan Carlos which squashed the fascist coup, led by Lieutenant-Colonel Antonio Tejero. In February 1981, a gang of civil guards burst into the Congress chamber and held the deputies hostage, shouting abuse and firing wildly. The King, however, refused to receive any of the coup leaders, and a few hours later appeared on television in his uniform as Captain-General of the Armed Forces, to denounce the coup in superbly forthright terms: 'Given the events taking place in the Palace of Congress, I hereby confirm that I have ordered the civil authorities and the joint chiefs of staff to take any and all necessary measures to uphold constitutional order within the limits of the law.' The coup fizzled instantly. That is Lawfulness and Diligence in action. No doubt Mussolini would have been a tougher nut to crack than the somewhat deranged colonel. But the King of Italy should have made the effort, as the King of Spain was to do.

Force, Intelligence, Eloquence, Lawfulness, Diligence: these five requirements are not of course separable; they have to blend into any successful reassertion of legitimacy after an attempted coup. What might be called FIELDwork is a delicate combined operation. But it is one which carries its own obvious dangers: of toppling over into brute reaction, of failing to learn the necessary lessons and not paying attention to the discontents which provided the upstart Caesar with a plausible platform. FIELDwork is only a set of techniques for seeing off a threat to the civil peace. It is not a blueprint for long-term governance. And that too we shall see as we look closer at our selection of failed coups.

Catiline on the Run

Lucius Sergius Catilina was just about the baddest man in the whole damn town. At least, that's how the Roman historians tell it. Sallust, who was about 20 years younger than Catiline, says that he had 'an evil and depraved nature. From an early age he delighted in civil wars, bloodshed, pillage and political dissension.'[1] A century later, Plutarch was no more forgiving:

> Lucius Catiline, in addition to other great crimes, had once been accused of deflowering his own daughter and of killing his own brother, and fearing prosecution for this murder, he persuaded [the dictator] Sulla to put his brother's name, as though he were still alive, in the list of those who were to be put to death under proscription . . . Moreover, Catiline had corrupted a large part of the young men in the city, supplying them continually with amusements, banquets and amours, furnishing without stint the money to spend on these things.[2]

In short, a Jeffrey Epstein of the first century BC, with added violence.

Yet even within these hatchet jobs other possibilities are to be glimpsed. Catiline was born in 108 BC to one of the oldest Roman clans, the *gens Sergia*, but their fortunes had been on the slide for generations. The last Sergius to make it to consul had done so as far back as 380 BC. Catiline's lifelong ambition was to restore both the family's political prominence and his personal cash flow. And he started off well enough. In the so-called Social War, the first of the civil wars that bedevilled the city throughout the period, he served with distinction under the young Pompey and the young Cicero. He then occupied one of the stepping stones to power as praetor and was appointed a proconsul in Africa, from which on his return in

66 BC he hoped to make the great leap to consul, but a delegation from Africa, who claimed to have suffered at his hands, came to Rome and managed to get him indicted for extortion. Sallust himself had suffered a similar prosecution after returning from service in Africa as Julius Caesar's quartermaster. Like Sallust, with the support of family friends in the Senate, Catiline got off – Cicero even briefly considered acting as his defence counsel.

Sallust also pays tribute to Catiline's great vigour of mind and body: 'his body could endure hunger, cold and want of sleep to an incredible degree. His mind was reckless, cunning, adaptable, capable of any form of pretence or concealment; covetous of others' possessions, he was prodigal of his own . . . His insatiable mind always craved the excessive, the incredible, the impossible.' Ever since the dictatorship of Sulla, he had been possessed by 'the greatest passion for seizing control of the government, and he did not consider it at all important by what means he achieved his objective, so long as he gained sovereignty for himself.'[3] In fact, he was the archetype of the would-be Caesar. Boris Johnson is only one of the many parallels that leap to mind.

After the indictment, Catiline was barred from standing for consul. His sense of grievance was by now red-hot, and immediately afterwards he was allegedly involved in a plot to murder the consuls-elect Cotta and Torquatus at the opening of the new Senate session on 1 January, to seize the *fasces* – the bundle of sticks that was the emblem of Rome's government – and take over the city. Considerable mystery clouds the details of this plot. Various prominent characters are said to have been involved, including the plutocrat Crassus and Julius Caesar. Knowledge leaked out, and D-Day was postponed to 5 February, but was then a total flop, according to Sallust, because Catiline gave the signal prematurely to his fellow plotters in front of the Senate House before enough of them had gathered. Suetonius in his life of Julius Caesar tells a different story: that the plot failed because it was Caesar who did not give the agreed signal – letting his toga fall from his shoulder – when Crassus failed to turn up at the rendezvous.[4] In fact, Suetonius doesn't mention Catiline at all in his account of what used to be called the First Catilinarian Conspiracy. Perhaps he was implicated by posterity only because of his undoubted leadership of the Second Catiline Conspiracy the following year. Sir Ronald Syme dismisses the whole story in any of its versions as 'a tissue of improbabilities'.[5] The various stories of this first failed coup are worth mentioning, though, if only because it shows the feverish atmosphere in these last years of the Republic, and how difficult it was then, let alone now, to sort out exactly who was up to what.

Sallust gives a detailed and vivid account of how this second plot was hatched. Catiline, we must understand, had this irresistible charisma for the young – he himself was by now in his early forties – and especially the spendthrifts and rakehells who had already pissed away whatever inheritance they had. He knew not only how to show them a good time, but also how to tickle up their self-pity. He first wooed his chosen confederates one by one. Look, he said, you and I are in the same boat, talented brave fellows from good families, impoverished and diddled and scorned by the fat cats of the day. Why should they have all the cash, take over two or three houses belonging to other men to build their villas, level mountains and build out over the sea to gain more living space and those fantastic views of the bay?

Resentment against the vast seaside villas springing up along the Naples coast was widespread at the time. Horace in his *Odes* mocks the pretentious palaces of these parvenus:

> Look where the builder with his horde of navvies
> Drives the stone pilings deep into the water
> (The cramped fish lose more sea)
> And tips in rubble for the millionaire
> Bored with dry land . . .[6]

Sallust himself shares this distaste for these ghastly edifices,[7] and sees them as part of the general degeneracy of the times. He admits, quite frankly, that the plot has considerable popular backing: 'This insanity was not confined to those who were privy to the plot, but the whole body of the commons out of eagerness for change approved Catiline's undertaking.'[8] Looking back a century later, Plutarch confirms this verdict:

> all Etruria was roused to revolt, as well as most of Cisalpine Gaul [that is, most of northern Italy]. And Rome was most dangerously disposed towards change on account of the irregularity in the distribution of property, since men of the highest reputation and spirit had beggared themselves on shows, feasts, pursuit of office and buildings, and riches had streamed into the coffers of low-born and mean men, so that matters needed only a slight

impulse to disturb them, and it was in the power of any bold man to overthrow the commonwealth, which of itself was in a diseased condition.[9]

Catiline then calls his chosen ones together to build solidarity, and harangues them in the same vein. Sallust does not claim to have a verbatim report of Catiline's words. He merely offers us the report of 'a speech of this sort' (huiusce modi). This was the technique of his Greek predecessor Thucydides, whom Sallust venerated. The famous funeral orations of Pericles in Thucydides' masterpiece The Peloponnesian War are reconstructions of what Pericles would have said in the circumstances. Sallust writes in much the same way as his master: crisp, direct, without tortuous subordinate clauses or orotund antitheses, sticking to the facts as far as he knows them; a unique quality much savoured in antiquity. Quintilian praises Sallust's paciness, his 'immortalis velocitas'.[10] His only quirk is his taste for the occasional archaism to add a bit of zest. Sallust may not be as profound as Thucydides, but he can lay claim perhaps to be the first reporter in the modern sense.

There is no doubt about the identity of the men to whom Catiline gave his homily. Sallust lists them all: Publius Lentulus Sura, Publius Autronius, Gaius Cethegus and half a dozen more senators and knights, as well as a selection of discontented aristos from various towns in Italy. These were to become leaders of the revolt, and Sallust makes clear that they stuck to Catiline right to the bitter end. In the Q&A that followed his harangue, Catiline offered them plenty of 'red meat issues', to use the term in vogue among Boris Johnson's inner circle: cancellation of their debts, a massacre of the wealthy, profitable priesthoods and military commands. One or two of them had done well out of Sulla's confiscations 15 years earlier, but had fallen into horrendous debt trying to keep up their new estates.[11] Catiline promised to see them right, and more of the same. At the end of the proceedings, it was claimed afterwards by Catiline's enemies, bowls of human blood laced with wine were passed round to seal the conspiracy, but Sallust leaves us to conclude that this story was merely black propaganda. Later on, Catiline seems to have widened his appeal from the dispossessed to those who never possessed anything to start with.

Even at this early stage, there was a mole at work in his inner circle. A seedy gambler by the wonderful Carry On name of Quintus Curius, who had been expelled from the Senate for immorality, had been having a longstanding affair with a noblewoman called Fulvia.

When he became too poor to show her a good time and she began to weary of him, this blabbermouth tried to impress her by boasting what a big shot he was going to be and spilling all the details of the conspiracy, which she, being equally indiscreet, in turn spilled to all and sundry.

As the gossip spread, so did public alarm, and voters looked for a safe pair of middle-class hands, rather than another of these unreliable Alcibiades types. Marcus Tullius Cicero had been struggling to overcome his background as a mere equestrian from out of town, one of the *novi homines*, but in the general panic the voters decided that a New Man was just what they wanted, and he and Gaius Antonius were elected consuls for 63 BC and Catiline was rejected.

Catiline was not deterred in the slightest. He continued to recruit soldiers and borrow money all over Italy. He dispatched reliable colleagues to drum up armies outside Rome: Manlius in Etruria (the area round Fiesole), Gaius Julius in Apulia. Inside Rome, he laid booby traps, prepared roadblocks, egged on the more slothful conspirators. On the night of 6 November, he summoned the other gang leaders to the house of Marcus Porcius Laeca for a pep talk and a sitrep. Everything was ready. Manlius and the other provincial armies were in place, and Catiline himself would set out to join them, just as soon as he had neutralized Cicero. He tasked two of his upper-crust collaborators to go and stab Cicero in his house, on the pretext of paying a courtesy call shortly before sunrise, a *salutatio*, rather like the Scottish custom of first-footing. When Quintus Curius heard the plan, he zipped round to Fulvia's, and she immediately passed the intelligence on to Cicero, who frustrated the assassins by the simple means of barring his door to them.

This early warning not only saved Cicero's life, but also gave him a head start in frustrating the rebellion, which was already the subject of popular gossip, not least because of the unrest being stirred by Manlius and his men up north in Etruria. The next day, Cicero laid all he knew before the Senate, and persuaded them of the great danger the state stood in. He was readily granted an SCU, or Senatus Consultum Ultimum, the Senate's ultimate decree, conferring emergency powers on the consuls. Under the SCU, the appointee could raise an army, wage war, exert all sorts of compulsion over the people, without needing to seek Senate approval.

Luckily, there were two generals camping with their armies just outside Rome. Both had scored notable recent victories, Quintus Marcius Rex in

Cilicia and Quintus Metellus Creticus by subduing Crete (hence his last name). It was not unusual for such war heroes to be kept hanging about for the Senate's permission to cross the sacred boundary of the city with their armies intact, in order to celebrate the Triumph that had been granted them (such permission was usually granted only after a few palms had been greased). These handy troops were now dispatched to Fiesole, and further armies raised in other troubled districts. Gladiators were parcelled out in commando squads across Roman territory; in Rome itself, watchmen were posted on every tower.

While Catiline's preparations had been impressive, Cicero, with the whole military machine of Rome behind him, was able to set up a prompt counter-force – largely as a result of the stream of intelligence provided by Quintus Curius. The interesting thing is that, apart from the granting of the SCU, both sides had so far been mostly operating off-stage. There had been, so far as we know, no public confrontation, certainly not in the place that really mattered, the Senate. The moral control over events, the narrative as one would call it now (the Romans would certainly have recognized the force of that idea), had yet to be established.

Catiline had now to go public. He had already been arraigned by Lucius Paulus under the Plautian Law, a piece of legislation covering the unlawful use of weapons and the occupation of public places by armed men – the sort of legislation which would have come in handy in many other times and places, in preventing Hitler's rise to power, for example. Now he had to clear himself and offer some high-sounding justification for the actions of himself and his friends.

So he came into the Senate on 8 November, two nights after the meeting at Laeca's house at which he had gingered up his gang for immediate attack. But before Catiline could speak, Cicero launched into the first of his famous four speeches against him. I cannot resist quoting at length his thunderous opening, which has resounded down the ages and inspired many imitators:

> In heaven's name, Catiline, how long will you abuse our patience? How long will that madness of yours mock us? To what limit will your unbridled audacity vaunt itself? Is it nothing to you that the Palatine has its garrison by night, nothing to you that the city is full of patrols, nothing that the populace is in a panic, nothing that all honest men have joined forces, nothing that the Senate is convened in this stronghold? [For security reasons, the Senate was meeting not in the Curia, but in the Temple of Jupiter at the

upper end of the Forum.] Is it nothing to see the looks on all these faces? Do you not know that your plans are disclosed? Do you not see that your conspiracy is bound hand and foot by the knowledge of all these men? Which of us do you think is ignorant of what you did last night, what you did the night before, where you were, whom you called together, what plan you chose? What an age! What morals! [In the original Latin, *O tempora, o mores!* – the most celebrated of tags, lamenting that the country has gone to the dogs.][12]

Then Cicero embarks on a devastating unknotting of Catiline's preparations: 'You were, then, at the house of Laeca on that night, Catiline, you apportioned the parts of Italy, you determined where you wished each man to go, you selected those whom you would leave at Rome, you parcelled out the parts of the city to be burned, you averred that you yourself would go presently, you said that you would delay a little while because I was still alive.'[13] Cicero goes on to describe how the two Roman knights were sent to kill him on his couch that very night just before dawn, and how he had barred his door to them. Then with everything laid before the Senate, he delivers the crunching dismissal: 'Since this is the situation, Catiline, go whither you had intended, depart at last from the city; the gates are open; get on your way! That camp you share with Manlius has awaited you, its commander, for all too long a time. Take with you all these friends of yours, if not all, then as many as you can; purge the city.'[14]

At the end of this unstoppable denunciation – it must have taken about an hour to deliver – Cicero sits down, and Catiline rises, we are told, with downcast eyes and a pleading voice. He begs his fellow senators not to jump to conclusions. He, Catiline, came from one of Rome's oldest families, he had worked his way up to his present eminence and done the state much service – why would he choose to throw it all away, especially when the city's purported saviour was Marcus Tullius, a mere resident alien in Rome (Cicero came from a relatively unknown family in Arpinum, about 60 miles south-east of Rome)? It was this snobbish gibe that brought the enraged senators to their feet. Cicero pointed out how they had already shrunk away from Catiline; now they started shouting 'Traitor' and 'Assassin' at him. In a fury, Catiline retorted: 'Since I have been cornered and am being driven to desperation by my enemies, I shall put out the fire besetting me, not with water but with a greater ruin.' (*Ruina* was the term for fighting an urban fire by demolishing the structures in its path, a firebreak used so effectively to halt the spread of the Great Fire of London.)[15]

Senators flee from Catiline as Cicero denounces him,
by Cesare Maccari (1840–1919).

With that, he dashed out of the Senate to his house, and paused there to calculate the odds. He had failed to bump off Cicero, the watchmen were stationed to prevent arson: his only future was to leave Rome and beef up his own armies before Rome's legions were enrolled. Which he did, leaving Lentulus, the hot-tempered Cethegus and several others to keep the unrest bubbling in the city.

We can see now – and I think it was obvious at the time – that the confrontation in the Senate had been decisive. Catiline had lost any chance of taking power from the centre. Rome was mobilized against him. He was now an exile, an outcast. Although the fluctuating strength of the troops at his disposal may have reached as high as 20,000, he was essentially on the run. Compare with this dismal outcome for Catiline the violence in the Senate on the Ides of March nearly 20 years later. The assassination of Julius Caesar was a decisive moment which transferred power into the hands of the self-styled Liberators, at the cost of a terrible civil war. There is no substitute for brisk and brutal seizure of the state's command and control centre.

The very next day, 9 November, Cicero takes the opportunity to hammer home the message. His second oration against Catiline is delivered, not in the Senate but out in the Forum, to the people. It is a sustained exercise in character assassination. Catiline has fled, 'blazing with audacity, breathing forth crime, wickedly plotting the destruction of his country'. Beyond question, Cicero declares, we have defeated the leader of this civil war. We have driven him from his post of advantage. Now we can carry on an open war against a declared public enemy.

And what a ghastly crew he has taken with him: ruined old men, boorish hellraisers, bucolic wastrels, bail-skippers, gamblers, parricides. Cicero only wishes Catiline had taken a few more of them: 'these persons whom I see flitting about the forum, standing near the Senate House and even coming into the Senate, who shine with unguents, who are refulgent with purple, I would prefer that he had taken with him as soldiers; if they remain here, remember that we should not fear so much his army as those who have deserted his army.'[16] Why don't these no-goods push off now? If they set off down the Via Aurelia, they will overtake him by evening. 'How happy our nation will be after evacuating this sewage!'

See how vividly Cicero conjures up the scene of the day before:

> Yesterday when I had almost been killed in my own home I summoned the Senate into the Temple of Jupiter. I reported the whole matter to the body of the Senate. When Catiline arrived, what senator addressed him? Who saluted him? . . . Nay, more, the leading senators left that part of the benches, where he had taken his place, unoccupied and deserted.

Catiline had remained silent as Cicero had unveiled the details of the meeting at Laeca's. Then he had inquired why Catiline hesitated to go 'where he had long intended going, where already arms, axes, the fasces, the trumpets, the military standards, and that silver eagle for which he had already prepared a shrine of crime in his own house had been sent in advance, as I knew'. Cicero brings the people into the picture, as vividly as the most gifted TV reporter.

Then he renews his demolition of the seedy chancers who have flocked to Catiline, his bosom friends: 'these are the men that you see with their hair curled, sleek fellows, either beardless or abundantly bearded, with tunics that reach to their ankles and the wrists, clad in sails, not togas. All of their interest in life and their waking hours are devoted to banquets that begin before evening.' (Respectable citizens stayed at work until nightfall.) He then outlines all the precautions he has already taken to safeguard the city. And he ends with a shameless flourish of self-advertisement: 'And all these things will be so done, citizens, that the most important things will be administered with the least disturbance, the greatest perils will be averted without any tumult and a rebellion and a civil war, the greatest and most cruel within the memory of man, will be suppressed by me alone, a leader and commander, wearing the garb of peace.'[17] Cicero's habit of self-praise was much mocked. He never ceased to boast of his heroic role in saving the city single-handed, long after the whole affair was over.

The Second Oration firmly entrenched in the minds of the citizenry both what a bunch of scoundrels Catiline's gang was and how heroic and timely Cicero's actions had been. Yet many of the leading conspirators had been elected to high office in the city. They may have been dissolute, but they were not nobodies. Publius Cornelius Lentulus Sura had been quaestor to the dictator Lucius Cornelius Sulla. When Sulla accused him of wasting public money, Lentulus ironically held out the calf of his leg, a gesture of ball players inviting punishment for an error (rather like modern footballers holding up their hands), for which he acquired the suffix Sura (calf). Lentulus was later praetor again and consul (in 71) and, though expelled from the Senate with a number of others for immorality, was now praetor again in 63. What was to be significant for Cicero was that Lentulus, at the time of these events aged 50 or 51, was also the stepfather of Mark Antony.

Another leading plotter, Publius Autronius, had been consul in 61 and had been a friend of Cicero's in youth. The hot-tempered Gaius Cornelius Cethegus was a senator who had joined the conspiracy in the hope of getting his debts cancelled. Lucius Cassius Longinus had been a rival with Cicero for the consulship. He was so corpulent that his adiposity became proverbial – *Cassii adeps*.[18]

They were a mixed and mostly disreputable bunch, and no doubt Cicero's eloquence further diminished them in public esteem, but they represented quite a slice of the Roman establishment, and Sallust tells us firmly that, in spite of the senatorial decrees, not a single individual deserted Catiline's camp. Catiline's mob might be lowlifes, but there were a lot of other lowlifes in Rome who had fallen into debt or had their property confiscated by Sulla: 'such men had all flowed into the city as into a ship's bilge'.

For days after Catiline's flight, Rome remained a feverish and divided city. Then Cicero had a marvellous stroke of luck. Catiline had complained that Lentulus was lazy and dilatory, but now his chief lieutenant bestirred himself to recruit fresh allies to the conspiracy. He detailed a businessman called Publius Umbrenus, who had dealings in Transalpine Gaul (roughly the South of France) to contact two envoys of the Allobroges tribe who happened to be in Rome to plead for remission of their debts and taxes. The Allobroges lived in the Rhône Valley, between Vienne and Grenoble, and Umbrenus was probably a *negotiator* involved in moneylending and tax-collecting in the region. He caught up with the envoys in the Forum and pretended great sympathy with their financial plight. After hearing them out, he said, 'I'll show you a scheme which will get you out of this hole, if only you are ready to be real men.' Taking them to the nearby house of an absent friend, he told them all the details of the Catiline plot, promised them huge rewards if only they agreed to join it. They did, and then set off home again.

But when they got back to the Côtes du Rhône, the Allobroges paused to think. Was it really wise to place all their bets on this dubious and risky enterprise as against the mighty resources of the Roman state? They opted for Rome. And they told everything to their official agent there, Quintus Fabius Sanga, who went straight to Cicero.

Now Cicero showed why he really deserved at least some of the praise he showered on himself. He told the Allobroges to make a big show of their enthusiasm for the plot, and to demand from each of the leading conspirators a sealed oath to take back to their countrymen, for they could not be expected to join so hazardous an enterprise without some sort of guarantee. Lentulus and the others happily complied. The trap was set.

Cicero sent two of his praetors to arrest the Allobroges delegates carrying the sealed oaths on the Milvian Bridge to the north of the city (centuries later to be the scene of the Emperor Constantine's famous victory). Messengers sped back to Cicero to tell him the job was done.

Yet Cicero's troubles were not over, as he instantly realized. He was delighted that the disclosure of the plot had averted the peril, but uncertain what should be done to citizens of such high standing who had been detected in such a serious crime. Punishing them would bring trouble to him personally, he believed, but failure to punish them would be ruinous to the state.[19] He turned out to be right on both counts.

Anyway, there was nothing for it but to round up Lentulus and the rest. Cicero himself led Lentulus into the Senate by the hand because he was a praetor, and the guards brought the others into the Temple of Concord. Then came Cicero's Third Oration against Catiline, on 3 December, delivered like the second before the people rather than just to the senators, and this time not a reconstruction, because Cicero had a written record kept and later published of the Senate's meetings on 3, 4 and 5 December.[20]

He opened with a vivid description of the events of the night before: the praetors' secret mission to the Milvian Bridge, their stake-out in the villas nearest the bridge, then at three in the morning the envoys beginning to cross the bridge, and the praetors falling on them. The Allobroges surrendered the letters with the seals unbroken.

The letters were brought to Cicero's house just before dawn. Then he had the plotters brought in. One by one, they were shown the letters. 'We cut the string. We read.' One by one, they acknowledged their own handwriting. The impetuous and violent Cethegus was questioned about the pile of swords and daggers found in his house; his excuse was, 'I have always been a collector of fine weapons.' Now he was overwhelmed by his conscience and confessed. And so, slowly, reluctantly, did the others, eventually even Lentulus.

If theirs was an attempted coup d'état, Cicero had certainly brought off a coup de théâtre. Even during this dramatic retelling of the events of the past 24 hours, he cannot resist recording the thanksgiving to the immortal gods that the Senate decrees in his honour – 'an honour which I am the first magistrate in the civil service to receive since the founding of the city'.[21] At the same time, he bigs up Gaius Cethegus as an opponent only Cicero could have floored:

> He alone was to be feared of all those, but only so long as he was within the walls of the city. He knew everything, he knew how to approach all men he could and dared summon, tempt and entice . . . He could bear cold, thirst and hunger. This man, so bitter, so bold, so ready, so clever, so watchful in crime, so diligent in iniquity, if I had not driven him from plots within the city to a bandits' camp (I shall say what I think, citizens), I could not easily have lifted this burden of disaster from your necks.[22]

Night is approaching now, and Cicero sends the people home, bidding them give thanks to the gods for their deliverance, and of course also to their vigilant consul.

But the drama is not over yet. The plotters have to be dealt with, and quickly, before their supporters launch a rescue attempt. The following day, 4 December, the Senate heard and rejected as false the rumour that Crassus had been involved in the plot. Rewards were voted to the faithful Allobroges, who turned out to have backed the right horse. And the arrested plotters were declared public enemies.

The day after that, the senators met again in the Temple of Concord to decide the fate of the prisoners. This was the occasion of a classic debate and of Cicero's Fourth Oration *In Catilinam*, although the target himself was now far away in what we would now call Tuscany. The consul-elect Junius Silanus kicked off by arguing that the five prisoners should be put to death. The other consul-elect agreed, and so did the other speakers until Julius Caesar, who said that they should be sentenced to life imprisonment and exiled separately to various provincial towns.

Caesar's speech, given at length by Sallust (he doesn't mention Cicero's), is a model of thoughtfulness. He argues against the death sentences, not because they would be too cruel – 'for what measure against such men can be characterized as cruel?' – but because they might turn out to be 'contrary to the best interests of our country'. Bloodshed would beget bloodshed, as it had after Sulla's death sentences (and would again after Caesar's own murder).

The argument rages on, and Caesar seems to be having the best of it. When Cicero takes the floor, he sets out to give weight to both points of view (as befits the consul supervising the debate), but he makes it clear that he favours the death sentence. Not, of course, before he has referred twice more to the unique thanksgiving conferred on him by the Senate.[23] What he does also, as great orators have a knack of doing, is to make palpable the febrile scene: 'All men are here, of every order, of all classes, even of all ages. The forum is crowded, the temples about the forum are crowded, all the approaches to this temple and place are crowded.'[24] He reminds the assembly of their sacred duty to preserve the city and not shrink from the harsh requirements of justice. He ends by recalling the heroes of past and present who have saved Rome – Scipio, Marius, and now Pompey, and he prophesies that 'certainly there will be amid the praise of these men some place for my glory.'[25] Even in this desperately serious crisis, Cicero's comic self-importance never falters.

It's not at all clear, though, that Cicero has won the Senate over. But then the austere figure of Cato the Younger gets to his feet, and with a grim homily persuades them to vote by an overwhelming majority for the death penalty. It was a classic debate, in the tradition of the Senate at its best; every argument deployed and listened to – from law, from precedent, from justice and mercy, from political prudence. All the qualities that were to be dimmed for ever when the Republic eventually died.

What followed was not the least extraordinary event in the whole drama. The five conspirators were fetched from the various places where they were being guarded by the praetors. Because Lentulus was himself a praetor, Cicero personally led him by the hand from the Palatine Hill, along the Via Sacra, through the middle of the crowded Forum, the people silent and shuddering at the sight, according to Plutarch, 'especially the young men, as though they were being initiated with fear and trembling into some ancient mysteries of an aristocratic regime'.[26]

It was twilight by the time Cicero escorted Lentulus into the Mamertine Prison. Sallust describes the scene:

> In the prison, when you have gone a little way up towards the left, there is a place called the Tullianum [nothing to do with Marcus Tullius Cicero], about twelve feet below the surface of the ground. It is enclosed on all sides by walls, and overhead is a vaulted ceiling formed by stone arches; but neglect, darkness and stench give it a hideous and terrifying appearance. After Lentulus had been let down into this place, the executioners who had been charged with the task, strangled him with a loop of rope.

The other four, Cethegus included, met the same fate.[27] Forty years earlier, the Numidian King Jugurtha (the subject of Sallust's other big surviving work) had been executed here. The great Gaul leader Vercingetorix was imprisoned here for years before being paraded through the city in Caesar's Gallic Triumph in 46 BC and then executed. St Peter and St Paul were both held here before being executed. No single site reminds us more potently of the cruelty of Rome. The Tullianum is still there today, just behind the Victor Emanuel Monument, aka 'the Wedding Cake'. If you buy a combined ticket for the Forum and the Colosseum, you can climb down into the cell.

When the job was done, Cicero went back up to the Forum and saw a huge crowd still gathered in the gloaming, according to Plutarch, many of them still fancying a rescue attempt. To forestall this, Cicero cried out to the crowd 'Vixerunt' – they have lived. Posterity has remembered this one-word newsflash as an example of Cicero's laconic brilliance. But Plutarch tells us that 'it is thus that Romans who wish to avoid words of ill omen indicate death.'[28] In other words, it was a standard euphemism. At any rate, Cicero walked home bathed in the cheers of all the Romans who were grateful that he had saved the city with so little bloodshed.

There was plenty of bloodshed at the final battle a month later near Pistoia in Tuscany, in early January 62, in which Catiline and his lieutenants died fighting to the end. Sallust gives generous coverage to Catiline's last speech, his pre-match rouser, though it's not clear how he obtained his material, as virtually all the rebels lay dead on the battlefield. Catiline explains with great frankness their desperate plight. They are surrounded and vastly outmanned, but he exhorts them all to fight to the end, for they have nothing to lose: 'we and our opponents are not subject to the same constraints; we are contending for our native land, for freedom, for our very lives; theirs is a pointless exercise to fight on behalf of the power of a few men.'[29]

Thus, from his beginning to his end, Catiline maintains the same line: we are fighting for the dispossessed masses against the selfish plutocrats. Naturally, historians who come from the comfortable classes do not see things that way. Neither did Cicero. By the time of his own death nearly 20 years later, Mary Beard tells us, Cicero owned some 20 properties in Italy: a town mansion on the Palatine, one of those seaside villas on the Bay of Naples, and his own family estates at Arpinum, the total being worth something like 13 million sesterces, enough to feed 25,000 poor families for a year.[30] Posterity has shown little sympathy for Catiline, but good historians – and Sallust with all his faults was a very good historian – make it clear how deeply Catiline's rhetoric resonated with the common people, and what a huge rhetorical effort Cicero had to deploy to discredit his cause. His Eloquence played a leading role in the outcome, but only after his Intelligence had given him a head start. Because Cicero played his hand so well, we must not succumb to the temptation to think that the Catiline Revolt was a mere skirmish which never stood a chance.

And the punishments? How far did the dangers of tit-for-tat revenge killings, as foretold by Julius Caesar, come to pass? It was the peremptory executions of the five plotters without a proper trial that enabled Caesar and his allies to force Cicero into exile four years later in 58 BC, on the grounds that he had broken the *Lex Clodia*, which decreed expulsion from Rome for anyone who had put a citizen to death without trial. Thus, in carrying out the execution so precipitately, Cicero for all his resourcefulness and brilliance had offended against the fourth of the FIELDwork principles: Lawfulness.

We need not rehearse here the fate of Julius Caesar, which he brought upon himself by his later lawless actions. But we do need to recall Cicero's own ghastly end: his head chopped off by hired assassins as he leaned out of his litter on his way to his seaside villa at Formiae. Those assassins were sent by Mark Antony, who had plenty of reasons to loathe Cicero – the 14 Philippics that Cicero delivered against him, for a start. But not the least of those reasons was that Mark Antony was the stepson of Publius Cornelius Lentulus Sura.

Gunpowder, Treason and Plot(?)

Lo what my country should have done (have raised
An obelisk, or column to thy name,
Or if she would but modestly have praised
Thy fact, in brass or marble writ the same)
I, that am glad of thy great chance, shall do!
And proud, my works shall outlast common deeds,
Durst think it great, and worthy wonder too,
But thine, for which I do't, so much exceeds!
My country's parents have I many known;
But, saver of my country, THEE alone.

This little verse is Epigram LX by Ben Jonson, entitled 'To William Lord Mounteagle'. At first glance, it seems like a conventional tribute – though a strangely contorted one, all brackets and exclamation marks – to a noble lord who has done his country some unique service. On closer inspection, though, the whole contrivance dissolves into a riot of question marks.

Lord Mounteagle, more often spelled Monteagle, is famous to this day as the man who spilled the news of the Gunpowder Plot to Robert Cecil, Earl of Salisbury, and so saved the Houses of Parliament from being blown to bits with all the peers and half the Royal Family, not to mention saving the nation from rule by some undetermined Catholic monarch to replace James I. For all this, the nation has remained extravagantly thankful from that day to this. The first bonfires in celebration of the event were lit in the twilight of that first November the Fifth, 1605.[1]

The questions start with the poet himself. Ben Jonson, that rackety genius, had begun writing for the theatre only after working for years as a bricklayer and then as a soldier fighting his way across the Low Countries. His almost immediate success in the theatre was interrupted when he was jailed for killing a fellow actor in a brawl. While in jail, he converted to Catholicism, and on his release in Elizabeth's last years, he began to associate with the young bloods of the Catholic aristocracy. Only a month earlier, on 9 October 1605, he had been a guest at a dinner at the Irish Boy in the Strand, given by the arch-plotter Robert Catesby, and including the other key plotters Francis Tresham and Thomas Winter or Wintour.[2] This, it seems, was not just a casual night out but the last in a series of warm-ups for the plot, other dinners being given at the Mitre in Bread Street and the Bull in Daventry.[3] By this time, according to Winter's confession after the plot was discovered, he and Catesby and a soldier of fortune called Guy or Guido Fawkes (despite his Italian soubriquet, he was originally from Yorkshire but had been serving abroad) had been tunnelling for months under the House of Lords.

The Gunpowder Plotters, from left to right: Thomas Bates, Robert
Winter, Christopher Wright, John Wright, Thomas Percy, Guido Fawkes,
Robert Catesby and Thomas Winter.

After the plot was rumbled, Jonson realized how perilous his personal situation was, and scurried to answer Salisbury's frantic appeal, as early as 7 November, to track down a certain Catholic priest who might induce Fawkes to make a full confession. Jonson couldn't find him but, as further earnest of his loyalty, a few months later he was received back into the Church of England by the Bishop of London. This recantation looks primarily tactical, for on his deathbed he returned to Rome.

On closer reading, the poet's dedication seems a somewhat devious, perhaps even ironic one. How wholehearted was his admiration for Monteagle's action, how sorry was he really that the plot had failed? There was, after all, no greater ironist in the English language than 'rare Ben'. But the dedicatee was twice as dubious. William Parker had been summoned to Parliament as Lord Monteagle for the first time only the year before. He had been brought up as a Catholic and knighted by the Earl of Essex in Dublin in 1599, one of the many dubbed during that ill-fated expedition. On his return he had joined Essex's rebellion in February 1601, along with Tresham and Catesby.

This really was a half-cock coup. Following his Irish disgrace, Essex was a ruined man in every sense. After repeated pleas to the Queen, he was released from house arrest, but the last straw was the removal of his juicy monopoly on the import of sweet wines. A bunch of discontented Catholics began to congregate and conspire at Essex House in the Strand. Ludicrously, their first move, on 7 February, was to go across the river to the Globe to ask the Lord Chamberlain's Men to stage a special performance of Shakespeare's *Richard II*, the scene of the King's deposition included, which the troupe promised to do on a special payment of 40 shillings. The same day, the Privy Council summoned Essex to appear before them. Hastily that evening, Essex and his coterie planned the rising. They started the next day by seizing the Queen's messengers who had called at Essex House and holding them hostage, while Essex and his 200 followers set off to rouse the City. But Salisbury had already warned the Lord Mayor, denouncing Essex as a traitor. Nobody in the City joined the rebels, who themselves began to melt away. Essex retreated to Essex House. By the time he got there, his hostages had gone too, and the House was besieged by the Lord High Admiral, the Earl of Nottingham. Essex surrendered and was executed less than three weeks later, with four accomplice knights also losing their heads. The other high-born plotters – including Tresham, Catesby and Monteagle – were let off with fines. And when King James came to the throne a couple of years later, Monteagle scurried to make his peace with the new regime. He told his friends that he had 'done with all former plots', and wrote to the new King promising to conform to the State religion, blaming his errors on his youthful upbringing – 'I knew no better.' But he remained a suspect character, not least because his wife Elizabeth was the sister of Francis Tresham, and she seems to have remained a recusant all her life.

Which is why the events at his house in Hoxton on 26 October 1605 have remained one of the most celebrated mysteries in English history. According to the official account given later in 'The King's Book', Monteagle had turned up, somewhat unexpectedly, to dine for the first time in months at the house (which had come to him from Elizabeth, who was the daughter of the fabulously rich Sir Thomas Tresham). At about seven in the evening, Monteagle's servant Thomas Ward had gone out in the street, perhaps to take the air, and was accosted by a stranger, 'a man of reasonable tall personage' (which rules out the dwarfish Salisbury), who gave him a letter to take to his master. On receiving the letter, Monteagle broke open the seal, but then gave the letter either to Ward or to another servant to read aloud to the company.

Now why would he do this? Because his fingers are sticky with food? Because he cannot decipher the handwriting (the original letter survives, remarkably, in the Public Record Office, and it doesn't look too illegible to me)? Or because Monteagle already knows what is in it, and wants everyone else to know too? This last possibility seems irresistible. After all, in those dicey times, a letter brought in from an unknown source might spell any kind of trouble – certainly to a dodgy figure like Monteagle – and would surely best be read by the recipient alone, preferably in the privacy of his closet. Among other things, Thomas Ward had close family connections with fellow Yorkshire Catholics, including Jack and Kit Wright, who had been at school at St Peter's, York with Guy Fawkes, and also Oswald Tesimond and Edward Oldcorne, who both became Jesuit priests and were deeply implicated in the plot (Oldcorne was executed, Tesimond escaped abroad to tell the tale). Once read aloud at the table, the contents of the letter would be quickly broadcast to the wider community of Catholic dissidents.

What the letter said was:

My Lord, out of the love I bear to some of your friends, I have a care of your preservation. Therefore I would advise you, as you tender your life, to devise some excuse to shift of your attendance at this Parliament; for God and man hath concurred to punish the wickedness of this time. And think not slightly of this advertisement, but retire yourself into your country where you may expect the event in safety. For though there be no appearance of any stir, yet I say they shall receive a terrible blow this Parliament; and yet they shall not see who hurts them. This counsel is not to be condemned because it may do you good, and can do you no harm; for the danger is passed as soon as you have burnt the letter. And I hope God will give you the grace to make good use of it, to whose holy protection I commend you.[4]

The letter was later described as 'dark and doubtful', but its meaning, like the handwriting, is plain enough: don't go to the opening of Parliament on 5 November (it had already been postponed several times, on account of the plague); go to the country instead; everything may look quite peaceful ('no appearance of any stir' – the vogue word for rebellion), but 'a terrible blow' is on its way and you won't see it coming – which refers, pretty obviously, to some sort of explosion.

What happened next is also clear and undisputed. Rather than burning the letter, and despite the darkness and the lateness of the hour, Monteagle decided to take the letter himself down to Salisbury at his home in Whitehall. There he found the great man at dinner with other leading members of the Privy Council: Worcester, Northampton and Suffolk – all of them as it happened, more or less Catholic in their sympathies, as opposed to the sternly Protestant Salisbury.

Some have thought it too convenient, even fishy, that Monteagle should have found this quartet at dinner, as though assembled to receive just such a warning. But it was dinner time, and Privy Councillors in those days, like Cabinet ministers in the eighteenth and nineteenth centuries, spent many evenings dining together, drinking deep as they discussed affairs of state. The importance, rather, it seems to me, is that the letter is known to have been openly received in this fashion. The Commissioners who were later appointed to investigate the Plot included these three Catholic-inclined noblemen as well as Salisbury and Nottingham, he who had rounded up the wretched Essex. It would have been impossible for Salisbury or anyone else to make up the whole story and falsify the confessions of the plotters without the connivance of these men.

Another supposed cause of suspicion is what Salisbury did next: i.e., nothing much. He did not trouble to inform the King about the letter. James was away hunting at Royston in Cambridgeshire and could easily have been contacted, but he did not like to be disturbed at the chase. Salisbury let him be and allowed the plot to ripen

over the next few days. Strangely lackadaisical behaviour for such a
hyperactive man of business? Not really. What else could he effectively
do on the basis of a single letter which might turn out to be, as
Monteagle himself wondered, 'some foolish devised pasquil' (piece
of nonsense)?[5] In any case, the plotters would surely not move into
position until just before 5 November.

On the other side of the fence, though, the effect of the letter was
instantaneous. The next day, 27 October, one of Monteagle's servants,
probably Thomas Ward, went to see Thomas Wintour:

> Two days after, being Sunday at night, in came one to my chamber,
> and told me that a letter had been given to my Lord Monteagle
> to this effect, that he wished his lordship's absence from the
> Parliament because a blow would there be given, which letter he
> presently carried to my Lord of Salisbury. On the morrow I went
> to White Webbs and told it to Mr Catesby, assuring him withal that
> the matter was disclosed and wishing him in any wise to forsake
> his country.[6]

In other words, all is known, fly for your life. Catesby was unmoved:
'he told me he would see further as yet and resolved to send Mr
Fawkes to try the uttermost.'[7] White Webbs was the country house,
only a few miles north of London in Enfield Chase, which had been
rented by the Catholic zealot Anne Vaux to shelter Catholic priests on
the run, notably Father Henry Garnet, who heard news of the plot
from Father Greenway alias Tesimond.

Within 24 hours of Monteagle opening the letter, therefore, both
Salisbury and the plotters knew all about its contents. Whoever wrote
the letter and for whatever purpose – to frustrate the plot, to give
the plotters time to escape or simply to save the country's elite from
destruction – must have been well pleased.

So who did write it? Ever since, Catholic apologists have been
understandably eager to clear their co-religionists (and indeed the Pope
and the Church as a whole) of plotting such callous mass slaughter,
and have fingered Salisbury as the plot's prime contriver. Somehow,
we are told, he inveigled Catesby into it, which is psychologically
improbable, Catesby being such a self-willed, charismatic hothead
who usually did the inveigling. Hilaire Belloc, for one, declares that
'we have evidence that he [Catesby] was secretly received by Cecil, and
we are justified in suspecting, but not in affirming, Cecil's use of him;

he could be used as imperiled adventurers and double-dealing men often are by those in power, as an agent.'[8] But, as Alan Haynes points out, would Salisbury really risk unleashing such an unguided missile, especially at a time when he was deeply embroiled in negotiating the long hoped-for peace treaty with Spain to bring decades of war to an end? Besides, the only evidence that Catesby had any dealings with Salisbury rests on the deathbed confession of one of Catesby's servants, retailed in some unreliable gossipy memoirs published half a century later.

Again, Father John Gerard, namesake of the Father John Gerard who is said to have administered the Sacrament to the plotters, wrote a supposed exposé of Salisbury's role in *What was the Gunpowder Plot?* (1897):

> It is unquestionable that the government consistently falsified the story and the evidence as presented to the world, and that the points upon which they most insisted prove upon examination to be the most doubtful. There are grave reasons for the conclusion that the whole transaction was dexterously contrived for the purpose which in fact it opportunely served, by those who alone reaped benefit from it, and who showed themselves so unscrupulous in the manner of reaping.[9]

The great Whig historian S. R. Gardiner found Gerard's argument utterly implausible and fired off a forensic demolition the same year, *What the Gunpowder Plot Was.* In particular, he argues that the confessions of Fawkes and Wintour hang together in an entirely credible fashion. There is a sense of spontaneity about them, which makes it incredible that they were written to order or dictated by government agents. In particular, what the Government was after was evidence against the priests, and no such evidence can be extracted from these confessions. What is more, Gardiner rightly declares, you cannot read them without having your estimation of the conspirators raised.

> Each touch as it comes strengthens the belief that the men concerned in the plot were patient and loyal, brave beyond the limits of ordinary bravery and utterly without selfish aims. Could this result have been attained by a confession written to order or dictated by Salisbury or his agents, to whom the plotters were murderous villains of the basest kind?[10]

Of course, this does not rule out the possibility that Salisbury had got wind of the plot and wanted to warn the plotters off by concocting the letter to Monteagle. In the letter he drafted to English ambassadors abroad, he remarks that the Monteagle letter had been 'in a hand disguised'. The Jesuit historian Francis Edwards, who spent half a lifetime trying to prove that there never was a plot (in his spare time he devoted himself to proving that the Earl of Oxford wrote the works of William Shakespeare), argues that Salisbury could know this for sure, only if he had himself written the letter or got the code master Thomas Phelippes to write it for him. Phelippes had been chief of ops to Salisbury's father's spymaster, Sir Francis Walsingham, and had helped to wreck the Babington Plot against Queen Elizabeth, but had fallen out with the new regime. Might he not, as Haynes speculates in his life of Salisbury, have been eager to worm his way back into favour, first by sharing the information he had gathered about the movements of various Catholic dissidents on the Continent, including Guy Fawkes, and then offering to do the writing of the Monteagle letter to smoke out or disarm the conspirators?[11]

That's quite possible, although a stratagem which alerted the conspirators and allowed them to slink off with impunity sounds to me altogether too generous for Salisbury, and in any case would leave them free to devise fresh plots. Far better to catch them red-handed.

A stronger possibility is that Monteagle himself had the letter written to be delivered back to him – which would explain why the tall stranger knew how to get the letter brought in via Thomas Ward loitering outside the Hoxton house, perhaps enjoying a pipe of the tobacco which King James so detested as a health hazard. (The plotters were keen smokers, like many young bloods of the day, and I like to think of the King's fury as he watched them from his spyhole puffing away during their interrogations.) Monteagle's motive would be plain: to win huge credit with the King and entrench his shaky credentials as a loyal subject. It is noteworthy that he did not stop at delivering the letter. He managed to get himself invited by Suffolk to join the first search of Parliament 'both above and below' on 4 November, together with other members of the Privy Council. In the words of the King, Suffolk merely 'cast his careless and reckless eye' over the various lodgings that surrounded the Parliament Chamber. But he did at least spot the enormous pile of firewood heaped up in the cellar, far too much for such a modest lodging. What this first search party also discovered was that the lodging was now let to Thomas Percy, an unreliable Catholic, kinsman and agent to the Earl of Northumberland. Quick as a flash, Monteagle told Suffolk that Percy must be the one who had sent the letter, not only because of his 'backwardness' in religion, but also because of the 'old dearness of friendship' between him and Monteagle. Rather slackly, the search party then left the premises, being 'loath and dainty' to make a more thorough search now they knew the lodging was being rented by the influential Percy.[12]

The King was not so dainty. He ordered a smaller party under Sir Thomas Knyvett back to comb the Westminster cellars. And there at around midnight on 4 November, or shortly afterwards, the legendary figure in cloak and dark hat, booted and spurred as though for instant flight, was discovered, claiming to be John Johnson, servant to Thomas Percy. It was 48 hours after his arrest before he admitted to the name of Guido Fawkes. The 36 barrels of gunpowder discovered under the firewood were removed to the ordnance department at the Tower of London, and so was Guy Fawkes. Experts then and now agree that the quantity of gunpowder was quite enough to blow the Houses of Parliament sky-high.

The first arrest warrant the government issued was for Thomas Percy, described as a tall man with sloping shoulders, having 'a great broad beard' grizzled with white, and near-white hair: 'privy to one of the most horrible treasons ever contrived'.[13] But most historians deny that Percy wrote the Monteagle letter. Surely, if he was going to warn anyone, it would be his cousin and patron Northumberland? The most likely candidate was and is Monteagle's brother-in-law Francis Tresham. Not only would he be keen to save the life of his sister's husband; he also claimed afterwards, not once but several times, to have warned the other plotters of the dreadful consequences of going ahead and to have implored them to postpone or abandon the plot. As Antonia Fraser argues, the obvious suspect is surely the right one.[14] Tresham did not need to write to his brother-in-law. He could warn him face to face, and Monteagle could do the rest. One theory is that the actual letter was written by William Vavasour, Tresham's secretary-valet, who often scribed for his master.[15] We know that Tresham was in London on 25 or 26 October, because Thomas Wintour received 100 pounds from him on one of those days at his chambers in Clerkenwell, only a short step from Hoxton. The other conspirators were convinced that Tresham was the traitor. At White Webbs, Catesby and Wintour interrogated him sharply, but Tresham stuck to the denial that he had written the letter – a denial he maintained right up to his painful death from the agonizing urinary blockage known as strangury, which saved him from execution (though he was then decapitated *post mortem*).

The authorship of the letter has been as much of a distraction to historians as it was to the plotters and indeed the whole of London, which was shaken by the news of the narrow escape. The essential point is that what Fraser calls the 'No-plotters' are clearly mistaken:

> Salisbury's penetration of the plot is one thing, but the deliberate manufacture of the entire conspiracy with the aim of damning Catholicism is quite another. There is far too much evidence of treasonable Catholic enterprises in late Elizabethan times for the Gunpowder Plot to be dismissed altogether as malevolent invention. It was, on the contrary, a terrorist conspiracy spurred on by resentment of the King's broken promises.[16]

Ironically, it was to Thomas Percy, in Scotland before Elizabeth's death, that James had made those vague promises of better treatment for the Catholics when he came to the throne.

The most absurd argument is that offered by Father Edwards: that the leading conspirators would be unlikely to try it on again, having got off so lightly for their part in the Essex revolt only four years earlier. This is to misunderstand the obsessive recidivism of plotters. They never stop trying. Even after hearing that Monteagle had taken the letter to Salisbury, Catesby persisted in going ahead. Which makes it all the more unlikely that the crafty Salisbury would have dreamed of trying to provoke such a fanatic into action.

To see how rebellious spirits could become incurably addicted to plotting, we have only to review the avalanche of plots that beset England and Scotland over the previous 30 years: first, the conspiracies to remove or assassinate Elizabeth and place Mary Queen of Scots on the throne: the Ridolfi Plot (1571), the Throckmorton Plot (1583), the Babington Plot (1586). Then, after Mary's execution, there was the Essex Conspiracy of 1601 and finally the barely less chaotic two plots of 1603, so slapdash that they are distinguished only by their loose connection to one another – the Main Plot (mostly English noblemen), and the Bye Plot (mostly Catholic priests and, for once, a few unhappy Puritans).

These plots were often linked together by blood and memory. Francis Throckmorton, executed in 1580, had been a cousin of Catesby and Tresham. His beautiful family seat, Coughton Court, with its statutory priest's hole, was now rented out to Sir Everard Digby, the glamorous 13th and final conspirator of 1605 (Tresham had been the 12th recruit). Catesby had asked Digby to take Coughton as a convenient staging post to the West Midlands, where the rebels' presumed strength lay, 'to be better able to do good to the cause'.

There had also come to light, as the interrogations of the plotters proceeded, nuggets about the so-called 'Spanish treason'. In questioning Tresham and Tom Wintour, the authorities learnt that they, together with Catesby, Monteagle and Father Garnet, had negotiated for a Spanish invasion of England before the death of Elizabeth. Wintour claimed that during his visits to Spain in 1601 and 1603, Philip III had personally offered him admittedly vague promises of military support.[17] All this was not included in the official account of the whole affair. Not only was Monteagle now the official hero of the hour, but the new peace treaty with Spain also made it wildly impolitic to reveal that, only a couple of years earlier, Philip III had been receiving overtures from English traitors. The truth remains that, *pace* Father Edwards, this coterie of plotters had been willing to call in Spanish troops as well as blow up Parliament.

The background to these events was vengeful and blind on both sides: first, the dreadful cruelty of the persecutions under Bloody Mary (whose personal guilt cannot be washed away), then the matching anti-Catholic severity of the Elizabethan settlement, followed by Pope Pius V's excommunication of Elizabeth in 1570, which licensed her deposition and/or murder. Then the hopes briefly raised by the accession of James, still a relatively unknown quantity south of the border, then the abrupt dashing of those never very realistic hopes. Seen from the Protestant viewpoint, great unease was stirred by the stream of Jesuit priests into England and the popping up of stately safe houses for Papists across the Midlands, roughly from Northants to the Welsh border, with their Jesuit confessors tucked away in the ingenious priest's holes constructed by the ubiquitous Nicholas Owen, 'Little John', to Protestants as sinister a figure as the equally dwarfish Salisbury was to Catholics. Owen was canonized in 1970 by Paul VI; Salisbury is revered in conservative circles as one of England's greatest statesmen. Posterity smoothes away the terror.

The fiendish ingenuity of the second Cecil in countering these plots became a legend in his lifetime. But his father was no slouch either, and neither was his dreaded spymaster Sir Francis Walsingham, who sent shivers down the spines of dissident Catholics in Elizabeth's reign – and how hard it was not to be a dissident to some extent when not only the ordinary practice of your religion but also most avenues of worldly advancement were barred to you.

Walsingham's greatest coup was carried out by his double agent Gilbert Gifford. Mary Queen of Scots, now in poor health, was under house arrest at the moated Chartley Hall in Staffordshire, and pining to send and receive letters. Gifford, who happened to be a Staffordshire boy, offered the French Embassy his help in getting their letters to her. Mary was overjoyed when the first letters she had received for a year reached her in a barrel brought by the local brewer from Burton-on-Trent. The letters to and then fro had been sealed in a leather jacket and placed in a waterproof tube inserted into the bunghole. The codes that Mary and her correspondents used, however, were easily penetrated by the code wizard Thomas Phelippes, who sometimes decoded the letters on the spot before having them expertly resealed and sent on to the French Embassy and thence eventually to Paris under diplomatic immunity. As Fraser points out, everyone was happy: Mary and her French contacts, because they thought they could now communicate freely and securely; Walsingham and his team, who could read every word long before the French; and the Burton brewer, because he was being paid by both sides.[18] By these delicious means, Mary was lured into making increasingly explicit her support for young Anthony Babington's plot. Her last letter, which sealed her doom, ended: 'Let the great plot commence.'

Thus it would be just as absurd to maintain that these plots never existed as it would be to deny the foreknowledge and the cunning provocations of the Cecils and their spymasters. These twin elements seem to recur in almost every attempted coup, from Catiline to the present day, whether abortive or successful.

It is now accepted by the latest generation of historians – the revisers of the revisionists – that the English Civil War was not simply a contest between parliamentary supremacy and the Stuart claim to the divine right of Kings; nor was it only 'a war of three kingdoms', as Conrad Russell called it. John Morrill, for example, concludes that 'the English Civil War was not the first European revolution; it was the last of the wars of religion.' Surely we can stretch this thought further back. The British Isles were never exempt from the sixteenth- and early-seventeenth-century wars of religion. The conflicts were simply managed at a lower level of violence, without the deployment of large modern armies, except in Ireland, which as always came off worst. These home-grown conflicts between Catholic and Protestant erupted periodically in conspiracy, repression and judicial murder. The Gunpowder Plot was simply the most picturesque and alarming of these eruptions.

To understand the modest scale of the whole affair, consider the course of events after the discovery of the 36 barrels of gunpowder. Fawkes was arrested, and his long interrogations began, five of them before they resorted to torture. He was wonderfully phlegmatic. Sir William Waad, the Catholic-hating Lieutenant of the Tower, described him as passing the night of 6 November 'as a man devoid of all trouble of mind', though he had been told forcefully what lay in store for him.[19] Nor did he attempt to hide what he had been up to. At his very first interrogation – we are still on 5 November; how quickly it all moved – according to the record prepared for Sir Edward Coke, the Attorney-General, who conducted the examination along with the ferocious Chief Justice Popham,

> he confesseth that when the King had come to the Parliament House this present day, and the Upper House had been sitting, he meant to have fired the match and have fled for his own safety before the powder had taken fire, and confesseth that if he had not been apprehended this past night, he had blown up the Upper House, when the King, Lords, Bishops and others had been there.[20]

He did not at this stage mention the tunnel, or 'mine', which he and his friends had been digging until they discovered the convenient large storage room, or 'cellar', under the Chamber, which was in fact at ground level. Some writers have concluded that this was because the mine was really a fabrication of the authorities, designed to make the plot sound even more frightening. It seems more likely, though, that Fawkes didn't mention it until he was tortured, because he didn't want to talk about his fellow diggers and preferred to shoulder all the blame himself.

The other conspirators were not all so stoical. At 11 a.m. on Monday, 4 November, Thomas Percy called at Syon House to see what rumours about the Monteagle Letter had reached his kinsman

Northumberland, who was a member of the Privy Council. This visit pretty well ruined Northumberland, as Percy ought to have realized if he had not been in such a self-centred panic, but he was relieved to hear nothing out of the ordinary and returned to central London to reassure the others. That evening, Catesby set off for the Midlands, where the planned rising was to kidnap James's daughter, the little Princess Elizabeth, and install her as queen. It is typical of the plotters' insouciance that they were unaware that, though she was only nine years old, the Princess did not share her mother Anne of Denmark's Catholic enthusiasm and was already showing signs of the devout Protestantism that was to mark her whole later life when she became Elizabeth, 'the Winter Queen' of Bohemia.

By daylight on the fifth, Ambrose Rookwood and Tom Wintour were the only plotters left in London. While the others were galloping along the roads to the Midlands, the plucky Wintour went down to Westminster to see what was cooking. At King Street, he was checked by a guard in the street, and then overheard someone saying, 'There is a treason discovered in which the King and Lords were to have been blown up.' By the evening, Catesby had reached his family home, Ashby St Ledgers in Northamptonshire, riding in under the gatehouse where in happier days he and his friends had first meditated the coup. By now he knew that all was discovered. He told Digby and Tom's brother, Robert Wintour, that 'Mr Fawkes was taken and the whole plot discovered.'

Yet even now he did not give up: 'if true Catholics would now rise, he doubted not that they might procure to themselves good conditions.' They rode on to the West, to Warwick where they raided the castle for some fresh horses. The dwindling party hurried on towards Staffordshire. All across the Midlands, priests were being dug out of their priest's holes and arrested. The trouble was that the true Catholics refused to stir. By the time the company reached the Lion at Dunchurch, Northants, there were about a hundred in Catesby's party, and when they heard the desperate news, they began to melt away, until by 10p.m. there were only 40 left. By the time they crossed into Worcestershire, there were 30 of them to hear Mass at Huddington House, administered by Father Nicholas Hart, who also heard their confessions.[21]

The last stand was made at Holbeach House, near Kingswinford in Staffordshire, the home of the Littleton family. The local sheriff's force surrounded the house. In the brief scuffle, Catesby and Thomas

Percy were killed, according to Tom Wintour, by a single bullet. The Littletons, Stephen and his uncle Humphrey (collateral forebear of the jazz trumpeter), were later executed, although they were not active members of the conspiracy. The grisly rituals of interrogation, trial and execution, followed by hanging, drawing and quartering, were played out under the merciless supervision of the Attorney-General. It is ironic that in his later years Sir Edward Coke was to gain an undying reputation as the deviser of the Petition of Right and founding father of our constitutional liberties.

The aftermath is remarkable in several ways. First, for the lack of 'stir' among the oppressed Catholics. We cannot tell how many of them joined in the general jubilation at the nation's deliverance, but civil unrest was conspicuous by its absence. The Oath of Allegiance, composed the following year by the King, Salisbury and Archbishop Bancroft, effectively quietened large-scale resistance, though over the next decade at least 13 Catholics lost their lives in one way or another because of the Oath. Catholics continued to be harshly repressed, as they were to be for the next 200 years, but there was no mass pogrom. Punishments were restricted to proven plotters and to those priests like Father Garnet to whom they had confessed, and who had refused to break the seal of the confessional, even if it might mean saving hundreds of lives.

The general atmosphere after the Gunpowder Plot was, if you like, one of grudging but peaceful silence. Compare with this the French experience of the Massacre of St Bartholomew's Eve, in 1572, in which somewhere between 5,000 and 30,000 Huguenots were murdered, egged on by Charles IX and his mother Catherine de' Medici. On hearing the news, Pope Gregory XIII ordered a Te Deum, and Philip II is said to have laughed for the only time in his life.

By comparison, the actions of Salisbury and James I resemble those of a modern Cold War, in which 'containment' is steadily and firmly pursued, rather than confrontation and military violence. An unlovely policy, no doubt, though one which may with luck and patience deliver more benign results over time. If we judge the Stuarts by the kind of calculus the American diplomat George Kennan applied to postwar East–West relations, we may come to the conclusion that the crucial error of Charles I was not so much his insistence on governing without Parliament as his determination to fight a religious war against the Scots Covenanters, so unleashing 20 years of religion-fuelled civil war which convulsed the entire British Isles.

Of course, it would have been far better had James I been able to follow his first instincts and offer some genuine hope of toleration to thousands of law-abiding Catholics. But this option was blocked by a rabidly Protestant Parliament and an inflamed anti-Catholic public opinion. What he and Salisbury did between them may be reluctantly accepted as the least bad option.

And what if 'the true Catholics' in that belt across the West Midlands from Northampton to the Welsh border had 'stirred'? How far would they have got? The rapidity with which the local sheriff's posse mopped up the remnants of Catesby's followers at Holbeach House suggests that any such rising would have been promptly and brutally squashed, with terrible long-term consequences for the Catholic population as a whole. Francis Tresham could see instantly then what we can see now: that, without a foreign power to back them, this bunch of high-spirited Catholic gentlemen lacked anything like a mass base beyond their own ostlers and serving men. On the day he was recruited, 14 October 1605, according to his later account, Tresham told Catesby: 'It would not be a means to advance our religion but to overthrow it, for the odiousness of the fact would be such as that would make the whole Kingdom to turn upon such as were taken for Catholics, and not to spare man or woman so affected.'[22]

Some coups are simply born to fail. But Francis Tresham signed up all the same. In the end, faith trumped prudence, and left common sense for dead.

The Dinner Party That Never Was

'The sons of corruption sigh for the evidence of a PLOT. Oh, how they sigh! They are working and slaving and fretting and stewing; they are sweating all over; they are absolutely pining and dying for a Plot!' So William Cobbett wrote to Henry 'Orator' Hunt in 1816.[1] He did not exaggerate. The verb 'foment' might have been invented to describe the activities of Sidmouth and Castlereagh and their spymasters in Bow Street during the turbulent 1810s. Seldom in the history of British espionage can senior ministers have got their hands quite so dirty. As E. P. Thompson grudgingly conceded in *The Making of the English Working Class*, 'Notions as to the traditional stupidity of the English ruling class are dispelled by an acquaintance with the Home Office papers.' In fact, he muses, you could write a convincing history of English Jacobinism and English radicalism in terms of the impact of espionage upon the movement.[2] Government spies penetrated and provoked, infiltrated and informed with unbelievable zeal – and success. The Cecils' networks had kept the Tudors and Stuarts safe from Papist plots. In the twentieth century, MI6 penetrated the Communist Party and the IRA with equal facility. But nothing surpasses Sidmouth. Before his elevation he was remembered only as Pitt's pallid stand-in – 'Pitt is to Addington as London is to Paddington' – but as Home Secretary he came into his own.

Bow Street's spy John Castle was on the action committee organizing the huge and supposedly peaceful meeting on Spa Fields to be addressed by the mellifluous Orator Hunt. Castle tirelessly whipped up the labourers who had just been laid off digging the Regent's Canal, while another member of the committee, Arthur Thistlewood, urged them to bring 'a spike-nail in the end of a stick or anything that would run into a fellow's guts'.[3] The riots that followed were the worst since the Gordon riots of the 1780s, and ended in chaos and humiliating failure to suborn the soldiers at the Tower. Half a dozen of the plotters were indicted for treason. Unsurprisingly, not Castle.

On the first day of these treason trials, 300 desperate stockingers and miners in Nottinghamshire and Derbyshire were persuaded by 'Oliver the spy' to march towards London to join a supposed armed uprising there. They were swiftly surrounded by forewarned troops and arrested at the village of Pentrich. Three of the Pentrich men suffered the traditional penalty for treason of hanging and decapitation; 14 more were 'pardoned', that is, transported to Australia. Sidmouth 'abused Oliver for a great fool for being detected'. Oliver's machinations had been exposed by the *Leeds Mercury* and retold by Sir Francis Burdett in the House of Commons, but the operation was another successful exercise in sending shivers down the spines of the respectable classes who had the vote, and in justifying further acts of repression.

The third, and most famous, would-be insurrection, launched from a dismal stable in Cato Street, just off the Edgware Road, was an even more scandalous set-up. Its leader, Arthur Thistlewood, had been banged up in the Tower of London for his part in Spa Fields. He had told Castle that the day had left him 'perfectly well satisfied that the people were not ripe enough to act'[4] – the excuse of failed insurrectionaries through the ages. But he had not learnt his lesson. This time he trusted an even more egregious government spy, a plaster-modeller going by the name of George Edwards. After the two men met, Edwards told his friends, 'Thistlewood is the boy for us, he's the one who will do our work.'[5] From the moment Thistlewood was released from jail, everything he did and said was immediately passed on to Bow Street and the Home Office.

In their Cato Street hovel and in the sleazy taverns where they rounded up a few dozen supporters, this small crew of underemployed shoemakers and loudmouthed drunks were endlessly bragging about how they were going to knock the blocks off Wellington, Sidmouth and the rest of the villains. Well, Edwards told them one evening, now's your chance – look at this announcement in the *New Times* that the Cabinet are going to meet for dinner at Lord Harrowby's house in Grosvenor Square tomorrow evening. What a golden opportunity to decapitate the lot of them! Edwards had of course inserted the announcement himself, and the Cabinet dined elsewhere, though Harrowby's staff was kept busy cooking and decanting all evening to maintain the deceit. Just as the plotters were tucking into their pre-match cheese and porter and loading their pistols, in charged the Bow Street constables, followed by heavily armed troops. The conspiracy was busted before they even left Cato Street.

The Arrest of the Cato Street Conspirators.

Vic Gatrell tells this sorry story with zest and sympathy. He is by inclination a social rather than a political historian, more concerned to recover the texture of life than to trace the course of governance. *Conspiracy on Cato Street* follows the trail of *The Hanging Tree* (1997) and *City of Laughter* (2009) in its search for Regency London in all its gaiety, violence, sexual sprawl and above all searing poverty. Gatrell's trigger finger trembles with passion as he takes aim at the romantic, curricles-and-crinolines view of the period. He might have included in his field of fire those optimistic economists such as Adam Smith, who remarks in *The Wealth of Nations* on 'the universal opulence which extends itself to the lowest ranks of the people'.[6]

Britain in the years before and after Waterloo was a chronically unsettled country. There were 200 sedition trials in the 1790s alone. Everyone was rioting: miners, tanners, weavers, debtors in their jails, young gents at Eton and Winchester. The comfortable classes, from the Iron Duke downwards, fretted that the country was tottering towards revolution. And out of taverns where the plots were hatched and dispatched pour the most extraordinary cast of desperadoes and craftsmen down on their luck, their life stories preserved verbatim, by the miracle of modern shorthand, in the accounts of their trials and the reports of the spies who befriended them. In his confession, Guy Fawkes was at pains to emphasize that his co-diggers under the House of Lords were 'all gentlemen of name and blood'. The same could not be said of the Cato Street plotters. William Davidson was a Black cabinetmaker of considerable eloquence (as his speech from the dock was to show), who had been born in Jamaica and run away to sea, and later once repaired furniture for Lord Harrowby, which he vainly pleaded to Harrowby as a reason for clemency. Four of the others were ex-soldiers, who were more or less starving and had taken to shoemaking with little success. The defiant James Ings was a butcher. Dr James Watson was an apothecary who happened to be in debtors' prison when the conspiracy erupted and so escaped arrest and trial. He had been an ingenious armourer for the plot, devising letter bombs and smoke bombs and also secret codes, which, alas, were cracked as soon as Edwards passed them on to Bow Street.

Unlike the rest, their leader Thistlewood had some pretensions to gentility and a few thousand from his two wives, which he spent partly on treating his skint cronies and buying ammunition for the cause, and rather more on reckless gambling binges. He lost £841 of his brother's money at hazard one night, then moved on to another dive in Pall Mall to lose £400 of his own. The many engravings done of him at his trial show him much as Gatrell describes him: 'a graceless, truculent and unforgiving figure, and as alienated, resentful and fantasy-laden as any modern jihadist.'[7] His ideas were as vague as they were violent: cut off a few heads, seize the Tower or the Bank of England, the troops will come over, and the people will rise. As Gatrell says, 'the last thing they had was an agenda.'[8] He seemed indifferent to the cause of land redistribution which was dear to the hearts of many reformers, nor were he and his little group – never more than 50 at best – class-conscious in the Marxist sense (which is why they were of so little interest to E. P. Thompson and later Labour historians). They were independent craftsmen rather than proletarians, unlike the masses of weavers and miners who marched behind Orator Hunt's more peaceable banner. All they did have were simple ideas of justice and democracy, sharing the allegiance of more moderate reformers to universal suffrage and the secret ballot. In his last day in court, just before his death sentence was delivered, Thistlewood rose to some eloquence (though he started quaveringly, being an awkward and rather timorous speaker):

> A few hours hence, and I will be no more, but the nightly breeze, which will whistle over the silent grave that shall protect me from its keenness, will bear to your restless pillow the memory of one who lived but for his country, and died when liberty and justice had been driven from its confines by a set of villains whose thirst for blood is only to be equalled by their activity in plunder.[9]

He went on to denounce the ministers, the court's failure to call the evidence of the spies who had helped to instigate the plot and the military force deployed against the people in their peaceful protests, most recently and shamefully at Peterloo. 'High treason was committed against the people at Manchester, but justice was closed against the mutilated, the maimed, and the friends of those who were upon that occasion indiscriminately massacred.' He then proceeded to justify the violence of their own actions: 'It was only when all else had failed, when all channels of peaceful protest had been barred to us, that the decision was made to embark on violent forms of political protest.'

Except these are not Thistlewood's words, of course, but those of Nelson Mandela. Thistlewood puts it more bluntly: 'Insurrection then became a public duty.' He did not possess a particle of Mandela's grace and generosity, but his argument is essentially the same. As the chief justice prepared to deliver the death sentence, Thistlewood took a pinch from his snuffbox, and looked around the courtroom 'as if he were entering a theatre'.

Gatrell remarks how quickly Cato Street tends to be passed over in histories of the period, on the Right because why should we care about these squalid brutes who were mercifully detected in time, and on the Left because the conspiracy seemed to lead nowhere, not to a growth in working-class consciousness or to an immediately renewed appetite for parliamentary reform. All it did was justify an intensification of the very repression it was protesting against. Sidmouth's notorious Six Acts were just becoming law, and Peterloo was fresh in the memory.

Nowhere were Sidmouth's preparations more painstaking than in the run-up to the great demonstration on St Peter's Fields on 16 August 1819. The crowds assembled to hear Orator Hunt address them on parliamentary reform have been variously estimated at between 35,000 and 150,000. Manchester magistrates had plenty of experience in dealing roughly with mass protests by desperate handloom weavers. Now they were fortified by an assurance from the Home Office that they would have a parliamentary indemnity in case of trouble – but please 'keep this delicate subject to yourself'. Sidmouth's undersecretary had also told the northern military commander of his master's belief 'that your county will not be tranquillized until blood shall have been shed either by the law or the sword', and that Sidmouth was 'confident that he will be adequately supported by the magistracy of Lancashire'.[10] In other words, the magistrates had carte blanche to call out the yeomanry, issue them with sharpened sabres and show no mercy. The horse artillery had even brought with them two long six-pounder cannon, the weapons of mass destruction that had done such damage at Waterloo. From Sidmouth's point of view, this was not an operation that got tragically out of hand, but rather one that went pretty much according to plan, and fully deserved the thanks from the Prince Regent that he forwarded to the magistrates a few days later.

Historians have been a little loath to examine quite how nefarious was the role of government, and sometimes reluctant to accept fully the claim made in court by one of those who was to be hanged and decapitated, James Ings, that 'Edwards was the instigator and author of all the atrocity I was going to commit . . . I am sold like a bullock driven to Smithfield-Market.' Even John Bew, in his excellent life of Castlereagh, asserts that Castlereagh genuinely believed that the whole Cabinet had come very close to being assassinated.[11] Yet in the letter to his brother that Bew goes on to quote, Castlereagh boasts that they had stage-managed the whole thing:

> You must allow that we are tolerably cool troops and that we have not manoeuvred amiss to bring it to a final catastrophe in which they are not only caught in their own net but that we can carry into a court of justice a state conspiracy which will be proved beyond the possibility of cavil, and which would form no inconsiderable feature in the *causes célèbres* of Treasonable and Revolutionary Transactions.[12]

In other words, Castlereagh only had to pretend that he was in mortal danger. He admits the set-up.

After all the eloquent speeches from the dock and in the House of Commons by Burdett and Alderman Matthew Wood and Byron's friend John Cam Hobhouse (all MPs elected from constituencies with a wide franchise), everyone who could read knew the score. Richard Carlile, the editor of the *Republican*, concluded that 'the ministers have been playing with Thistlewood . . . they brought the Cato Street affair to maturity, just to answer their purposes for striking terror into the minds of the people on the eve of a general election.'[13] And answer their purposes it did. Lord Liverpool was returned for the third time, with a nice majority. Shelley too was fully up to speed:

> Thus much is known, that so soon as the whole nation lifted up its voice for parliamentary reform, spies were sent forth. These were selected from the most worthless and infamous of mankind and dispersed among the multitude of famished and illiterate labourers. It was their business, if they found no discontent, to create it.[14]

Only a few days after the five Cato Street plotters were executed, Charles Lamb in 'The Three Graves' was reserving a special place in hell for the spies:

> I ask'd the fiend, for whom these rites were meant?
> 'These graves', quoth he, 'when life's brief oil is spent,
> When the dark night comes, and they're sinking bedwards,
> – I mean for Castle, Oliver and Edwards.'

The Sidmouth strategy was in its own terms triumphantly successful. The cause of moderate reform was besmirched by the stain of terrorism, and, despite huge popular support, effectively remained outlawed throughout the four decades of uninterrupted Tory rule from 1784 to 1830. The comfortable classes had taken fright, just as they were meant to. Byron prophesied to Hobhouse that 'the king times are fast finishing. There will be blood shed like water, and tears like mist; but the peoples will conquer in the end.' On the other hand, from Byron's own personal point of view, 'born an aristocrat, and naturally one by temper, with the greatest part of my property in the funds, what have I to gain by a revolution?'[15]

Vic Gatrell freely admits that 'when all is said and done, the Cato Street men did propose the most violent and precisely aimed assault on the British political order since Guy Fawkes and friends had tried to blow up Parliament in 1605, and then since the Cromwellian regicide.'[16] Ministers were fully entitled to take precautions to save themselves from having their heads chopped off. But it can be said equally that the ferocity of the conspirators is explained, if not excused, by the Tory government's refusal, ever since Pitt abandoned the attempt in the 1780s, to contemplate any parliamentary reform at all.

Gatrell reminds us too of the systematic reinforcement of repression. The peacetime army after Waterloo still numbered 150,000 – twice the size of the army today, with a far smaller population then. With no foreign enemies to worry about, thousands of troops could be ordered up at short notice to quell any disturbance, usually from near at hand. The eighteenth century had seen Ireland turned into a huge military camp – 270 barrack sites constructed across the island. Now the same thing happened in London. The barracks familiar to us today – Knightsbridge, Regent's Park and so on – mostly date from this period. Daniel Defoe had noted long ago that Britain had more prisons than any other nation in Europe. Now further Bastilles were added. London also had the highest rate of executions in Europe, although this dropped markedly with the opening of the Australian penal settlements in 1788. Often the plotters prospered after being transplanted, ending up as leading citizens in several towns. One of the Cato Street shoemakers, John Shaw Strange, finished as Chief Constable of Bathurst. Their success was paralleled by the respectable later lives of the spies who fled to South Africa to escape public obloquy. 'Oliver the spy' (real name W. J. Richards) became Inspector of Buildings in Cape Town.

Historians of a conservative disposition have tended to downplay the extent of the 'Alarm' (the political vogue word of the time) that animated Lord Liverpool and his ministers. R. J. White, for example, in *Waterloo to Peterloo*, declares that 'Lord Liverpool and his colleagues lost far less sleep over the dangers of revolution than might seem probable to the historian who spends laborious days among the packets marked "Disturbances" in the Public Record Office.'[17] J. C. D. Clarke in *English Society 1668–1832* refers dismissively to Peterloo as 'the St Peter's Fields incident' and omits it from his index.[18] This insouciance is tenable only, if at all, because the British state was so heavily buttressed by the forces of law and order.

With all the heavy machinery of repression already in place, it may seem superfluous that the government should have gone to the trouble of pushing the Six Acts through Parliament. Why bother to toughen the existing laws against seditious libel? Or further extend the punitive taxes on newspapers? Or tighten the conditions for bail and speed up court proceedings (already most Old Bailey trials were over in a matter of minutes)? Or give local JPs more powers to search for or seize arms? Or ban public meetings of any size, when the authorities could already take steps to prevent any breach of the peace? Or introduce a special law to prevent Thistlewood and his friends from doing their absurd drilling on Primrose Hill?

The Six Acts have slightly baffled those few historians who bothered to examine them closely. The conventional view used to be that of Elie Halévy, that they were a panic-stricken extension of the counter-revolution. But more recent historians have tended to downgrade them as rather mild measures, only sporadically enforced and in any case watered down by Liberal amendments which the government seemed quite ready to accept.

But surely the Six Acts are perfectly explicable in terms of low politics. Gatrell says at the beginning of his delightful, salutary and often startling book on the Cato Street Conspiracy that 'A book of this kind cannot help speaking to the present.' By speaking from the present and referring forward as well as back, we may find it easier to understand the Six Acts and the whole Sidmouth strategy. For they cannot help reminding us, rather forcibly, of the Five Acts that Boris Johnson's government passed in March and April 2022. In both sets of laws, the justification is nugatory, the likely effect questionable and the side effects shameful; but the politics of them are blatant. As we have already seen, each of those five acts is intended to increase government control: over Parliament itself, over elections, over the courts, over immigrants and over public demonstrations. How it all brings back the dear, dead days of 1819 – the hulks, the sabres, the Bastilles, the transportation of illegal males without a chance to say goodbye, let alone take their families with them!

For Boris Johnson, the outrage these Acts generated in Lefty circles was not a drawback but a brilliant success. The whole thing was a deliberate strategy to enthuse his core vote, to heighten their sense of imperilment. We may wonder whether Professor Bew, who became ensconced in No. 10 as Boris Johnson's adviser on foreign policy, recognized some echoes of the Castlereagh years. He would have encountered one of Downing Street's newer recruits, David Canzini, a former colleague of the redoubtable Lynton Crosby. Canzini's instructions to his cohorts had a daunting clarity: 'Find the wedge issues in your department and hammer them.'

The concept of the 'wedge issue' has been familiar in Australia and the US for 20 years or so, but is rather new in the UK. The trick is to find a policy which repels the minority who were never going to vote for you, but which will harden and broaden your support with the majority, who are no longer the silent majority because you are speaking up for them. This is the technique practised by populists everywhere – Trump, Bolsonaro, Erdoğan, Orbán. Whether the proposed policy actually works is beside the point; the question is whether it drives the wedge in the right place. Lord Sidmouth would have understood perfectly. He lacked only the name for it.

The Beer Hall Putsch

THE FALLEN

This is how *Mein Kampf* begins:

> On 9 November 1923, at 12.30 in the afternoon, in front of the Feldherrnhalle as well as in the courtyard of the former War Ministry, the following men fell, with loyal faith in the resurrection of their people:

Alfarth, Felix, businessman, b. 5 July 1901
Bauriedl, Andreas, hatter, b. 4 May 1879
Casella, Theodor, bank clerk, b. 8 August 1900
Ehrlich, Wilhelm, bank clerk, b. 19 August 1894
Faust, Martin, bank clerk, b. 27 January 1901
Hechenberger, Anton, locksmith, b. 28 September 1902
Körner, Oskar, businessman, b. 4 January 1875
Kuhn, Karl, head waiter, b. 26 July 1897

Who exactly are all these people, and why should we care about them?

Laforce, Karl, student of engineering, b. 28 October 1904
Neubauer, Kurt, valet, b. 27 March 1899
Pape, Claus von, businessman, b. 16 August 1904
Pfordten, Theodor von der, judge of the Bavarian Supreme Court, b. 14 May 1873

Rickmers, Johann, retired cavalry captain, b. 7 May 1881
Scheubner-Richter, Max Erwin von, doctor of engineering,
b. 9 January 1884
Stransky, Lorenz, Ritter von, engineer, b. 14 March 1889
Wolf, Wilhelm, businessman, b. 19 October 1898

So-called national authorities denied these dead heroes a common grave.

It is the strangest beginning to any world-famous or infamous book. It is a dedication certainly, because the author concludes: 'Therefore I dedicate to them, for common memory, the first volume of this work. As its blood witnesses, may they shine forever, a glowing example to the followers of our movement.' And he proudly signs himself off: 'Adolf Hitler, Landsberg am Lech Fortress prison, 16 October 1924'. So this is more than a dedication. It is a grandiose and bitter summons to a national uprising, and thus an integral part of that self-appointed mission which the whole book is to promote. These 16 corpses are being weaponized before the reader's eye.

Mein Kampf must be one of the most loathed books ever published. The historian Donald Cameron Watt, in his introduction to the English edition, describes it as 'lengthy, dull, bombastic, repetitious and extremely badly written'.[1] Most of its statements of fact are 'demonstrably false', and its author is 'a master of the inept, the undigested, the half-baked and the untrue'. Michael Burleigh, in his new history of the Third Reich, describes the book as 'a poisonous and turgid concoction'.

In the same way, the failed coup in which Hitler's 16 heroes died is frequently written off as a squalid scuffle in a tavern. Joachim Fest, in his masterly biography of Hitler 50 years ago, warns us against 'the tendency to make the operation seem ridiculous by the use of such terms as "Beer Hall Putsch", "Political Fasching" [Munich's Shrove Tuesday carnival], and so on'.[2] I shall stick to 'Beer Hall Putsch' for the sake of familiarity, but the whole thing was both more horrible and more daring, more momentous at the time and more consequential afterwards. And, disgusting as it undoubtedly is, *Mein Kampf* too deserves our closer attention.

A closer look at the men who died in the crossfire in front of the Feldherrnhalle will tell us quite a lot. Four of them were Bavarian policemen. Unsurprisingly, they find no place in Hitler's list. The other 16 were a typical sample of the embittered nationalists who were swilling around Germany, especially Bavaria, after the great defeat of 1918, seeking vengeance for the 'stab in the back' which had allegedly kept the Reich from victory. They range in age from 19 to 50, and in class from clerks and industrial workers to noblemen and even a high court judge.

Felix Alfarth was a former apprentice at the Siemens works. He was shot down by the police as he was singing 'Deutschland über alles'. During the Nazi era, four streets across the Reich were named after him. The hatmaker Andreas Bauriedl had a lot more streets named after him, 14 in total. This was because his blood happened to soak the flag the Nazis were carrying, which was thereafter hallowed as the Blutfahne and paraded at Nazi rallies. As the storm troopers passed, they sanctified their standards by dipping the tips in the Blutfahne. The blood of Anton Hechenberger, the locksmith, was also said to have soaked the flag, ditto that of the Bavarian nobleman Lorenz Ritter von Stransky. The giant swastika on the flag must have been saturated.

As with other coups – Cato Street, the Gunpowder Plot – many of the fallen had a previous record of violent opposition to the regime. These bank clerks were scarcely meek commuter types. Casella and Ehrlich had both joined the Freikorps after the Armistice, both of them having won the Iron Cross in the war as Hitler himself had. So had the retired cavalryman Johann Rickmers, who came from a well-known Bremen shipbuilding family and kept an arms depot on his country estate for the use of potential putschists.

Kurt Neubauer was Ludendorff's valet and reputedly the youngest volunteer to join the German army in the war, at the age of 15. He too won the Iron Cross but, according to Frau Ludendorff, he was a dreamy soul at his happiest fattening the pigs in her garden. She tried to deter him from going on the march, but he insisted on climbing into his uniform and rushing off to take part with his master.

The most poignant of the victims was Karl Kuhn, a head waiter at the Café Annast on Odeonsplatz. He was hit by accident when he stepped outside onto the square to watch the drama. Though he appears to have had no known political affiliation, he was to have seven streets named in his honour between 1933 and 1945 (when they all reverted to their original names).

The most prominent of the casualties was Scheubner-Richter, who had joined the Baltic Freikorps and taken part in the Kapp Putsch of 1920, which attempted to overthrow the government in Berlin and for a few days looked as if it might succeed. Scheubner-Richter was marching arm-in-arm with Hitler, and he seems to have fallen on top of the Führer (as he was already being called), dislocating Hitler's shoulder but perhaps saving his life. Hitler described him as 'the only irreplaceable loss' in the Beer Hall Putsch. He was also an invaluable source of funds from his rich contacts. Little more than a month earlier, Scheubner-Richter had given Hitler a blueprint which argued that 'the national revolution must not precede the seizure of political power.' The thing was 'to lay hands on the state police power in a way that is at least outwardly legal'. This was the lesson the failure of the Beer Hall coup taught them, and which guided Hitler's tactics ever afterwards. Indeed, after the failure of other earlier coups, including an abortive effort of his own in May, he scarcely needed telling.

Also among the fallen was Oskar Körner. Now in his late forties, he had started out working in a toyshop near the food market, then taken over the shop and donated half the profits to the infant NSDAP. He quickly became a key figure in the party as head of advertising and propaganda. He helped raise funds for the purchase of the *Völkischer Beobachter* as a party newspaper. He was also instrumental in designing the insignia that the Nazis delighted in, including the adoption of the swastika. Körner preferred the left-facing version of the hooked cross, but was outvoted. In the march to the Feldherrnhalle, he is reported to have jumped in front of Hitler as his own skull was shattered, his death showing, like Scheubner-Richter's, what a close shave Hitler had.

If Körner's career in the party reminds us how unlike other parties the Nazis were – so focused on professional advertising techniques and so keen to adopt the latest media, radio and film – the fatal participation of Theodor von der Pfordten reminds us how far up the social scale the appeal of the Nazis sometimes reached. Von der Pfordten was a judge in the Bavarian Supreme Court and the author of high-flown essays such as 'The Official Ideal in Plato and its Importance for the Present Day' and, rather less savoury, 'Appeal to the Educated German Blood'. If it was startling to find a Justice of the Supreme Court among the corpses, it was even more startling to find in his pocket the copy of an 'emergency constitution', apparently intended as a working document for the national dictatorship planned by Hitler and Ludendorff and probably a variant on previous documents drafted by Heinrich Class and the Pan-German Association. It went way beyond the official NSDAP programme of the moment, calling for the dissolution of all parliamentary bodies, the prohibition of strikes, the dismissal of all Jewish officials and confiscation of Jewish property, plus the transfer of dangerous persons and 'useless eaters' to concentration camps. The penalty for most offences was to be death. Because of the soft attitude of the prosecuting authorities, this document was not produced at the trial of Hitler and the other putschists. When it came to light later in the 1920s, it was denounced as 'the most bloodthirsty document that political history has ever known'. It was of course pretty much the programme followed by the Nazi regime.

In the records of the fallen putschists, we see striking continuities with the welter of hyper-nationalist organizations and violent uprisings that had plagued Germany over the previous five years. But in the personnel of the putschists who didn't fall, we see even more remarkable continuities with the whole subsequent Nazi period. Hermann Göring, Alfred Rosenberg, Rudolf Hess, Julius Streicher, Hans Frank, Wilhelm Frick and Heinrich Himmler were all either with Hitler at the Feldherrnhalle or helping Ernst Röhm and the SA to take over barracks and government offices. They were all in the dock at Nuremberg 20 years later.

THE FÜHRER

More remarkable perhaps than the events of the Beer Hall Putsch itself was the identity of its undoubted leader. Adolf Hitler was always sensitive about his background and his early life: 'These people must not be allowed to find out who I am. They must not know where I come from and who my family is.'[3] That was in 1930, but by then everyone knew roughly who he was and where he came from. That he was born in 1889 in the pretty little Austrian town of Braunau am Inn, on the border with Bavaria, the son of a customs officer, himself born Alois Schicklgruber, to an unmarried servant girl. She later married an unemployed miller, Johann Georg Hiedler or Hüttler, whose family were 'so poor they did not have a bed and slept in a cattle trough'. I cannot trace how soon it was before the enemies at home and abroad of Adolf Hitler (his preferred spelling) started calling him Schicklgruber, but there really wasn't much that was obscure about the obscurity of his origins. And of course, in a cleaned-up version, Hitler was always proud of coming from nowhere and contemptuous of idle toffs. He made no secret, either, that he got on badly with the pompous, bad-tempered Alois, especially when his father was drunk.

But he was clearly proud of the way his father had risen as high as he could in the customs service, and he appreciated that Alois should wish him to follow in his footsteps, which he violently rejected, just as violently as his father objected to Adolf's ambition to become an artist. To the unprejudiced reader, these opening pages of *Mein Kampf* read as normally as the recollections of any would-be artist arguing with a stubborn philistine father. So too does the description of his repeated failures at school.

Adolf was not the only school drop-out loafing around Vienna after failing to get into the Academy, and not the only embittered youth who took refuge in the poisonous anti-Semitism and nationalism that were in the air, and who hitched on to the horrible Georg Ritter von Schönerer and the equally horrible, though rather more calculating, Karl Lueger, the city's mayor. 'From a purely human standpoint they both tower far above the scope and nature of so-called parliamentary figures,' he gushes in *Mein Kampf*. 'Amid the morass of general political corruption their whole life remained pure and unassailable'.[4]

In reality, von Schönerer was a drunken psychopath – anti-Semitic, anti-liberal, anti-Catholic, anti-socialist, anti-Habsburg. He adored Bismarck and agitated to reunite Austria with the German Reich. He bestowed the title of Führer on himself and demanded that his followers greet him with a 'Heil' salute. Pretty much the full deal, in short. But by the time Hitler came to Vienna, von Schönerer was on the slide, and Lueger was the new star. Unlike von Schönerer, with his crude '*los von Rom*' sloganizing, Lueger understood the need to conciliate the Catholic Church, a lesson that the equally anti-clerical Hitler never forgot. He called Lueger 'the greatest German mayor of all time.'[5]

There were plenty of other rabble-rousers peddling the same toxic brew. Biographers disagree whether the young Hitler also visited the rabid former Cistercian monk Jörg Lanz von Liebenfels (born plain Adolf Lanz) in his ruined castle on the Danube between Linz and Vienna, where he ran his 'New Templar Order', adorned with a bunch of kabbalistic insignia, including the swastika, adopted quite contrary to history as an exclusively Aryan symbol. Lanz looked forward to the coming struggle for supremacy between the blond Aryan Germans and the dark beast-men, and the sterilization of the lower orders of humanity. Notoriously unreliable, Lanz claimed that Hitler visited him to beg a few back numbers of his magazine *Ostara*, but even if he didn't, Hitler tells us that after his conversion to the anti-Semitic cause he began devouring anti-Semitic pamphlets – in other words, the racist junk like *Ostara* that was for sale on every Vienna bookstall.[6]

Hitler described his time in Vienna as

> five years of hardship and misery. Five years in which I was forced to earn my living, first as a day labourer, then as a small painter; a truly meagre living which never sufficed to appease even my daily hunger. Hunger was then my faithful bodyguard; he never left me for a moment.[7]

This is only half the truth. He was indeed mourning the early death of his mother, a sweet-natured woman and probably the only person he ever really loved. And he did partly exist on a stream of small artistic commissions, including posters advertising a hair tonic and a feather-bed shop, also one for an anti-perspirant sold under the brand name of 'Teddy' – a copy of which has been found with Hitler's signature in a corner, although like many Hitler artefacts it could well be a forgery.[8] Hitler knocked out these and copies of postcards and Vienna scenes, while resident in a hostel for homeless men in Meldemannstrasse. His fellow lodgers remembered him as sullen and cantankerous, inclined to unstoppable rants against Jews, Slavs, Social Democrats and Habsburgs.

But he wasn't as badly off as he makes out. He had his share of his father's inheritance, a legacy from his mother and an orphan's pension. Even without counting his earnings, he had somewhere between 80 and 100 crowns a month, the salary of a junior magistrate at the time. So he was well able to loaf around in the cafés and buy a ticket to hear his beloved Wagner at the opera (he claimed to have clocked up 30 or 40 performances of *Tristan and Isolde*).

There is, though, no reason to doubt his overall claim in *Mein Kampf* that he was miserable in Vienna:

> An oppressive discontent had seized possession of me, the more I recognized the inner hollowness of this state and the impossibility of saving it . . . I was repelled by the conglomeration of races which the capital showed me, repelled by this whole mixture of Czechs, Poles, Hungarians, Ruthenians, Serbs and Croats, and everywhere, the eternal mushroom of humanity – Jews and more Jews. To me the giant city seemed the embodiment of racial desecration.[9]

There is nothing in this terrible book that equals the shudder of horror that Hitler experiences at his first encounter with an Orthodox Jew in the Inner City, 'an apparition in a black caftan and black hair locks'.[10]

But when he moved to Munich in May 1913, it was not primarily to escape the vile sights of Vienna or even, as he claimed, to earn his living as an architect, but rather to dodge the Austrian military draft. He was damned if he was going to fight for the Habsburgs, who he loathed almost as much as the Jews. For a time, the Austrian authorities searched in vain for him, but they caught up with him at 34 Schleissheimer Strasse, Munich, and he was arrested. A conviction might have ruined his whole career. Who would follow a convicted draft dodger? But by writing a long oleaginous letter of excuse to the authorities, he escaped being charged, on condition that he took a medical before the draft board on 5 February 1914, which recorded that he was 'unfit for military and auxiliary service; too weak, incapable of bearing arms'.[11]

Only a few months later, Hitler was amongst the cheering crowds on 2 August 1914, in Odeonsplatz, Munich, when war was declared. He can clearly be identified in the photograph, chortling and bright-eyed. He did not hesitate before enlisting to fight for the Reich. When he received the summons to report to the 16th Bavarian Reserve Regiment, known as the List Regiment after its CO, Colonel List, 'My joy and gratitude knew no bounds. A few days later I was wearing the tunic which I was not to doff until nearly six years had passed. For me, as for every German, there now began the greatest and most unforgettable time of my earthly existence.'[12]

Hitler really did adore being a soldier. The camaraderie of the barracks and the dugout was as near as he came to being at ease in the world. In no man's land, he felt at home, as Fest puts it. He spent the entire war as a courier between regimental HQ and the front line, an extremely dangerous posting. He was awarded the Iron Cross Second Class for bravery under fire in December 1914 and the Iron Cross First Class in May 1918. In between, he served in most of the great battles from the Menin Road to the Somme and back. While resting, he alternated between silent brooding and occasional unstoppable harangues about his fears that the rightful victory would be lost and the German nation betrayed. The fear of the *Dolchstoss* seemed to obsess him, even while Germany still appeared to be winning the war.

The Reichswehr gave Hitler a home, but it also gave him his crucial break. He emerged from the war sharing all the rancid obsessions of the German nationalists: hatred of the Jews and to an only slightly less extent of the Slavs; loathing of the 'November criminals' who had signed the Armistice, brought in the Weimar Republic and allowed the humiliating Treaty of Versailles; anxiety for the purity of the German race; loathing of parliaments and of democracy generally; belief that Germany's population was being stifled by her cramped borders and that the nation had the right to seek more living space in the East. All these obsessions were fully formed in the minds of thousands of troops returning from the trenches, and in poisonous combination they animated the disturbances and coups that began to plague Germany almost from the day of the Armistice. These feelings were passionate and widespread, but there was no earthly reason to expect that Corporal Adolf Hitler of the 16th Bavarian Regiment would be the man to voice them on behalf of the masses. Hitler had, after all, been expressly denied promotion from the ranks because of his 'lack of leadership skills'. Who would select as their saviour a former third-rate commercial artist lodging in a tailor's attic?

Here enters a key figure in the creation of the Führer, but an unsung one: Captain Karl Mayr. Despite his modest rank, Mayr had been put in charge of the education of Bavarian troops in the correct anti-Bolshevist, nationalist attitudes. Hitler had already done some propaganda work in his barracks, though ironically on behalf of the socialists, and when Mayr first met him, he said Hitler was 'like a tired stray dog looking for a master . . . ready to throw in his lot with anyone who would show him kindness.'[13] He sent Hitler to receive some political education at Munich University and then deployed him as a *Bildungsoffizier*. Hitler instantly became a star lecturer. He himself was delighted to discover that 'I could "speak".' All the qualities that made him a liability in ordinary society – the unstoppable rants, the sudden rages, the brooding pauses – all these turned out to be crowd-pullers on the platform. Mayr was soon describing him to the exiled putschist Wolfgang Kapp as 'a popular speaker of the first rank who had already helped to recruit 2,000 members to the new NSDAP by September 1920'. Mayr later claimed to have *ordered* Hitler to join the German Workers Party and paid him 20 gold marks a week out of army funds, while allowing him to stay in the army – an embarrassing fact if it had become known at the time. It made nonsense of Hitler's claim to have been a founder member with party number 7 – in fact, according to the infant party's chairman Anton Drexler, Hitler was member No. 555. Anyway, Drexler was deeply impressed: 'Goodness, he's got a gob on him. We could use him.'[14]

And use him they did. But it was not long before he was using them. Ironically, we must record here that Captain Mayr, the Svengali who had found his voice for him, went on to be darkly disillusioned with the Nazis, becoming an active figure in the Social Democrats and in 1933 fleeing to France, where he was later captured by the Nazis. He died in Buchenwald in February 1945.[15] Adolf seldom forgave anyone who had done him a good turn.

Hitler freely admitted that he was the drummer (der Trommler) in the band, the propagandist, not the thinker or the organizer. 'Not from modesty did I want at that time to be the drummer. That is the highest there is.'[16] At a crucial moment in the Beer Hall Putsch, Hitler was to declare, 'Propaganda, propaganda, now it all depends on propaganda!'[17] For Hitler it always did. As Ian Kershaw points out in his monumental life, there was nothing original or distinctive about the ideas Hitler was peddling in these early years in the beer halls. Not only were they common to all the völkisch sects of the time, but they had also already been advanced in their essentials by the pre-war Pan-Germans. It was less what he said than how he said it, in a rasping popular style, blasting the same scapegoats hour after hour. He became a dedicated orator, but only to the masses. When asked to say a few words at a comrade's wedding party, he refused: 'I must have a crowd when I speak. In a small intimate circle I never know what to say.'[18] To a lesser degree, this is true of many other politicians I can think of, who are awkward in private conversation, but Hitler was an extreme case.

In front of a big crowd, however, he was a knock-out. Hans Frank, while awaiting the hangman at Nuremberg, recalled the moment in January 1920 that at the age of 19 he first heard Hitler speak:

> I was strongly impressed straight away. It was totally different from what was otherwise to be heard in meetings. His method was completely clear and simple. He took the overwhelmingly dominant topic of the day, the Versailles Diktat, and posed the question of all questions: What now, German people? What's the true situation? What alone is now possible? He spoke for over two-and-a-half hours, often interrupted by frenetic torrents of applause – and one could have listened to him for much, much

longer. Everything came from the heart and he struck a chord
with all of us . . . From that evening onwards, though not a party
member, I was convinced that if one man could do it, Hitler alone
would be capable of mastering Germany's fate.[19]

As early as 1921, to the Munich public Hitler already *was* the Nazi
Party. It was Hitler who was expected to lead the next putsch. And it
was Hitler that the right-wing monarchist, newly appointed as head
of the Bavarian government, Gustav Ritter von Kahr, asked to see in
May 1921, hoping to conscript and control 'the impetuous little
Austrian'.

It was an amazing rise to fame for the drop-out no-hoper. And it
was an extraordinarily fateful meeting, which illustrates the ghastly
demoralization of Bavarian politics and indeed of the whole Reich
at the time. We must not think that because Kahr was a reactionary
old monarchist he was therefore a respectable, law-abiding operator.
On the contrary, he was as eager as Hitler to destroy the Weimar
regime, if necessary by illegal or violent means – and preferably with
the assistance of Hitler and his mob, who could then be discarded
after use.

THE PUTSCH

The bizarre thing about the whole episode was that it was a coup
to pre-empt another coup. Kahr, together with the local Reichswehr
commander General Otto von Lossow and the chief of the
Landespolizei Colonel Hans von Seisser, formed an all-powerful
triumvirate in Bavaria. Their somewhat hazy plan was for a Bavarian
march on Berlin, modelled on Mussolini's march on Rome the
year before, which had proved such a pushover for the Fascists. The
triumvirate would overthrow the hated Weimar regime and set up
a conservative authoritarian government, either in the whole of
Germany or in Bavaria, possibly restoring the monarchy. '*Los von Berlin!*'
– free from Berlin – was their slogan. Hitler's Kampfbund certainly
shared their loathing of the decadent bohemianism of Berlin and
were agreed on chucking out 'the November criminals', but they
wanted a united Nazi Germany, including Bavaria. And they wanted
to get in first and run the show.

It is doubtful whether Kahr's team had the stomach for an
actual march, as opposed to deploying the threat of one to secure
concessions from Berlin and greater independence for Bavaria. What

they were certainly determined to do was to squash the counter-threat of the Nazis. There were to be no 'private initiatives'. And to show they meant business, the triumvirate fixed the date of 15 November for their March on Berlin.

On their side, Hitler's storm troopers were impatient for action, and Hitler had no option but to egg them on. 'This November Republic is nearing its end,' he had declared as early as 12 September. 'We begin to hear the soft rustling which heralds a storm. And this storm will break, and in it this Republic will experience a transformation one way or another. The time is ripe.'[20]

The trigger was to be Kahr's speech in the Bürgerbräukeller on the evening of 8 November. This was one of the cavernous great halls much used for public meetings in Bavaria, not a low dive but rather the city's equivalent to London's Olympia or the Ulster Hall in Belfast. Kahr's address was to mark and lament the fifth anniversary of the November Revolution. It was certain that he would denounce Marxism and all its works, but would he also take the opportunity to proclaim some sort of independence for Bavaria, perhaps the restoration of the monarchy? Hitler could not afford to give him the chance. Kahr had been speaking for about half an hour to his 3,000 supporters. Much of what he was saying would have been rather to Hitler's taste, stuff about 'the new man' as 'the moral justification for dictatorship'.[21]

Then, at around 8.30 p.m., a bunch of Hitler's storm troopers in steel helmets burst into the hall, led by Hitler in an evening tailcoat with his Iron Cross pinned to his chest, flanked by two bodyguards pointing pistols at the ceiling. Hitler held up a beer stein, took a slurp, then jumped up on to a chair or a table, fired a single shot into the ceiling to quieten the hubbub, and shouted:

> The national revolution has begun. The hall is surrounded by 600 heavily armed men. No one may leave the premises. Unless quiet is restored immediately, I shall have a machine gun placed in the gallery. The Bavarian government and the national government have been overthrown, and a provisional national government is being formed. The barracks of the Reichswehr and the state police have been occupied; the Reichswehr and the state police are approaching under the swastika flag.[22]

After this stream of impudent fabrications, he then ordered Kahr, Lossow and Seisser into an adjoining room, gesturing wildly with his pistol as he made them an offer they could not refuse. In his *coup accompli*, he himself was to be president of the new national government, Ludendorff, his prize new ally, was to lead the national army on the march to Berlin, Kahr was to be the state administrator, Lossow chief of the Reichswehr, Seisser the chief of police. There was to be no argument.

> Each of you must assume his allotted position; whoever fails to do so has forfeited his right to exist. You must fight with me, triumph with me, or die with me. If things go wrong, I have four bullets in this pistol: three for my collaborators should they desert me, and the last bullet for myself.

Kahr, Seisser and Lossow seemed unimpressed by these theatrics. Hitler left them in the room to make up their minds, while he returned to the hall to announce the new government. Eventually, the triumvirate yielded, Kahr the last to give in. They even muttered a few words to the crowd in the beer hall about loyalty to the nation.

Then Hitler made his first tactical mistake. Hearing that the planned simultaneous uprisings across the city were running into trouble, he rushed out of the Bürgerbräukeller, leaving Ludendorff in charge of the triumvirate. Believing the word of officers and gentlemen, at about 10.30 p.m. Ludendorff let the triumvirate go free. Whereupon they immediately recanted their assents to Hitler's proposals, arguing that they had been extracted at gunpoint (Hitler was predictably furious at this 'breach of honour'). By 2.55 a.m., Lossow had informed all German radio stations that they repudiated the putsch, and more importantly so did the Reichswehr and the state police. Although there were placards on the streets proclaiming Hitler as the new Chancellor, the coup had effectively failed.

By concentrating on Hitler's own movements, his earlier biographers have tended to underplay the counter-attack by the authorities. It is not just that 'neither the army nor the state police joined forces with the putschists.'[23] They were actively ordered by their commanding officers to put down the uprising. Major-General Jakob von Danner loathed 'the little corporal' and 'the Freikorps rowdies'. He and Captain Karl Wild set up command posts to protect government buildings and, as early as 11 p.m. that evening, compelled their superior officer, Lossow, to repudiate the coup.

Another state official who received early intelligence of the coup was the Vice-Premier of Bavaria, Franz Matt. A devout Catholic, he happened to be having dinner with Cardinal Michael von Faulhaber, the Archbishop of Munich, and Archbishop Eugenio Pacelli, the Papal Nuncio and later Pope Pius XII. We are reminded of the Earl of Salisbury at dinner with his Privy Council colleagues when receiving the Monteagle Letter. Posterity has slammed both Faulhaber and Pacelli for their later equivocations in the face of Nazi terror, but on this occasion their behavior was faultless. In case the coup began to succeed, Matt immediately set up plans for a government-in-exile in Regensburg and issued a proclamation calling on all policemen, civil servants and members of the armed services to stay loyal to the government. The next day, Faulhaber and Crown Prince Rupprecht visited the wretched Kahr and persuaded him publicly to repudiate the putsch.

So the coup did not just fizzle out. It was actively suppressed by the forces of law and order.

By 5 a.m. on 9 November, Hitler was still declaring that he was ready to fight and die for the cause, a sure sign that he knew he was losing. What next? There were still hundreds of sleepy storm troopers dossing down in the hall, inhaling the stale tobacco smoke and beer fumes. As dawn broke, Hitler and Ludendorff were still bickering about the next move. The only practical action Hitler took was at 8 a.m. to send some SA men out to grab bundles of 50 million Mark notes hot from the printing press to pay his tired and despondent men – an indication both of Hitler's incurable lawlessness and the rampant inflation. This gross theft was another circumstance skated over at Hitler's trial.

In the end, either Hitler or Ludendorff came up with the standard Nazi answer to any problem: 'Wir marschieren.' A march through the city would rally morale and convince people that the coup had succeeded after all. Long afterwards, Hitler continued to insist that the spectacle of the march would cause jubilation to break out across the Reich. And so at around midday, about 2,000 men, most of them exhausted and hungover, set out from the Bürgerbräukeller across the River Isar to the city centre, pistols at the ready. There were some encouraging shouts from the crowds, but quite a few of the posters announcing the revolution had already been torn down. The marchers broke through one scanty police cordon on the Ludwigsbrücke, but as they came down Residenzstrasse into the Odeonsplatz, singing the *Sturmlied*, they ran into a much heavier police presence.

Shots rang out. Nobody is quite sure who fired first – probably the putschists. But after about half a minute, a minute at most, the firing stopped. Sixteen putschists and four policemen lay dead, most of them in front of the Feldherrnhalle, the fine early-nineteenth-century memorial to Germany's dead in the Thirty Years War and the Napoleonic Wars and, added on later, the Franco-Prussian War too. It was and is just the sort of airy classical building that Hitler adored.

As we have seen, most of the prominent leaders of the coup survived, quite a few of them until they met their ultimate fate at Nuremberg. But in most cases, their survival was scarcely glorious. The hagiographers had to suppress the way in which the Führer himself took to his heels, his shoulder dislocated, having to be scooped up by a doctor who drove him at high speed from the scene of the crime. Ludendorff, in painful contrast, disdained flight and stood among his fallen comrades waiting to be arrested. Later, Hitler concocted a myth that he had only left the scene to carry a child to safety, even producing a child to fill the bill. Ludendorff and his friends lost no time in demolishing this fantasy. Hitler's behaviour throughout the proceedings must have been the beginning of Ludendorff's disillusion, culminating with the scorching telegram he sent to President Hindenburg after Hindenburg had reluctantly appointed Hitler Chancellor in January 1933: 'I solemnly prophesy that this accursed man will cast our Reich into the abyss and bring our nation to inconceivable misery. Future generations will damn you in your grave for what you have done.'[24]

Spot on. On the other hand, it was Ludendorff who had betrayed his own heroic status to give Hitler credibility in the first place, under the illusion shared by many in the Establishment that they could 'box in' the vulgar little man. By the time Hindenburg took his fateful decision, he had little alternative. Although the Nazis, Goebbels in particular, had frankly stated that they only wanted to get into the Reichstag in order to smash it, they had, after all, come out top in two Reichstag elections. If the German people could not be said to have actively voted for a dictatorship, there were relatively few objections when Hitler introduced one within months of coming to power.

In his remarkable memoir, *Defying Hitler*, the young lawyer Sebastian Haffner described how people around him were shell-shocked by the events of February and March 1933.

Daily life also made it difficult to see the situation clearly. Life went on as before, though it had now definitely become ghostly and unreal, and was daily mocked by the events that served as its background. I still went to the *Kammergericht*, the law was still practised there, as though it still meant something, and the Jewish judge still presided in his robes, quite unmolested. However, his colleagues now treated him with a certain tactful delicacy, like one does somebody suffering from a serious disease.[25]

He went dancing with his girlfriend, took her to the cinema, celebrated family birthdays. 'It was just this automatic continuation of ordinary life that hindered any lively, forceful reaction against the horror.'

AFTERWARDS

Hitler was taken to his friend Putzi Hanfstaengl's house on the Staffelsee outside Munich (Putzi himself had fled to Austria). There he was arrested on the evening of 11 November and shut up in the old fortress-prison of Landsberg am Lech, 40 miles west of the city. To many outside observers, it seemed he was finished. He would surely be tried and jailed, perhaps deported back to Austria after he had served his sentence. We would hear no more of the little corporal.

It did not turn out that way. And the central reason was quite simply that public sentiment in Bavaria was largely in sympathy with Hitler's aims. The putsch failed not because it lacked public support, but because the legitimate authorities still had a stern conception of their duty to uphold the law. Yet even after the putsch, both in the Landtag elections of April 1924 and the Reichstag elections of May, the *Völkisch* block gained around 30 per cent of the vote, well ahead of the rest. Hitler had only to tell a good story in court to become the hero of what had appeared a fiasco.

And he did. Indulged with a four-hour oration by the judge, the nationalist sympathizer Georg Neithardt, the same judge who had let him off lightly two years earlier when he'd been up for a breach of the peace,[26] he turned the tables on his accusers, relying on the undeniable fact that he had been acting in cahoots with the triumvirate, in trying to realize the dearest wishes of the huge mass of nationalist voters:

I cannot declare myself guilty. True, I confess to the deed, but I do not confess to the crime of high treason. There can be no question of treason in an action which aims to undo the betrayal of this country in 1918 . . . And if we *were* committing treason, I am surprised that those who at the time had the same aims as I are not sitting beside me now. At any event, I must reject the charge until I am joined by those gentlemen who wanted the same action as we, who discussed it with us and helped prepare it down to the smallest details.[27]

Kahr and Seisser had no answer to that. Lossow at least had the guts to accuse Hitler of being a habitual liar and a German Mussolini. But Hitler shouted him down, to the cheers of the crowd inside and outside the court. To us nothing is more jaw-dropping than the greasy deference the chief prosecutor paid to him, remarking on his 'unique gifts as an orator', refusing to describe him as a demagogue and paying tribute to his impeccable private life: 'Hitler is a highly gifted man, who has risen from humble beginnings to achieve a respected position in public life, the result of much hard work and dedication. He has devoted himself to the ideas he cherishes, to the point of self-sacrifice.'[28] The sentence of five years under little more than house arrest in Landsberg was lenient enough, but the release on parole after a mere five months could not help giving the impression that his conviction had been unfair – an impression Hitler lost no time in capitalizing on. He was not simply comforting himself when he later claimed that the defeat of 9 November 1923 was in reality 'perhaps the greatest stroke of luck in my life'.

His short time in Landsberg, surrounded in comfort by his acolytes, may have taken him away from the political action and temporarily weakened the party which relied so much on its star orator. But it gave him time and space to develop his narrative.

Which brings us back to *Mein Kampf*. Much revised before publication by more experienced literary hands, it retains Hitler's driving purpose. There are at least three aspects to the book which still demand our attention.

First, in it he answers the movement's need to dignify itself, to raise it above the other street fighters who misspent so much of their time fighting one another – the Stahlhelm, the Reichskriegsflagge, the Vikingbund, the assorted Freikorps. Hitler needed martyrs, and he manufactured them on page 1 out of the weary and hungover thugs who had fallen so conveniently in front of the national memorial to the nation's heroes. Every year on *Der Neunte Elfte* – the first 9/11 atrocity to enter a nation's consciousness – the putsch was commemorated nationwide, but most especially in Munich. On the night of the 8th, Hitler would address the *Alte Kämpfer* in the Bürgerbräukeller with a re-enactment the next day of the march across the river down the Residenzstrasse, but now going on beyond the Odeonsplatz to the Königsplatz, where two sizeable *Ehrentempel* (in the classical style, of course) had been erected, each receiving eight of the dead bodies, including that of poor Karl Kuhn, who had only stepped out from the café for a moment to see the fun.

Hitler, Göring, Streicher and the doomed Scheubner-Richter
(far left) lead the march to the War Ministry, 9 November 1923.

These 'honour temples' were carefully located in front of the Glyptothek, the museum which contained – still contains – Ludwig I's great collection of Greek sculpture and was one of Hitler's favourite haunts in his loafing days. He loved the Norse myths when Wagner brought them to life, but it was ancient Greece rather than medieval Germany that he worshipped (although he did give his invasion of Russia the code name of Barbarossa after the fearsome Emperor Frederick I).

In future years, the *Neunte Elfte* also acted as a magnet to would-be assassins, most notably in 1939 when the carpenter Georg Elser placed a time bomb in the Bürgerbräukeller, killing eight and wounding 62, not including Hitler, who had left earlier than expected. It is a myth that there were no attempts on Hitler's life until the Germans realized they were losing the war. At a rough count, there were over 40, about half of them before 1940. During the war, Allied bombers planned raids on downtown Munich to coincide with the *Neunte Elfte*, in the hope of killing prominent Nazis.

Secondly, what *Mein Kampf* does is to knit together the various elements of the Hitler programme into a single terrible crusade: the unification of the German people, the extirpation of the Jews, the undoing of the Versailles Treaty, the final defeat of Marxism and the expansion of the nation's borders in search of Lebensraum. Some writers have talked of the 'development' of Hitler's ideas, but really there was no such thing, only a wholesale adoption of the current *völkisch* programme, which was itself only an elaboration of the Pan-German programme before 1914. Hitler simply added a venomous and ruthless intensity, insisting on the need for terror and deception, and also on the need to make haste if the German nation was not to disappear. The idea that Hitler somehow stumbled into the path that he followed, common among English-speaking historians such as A. J. P. Taylor, cannot survive even a cursory reading of *Mein Kampf*.

If the quest for Lebensraum may seem like a latecomer to the agenda, that is only because it had no realistic place there until the first goals had been accomplished: the reoccupation of the Ruhr and the Rhineland, the abrogation of Versailles, the Anschluss. In Hitler's last years, Lebensraum became a mania: a hundred million Germans were to be settled on the Eastern plains; there would be palaces for the German overlords, huts for the helot Slavs; the Crimea was to be completely cleansed of its inhabitants and transformed into a great German spa; all the grainfields of the Ukraine were to be seized for the Reich. The mineral and agricultural deficits which had plagued Germany since 1914 would be a thing of the past. With the Red Army already in Berlin, Hitler's last message from the bunker ended: 'The aim must still be to win territory in the East for the German people.'[29]

But these were not new ambitions. They permeate Bethmann-Hollweg's statement of war aims in September 1914. And their outline is already present in *Mein Kampf*, where 'the soil policy of the future' is described as a revival of the medieval *Ostsiedlung*: 'And so we National Socialists consciously draw a line under the foreign policy tendency of our pre-War period. We take up where we broke off 600 years ago. We stop the endless German movement to the south and west, and turn our gaze towards the land in the east.'[30]

Thirdly, and most crucially, *Mein Kampf* is all about propaganda. Where Hitler can, I am afraid, be said to be original was in his unwavering insistence on the importance of propaganda, regardless of truth or decency: the first writer to do so as flagrantly since Machiavelli, and with a greater intensity. Again and again in *Mein Kampf* he returns to the subject. It was, he tells us, the superiority of Allied propaganda about imaginary German atrocities that had destroyed German morale in the Great War and eventually led to revolution in Germany. It was the obsession with propaganda that had made the Marxists such a menace; not their economic ideas, which were rubbish, but their campaigning methods. It is from the Social Democrats that

> I achieved an equal understanding of the importance of physical terror towards the individual and the masses. Here, too, the psychological effect can be calculated with precision. *Terror at the place of employment, in the factory, in the meeting hall, and on the occasion of mass demonstrations will always be successful unless opposed by equal terror.*[31]

From the dawn of his career, when he was addressing dozens of meetings every week, he insisted that 'we need force to win our battles. Let others stretch out in their easy chairs. We are ready to climb on the beer table.'[32] In his subsequent career, he never wavered from this insistence – for example, in the bullet points of his address to the High Command on 22 August 1939 at Obersalzberg: 'Close heart to pity. Proceed brutally. Supreme hardness.'[33]

And this mission could be carried out only by a dedicated hard core of loyalists. He was always anxious that the party's will should not be weakened by a suffocating influx of half-hearted new members. He openly admitted that it was from Lenin he had learned that a revolution demands a quasi-religious faith promoted by a dedicated core of fanatical supporters. The word 'propaganda', after all, came from the *congregatio de propaganda fide*, the Papal organization for foreign missions, and the German revolution too demanded its own ruthless and dedicated *congregatio*.

Never was this hardness more savagely demonstrated than in the Night of the Long Knives, on 30 June 1934, codenamed Operation Hummingbird, when Ernst Röhm, the prime creator of the SA and for years Hitler's closest ally, was murdered, along with Hitler's predecessor as Chancellor, Kurt von Schleicher, his oldest party colleague Gregor Strasser, and the poor old 'strong man' of the Beer Hall Putsch, Gustav Ritter von Kahr, together with about 150 other former colleagues or rivals in what Hitler called 'a cleansing operation'. Thirteen years earlier, Hitler had been respectfully negotiating with Kahr about collaboration. Now Kahr was dragged away by SS men and later found hacked to death near Dachau. Talk about clearing the decks. In sheer numbers, the victims of 30 June do not begin to compare with the six million Jews who were to be murdered in the Holocaust, but in terms of personal inhumanity their fate does add something to what we know of Hitler's character. This truly was the 'propaganda der Tat'.

Brutality, but also vulgarity. Propaganda, Hitler tells us,

> must be addressed always and exclusively to the masses . . . All propaganda must be popular, and its intellectual level must be adjusted to the most limited intelligence among those it is addressed to . . . The receptivity of the great masses is very limited, their intelligence is small, but their power of forgetting is enormous. In consequence of these facts, all effective propaganda must be limited to a very few points and must harp on these in slogans until the last member of the public understands what you want him to understand by your slogan . . . only after the simplest ideas are repeated thousands of times will the masses finally remember them.[34]

The Third Reich collapsed in the most appalling degradation and slaughter known to history. But it did leave perhaps one legacy. The democratic nations vowed never to be caught napping again. Whatever it took, they would in future match the intensity of the enemy's propaganda. And there, huge and hideous and endless, is the shape of modern political debate at its worst. The deliberate degradation of public discourse is not the least of the evils that Hitler unleashed upon a dozy world. From Hitler, even if they do not admit it or are even unaware of it, the organizers of any modern coup have learnt the importance of crude, relentlessly repetitive propaganda. It is now our daily fodder: the babble of tweets from every MP and congressman; the huge 'comms' teams in Downing Street and the White House, working day and night, '24/7', to 'control the narrative'; the shameless fabrications of Donald Trump and Boris Johnson. The Führer did it all first.

Mrs Gandhi's Emergency

It is, of course, easier to stage a coup if you are already on the stage. An incumbent Prime Minister or President has all the machinery of state at his or her command: the police, the army and the civil service. If he or she itches to change the rules to consolidate personal power, a compliant parliament may make the necessary amendments. The judges in the Supreme Court may object if the constitution is blatantly perverted, but judges can be browbeaten or replaced. Louis-Napoleon, Benito Mussolini and Adolf Hitler are our prime instructors in how to construct a dictatorship only after you have come to power by legitimate means. In more recent times, Park Chung Hee in South Korea and Ferdinand Marcos in the Philippines are good examples of the self-coup or *autogolpe*, both having been elected democratically and then installed themselves as dictator nine and seven years later respectively.

The path to absolute rule is all the smoother when the public aren't expecting it. The later in the process that they suspect the intentions of a would-be dictator, the less trouble the coup is likely to provoke. If nicely done, it won't look like a coup, in the classic frightening sense, at all. Softer words may seem appropriate, such as 'Emergency'.

Everyone in India knew who Indira Nehru was, from the moment she was born on 19 November 1917, the only child of the resistance fighter Jawaharlal Nehru and the granddaughter of the plutocrat leader of the Congress Party Motilal Nehru. When not yet three years old, she travelled from Allahabad to Calcutta to attend her first Congress meeting, at which Gandhi launched the non-co-operation movement and called for *Swaraj* – self-rule – within a year. She visited Gandhi in jail at Yeravda and when he broke his 'fast unto death', it was the 15-year-old Indira who squeezed and gave him the orange juice that was his first nourishment. For as long as the Mahatma lived, she was on the receiving end of his advice, much of it unwanted: to wash the lipstick off her face and wear homespun instead of the gorgeous silk saris she loved, and, most irritating of all, to remain celibate after her marriage. When Gandhi was shot in 1948, it was Indira who rushed to be beside his unconscious body. Her husband, the rumbustious womanizing Parsi, Feroze Ghandy, even changed the spelling of his name because he so admired the Mahatma, leading the outside world to think that Mrs Gandhi must be some relation of the great man, adding to the aura of chosenness which hung around her through her life.

It was, to start with anyway, a rich inheritance in the material sense too. Motilal had made a huge fortune as a lawyer in Allahabad. His 42-room mansion, Anand Bhawan, 'the Abode of Happiness', had a tennis court, indoor swimming pool and riding ring, as well as the first electricity and running water in Allahabad, plus the first motor car, with an English chauffeur. Jawaharlal was sent off to Harrow and Cambridge. But then in 1920, Motilal signed up to Gandhi's boycott of everything British, and there was a huge bonfire of the vanities at Anand Bhawan. Indira's first memory was of seeing the flames on the lawn consume the Savile Row suits and French frocks.

Her life, then and later, was both enormously privileged and weirdly deprived and demanding, surrounded by servants and sycophants but also desperately lonely and with much expected of her. She was sent off to boarding schools in the Alps and in England, and then to sanatoria as she contracted TB, almost certainly from her mother, who died of it in 1936 when Indira was 18. For much of her childhood and adolescence, her father was in jail, as her grandfather had also been. Years later, she too was jailed for eight months, and felt proud to share the family fate. Jawaharlal wrote endlessly to her, warm and touching letters confiding his own doubts and anxieties. But he also wrote a series of didactic letters, subsequently published under the title of *Letters from a Father to His Daughter*, which must have been quite something for a 13-year-old girl to take in, an odd compendium of lectures about fossils and evolution and the self-indulgence of maharajas, and composed 'in the hope that it will interest you and make you think of the world and of the other people in it as your brothers and sisters'. This unspoken assumption that Indira was the heiress of the nation's destiny did not diminish with the coming of independence. The widowed Prime Minister made 24 foreign trips with his daughter as his quasi-hostess. She met everyone from Truman and JFK to Chou-en-Lai and W. H. Auden.

Yet it was not until 1959, when she was already in her 40s and her marriage had broken down (Feroze died of a heart attack a year later), and her two sons were almost grown up, that she took any active part in politics. She was persuaded to become President of the Congress Party, and even this was more because of who she was, not what she was: a figurehead in the precise sense of the word. Almost without exception, the editorials and the columnists argued that she was not up to the job.

Much the same thing happened, on a grander scale, after the death of her father and the death of his successor as Prime Minister, Lal Bahadur Shastri, less than two years later. The ruling 'Syndicate' of the Congress Party chose her as Prime Minister, not to lead them but so that they could lead her. In the words of a later PM, Narasimha Rao, she was merely 'a vote-catching device'; after the elections, 'she would take or they would make her take a back seat,' and a more experienced leader would take over and run the country.[1] The remarkable truth is that, as Ramachandra Guha points out in India After Gandhi, nobody really knew what she thought about anything: 'Her core beliefs had not been revealed to either party or public. They knew not what she really thought of the market economy, or the Cold War, or the relations between religions, or the institutions and processes of democracy.'[2] The many volumes of Nehru's writings are stuffed with his views on these subjects. But, before 1967, his daughter had scarcely uttered a word on them, in public at least. All the years she had been bringing up the boys and trying without success to cope with her wayward husband, she had steadfastly refused to enter Parliament. She was 50 before she was finally elected to the Lok Sabha, and her first halting speeches confirmed the view of the cynics. She couldn't think on her feet, she was 'a dumb doll'.[3]

What neither her patronizing detractors nor her equally patronizing backers had hauled in was how dauntless Indira was. In her long solitudes, she had learnt to rely on herself. All through those years of unearned prominence when she was always on show but never consulted, she had forged an inner steel. She would never be a deep thinker or widely read, she had never completed any course of study (at Oxford she had failed Pass Mods twice), but she had willpower. Aged 19 at Badminton School, when the headmistress had asked if she was homesick, she replied, 'I don't like being away from India at this time, but I must get to know the British [in order] to fight them.'[4] On a brief visit to South Africa in 1941, she had stunned the Indian community by blasting their indifference to the plight of the black majority – something that Gandhi, in all his years in South Africa, never dreamed of doing.[5] She was scornful of Chamberlain at Munich, ferociously hostile to the Americans in Vietnam.

And she was fearless. During the terrible days of Partition, she plunged into the refugee camps and worked eight to ten hours a day. When the Chinese invaded India in 1962, she flew straight to the Chinese border ferrying supplies with the Indian Red Cross. She was, as she said herself, at her best in a crisis. More like a tigress than a dumb doll.

And as Prime Minister, it did not take long before she showed her claws. She devalued the rupee by a huge 57.5 per cent, she nationalized the banks, she shifted the obdurate Morarji Desai away from the Finance Ministry, and she chose the pliable V. V. Giri to be the next President in preference to the Syndicate's candidate. The enraged old sweats of the Syndicate, who opposed everything she was doing, expelled her from the Congress Party, and the party split. She could not have cared less. Three years earlier, she had told Ved Mehta that 'the Congress Party is moribund.' More ominously, she added, 'sometimes I feel that even our Parliamentary system is moribund. Everything is debated and debated and nothing gets done.'[6] As PM, she attended Parliament less and less, and withdrew into a circle of reliable civil servants who shared her bias towards a largely nationalized, socialistic type of economy. Her wing of Congress, known as Congress (R), became all-powerful. India was supposed to have a scrupulously federal system, but Indira ruthlessly eased out any Chief Minister who failed to support her against the Syndicate. In Rajasthan, Andhra Pradesh, Madhya Pradesh and Maharashtra, she installed her placemen. In the 1971 election, when asked what the issues were, she said proudly, 'I am the issue.' Her publicists puffed her as *mataji*, the Mother of the Nation, but she was an unnerving sort of mother. Hours before declaring the Emergency, she remarked: 'I feel that India is like a baby, and just as one should sometimes take a child and shake it, I feel we have to shake India.'[7]

Another Congress landslide followed, and so did the first repressive measures: the Maintenance of Internal Security Act of 1971, which sanctioned indefinite preventive detention, search and seizure of property without warrant, and wiretapping; the 24th Amendment of August 1971, which enabled Parliament to dilute the fundamental rights spelled out in the Constitution; and the 25th Amendment of December 1971, which gave Parliament, rather than the courts, the right to determine the amounts of compensation to be paid when the government acquired private property. The legal expert V. G. Ramachandran described the 24th and 25th Amendments as not a case of 'tinkering with the Constitution' but rather 'a veritable slaughter of the Constitution'. Mrs Gandhi dismissed the Amendments as simply 'milestones on the progress of democracy' – which she defined as 'the right of the largest number of people'.[8]

The judges essayed a fightback of sorts. When these Amendments came before the Supreme Court, it endorsed Parliament's right to alter the Constitution, so long as it did not alter its 'essential features' – namely, that India was a democratic, secular, federal republic. But it was still for the courts to decide exactly what these 'essential features' entailed. In other words, judicial review still applied. Mrs Gandhi was furious and, when the Chief Justice happened to come up for retirement the following year, she excluded the next three judges by seniority, who had all voted to put this brake on Parliament's power, and chose the pliant A. N. Ray instead. The three passed-over judges resigned in protest at the attempt to secure 'a committed judiciary'.

All these measures preceded the actual Emergency by nearly four years. Mrs Gandhi was already well launched on her road to populist dictatorship. The Congress Party – now Congress (I) for Indira and then simply Congress again – had been brought entirely under her control. Cash donations went straight to Indira and her increasingly influential younger son, Sanjay, at their government bungalow, No. 1 Safdarjung Road. Corruption, an abiding sore in what was derided as the 'Licence Raj', had reached huge proportions, now that the banks and access to funds were controlled by the government. Indira's Principal Private Secretary, P. N. Haksar, shared her socialist inclinations and her desire for a committed judiciary, but he told her that Sanjay's antics were destroying the government's credibility, and she should send him away. It was Haksar who was sent away.

The crux, when it came, had a relatively trivial cause. On 12 June 1975, the High Court in Allahabad found that Mrs Gandhi's election campaign had broken electoral law in two respects: the state government had paid for high rostrums to allow the little PM (only 5ft 2in) to address election meetings from a dominating position, and her election agent had still been a government employee for a couple of weeks after the campaign had started. Justice Sinha therefore declared her election null and void, but granted a stay of 20 days on his order, to allow an appeal to the Supreme Court. The judge who heard the interim appeal issued a further conditional stay; Mrs Gandhi could attend Parliament but not vote until her appeal was fully dealt with.

Embarrassing, of course, but such election suits are commonplace in all democracies. The Allahabad judgment was undoubtedly a tiny revenge by the judges for all the flak they had endured from Mrs Gandhi over the amendments to the Constitution. Most lawyers believed that the Supreme Court would reverse the Allahabad judgment. Could the height of a rostrum really count as a serious 'electoral malpractice'? Mrs Gandhi pooh-poohed the judgement, and noted that the *Guardian* in London had compared the charge to a traffic violation. But P. N. Dhar, who had succeeded Haksar as Indira's PPS, pointed out that the opposition had succeeded in making the charges part of their campaign against corruption: 'in view of that, it would be better to await the verdict of the Supreme Court, which, I hoped, would go in her favour. I cautioned against letting the Congress Party launch a counter-agitation against the judgement.'[9]

Mrs Gandhi paid no more attention to Dhar than she had to Haksar. Sanjay's word was law. He was already bussing in large numbers of Indira supporters at taxpayers' expense to shout 'Indira Zindabad' all day long outside her bungalow. The chaos thus manufactured gave mother and son the pretext they had been angling for. Several days earlier, Sanjay and his cronies had begun drawing up a list of those to be detained, including Morarji Desai and J. P. Narayan, the veteran hero of independence who was leading the anti-government protests. For form's sake, she now summoned the Chief Minister of West Bengal, who happened to be in Delhi, to give her legal cover to ask the President to proclaim a state of emergency under Article 352 of the Constitution. The beauty of Article 352 was that nested within it were eight further articles which gave teeth to the Emergency: for example, powers to extend the life of a parliament and to prevent citizens from appealing to the courts to secure their fundamental rights. The Chief Justice was rather slow to pick up his cue, but eventually gave his approval. She undertook only to consult the Cabinet retrospectively, for fear of leaks. She needn't have worried. The Cabinet meeting, held the next morning at 6 a.m., lasted less than half an hour. There was no discussion and no vote. In her broadcast to the nation on All India

Radio, Mrs Gandhi opened by saying: 'The President has proclaimed an Emergency. There is nothing to panic about.' And unless you were one of the thousands who were rounded up and slung into jail alongside common criminals, nobody much did.

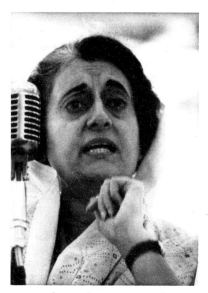

Indira on the campaign trail.

In its early months, the Emergency was undoubtedly popular. Life in the streets was more peaceful than it had been for ages. The day after it was declared, Jonathan Dimbleby reported in *The Sunday Times* that the streets of Delhi were 'uncannily normal'. The jingling flotilla of cyclists set off for work in the morning; shops and factories opened as usual. The middle classes were mostly delighted. So were the rich. The industrialist J. R. D. Tata felt that 'things had gone too far. You can't imagine what we've been through – strikes, boycotts, demonstrations. Why, there were days when I couldn't walk out of my office into the street. The parliamentary system is not suited to our needs.'[10] The Birlas and the Oberois rejoiced. 'The Emergency is just wonderful,' remarked one of the Oberoi hotel-owning clan. 'We used to have terrible problems with the unions. Now when they give us any trouble, the government just puts them in jail.'[11] We are reminded of the peaceful atmosphere in Germany after January 1933, as described by Sebastian Haffner – the same feeling of reassurance, of responsibilities parked, difficulties shelved.

Few officials resigned. By contrast, Guha points out that Gandhi's call to non-co-operation with the British Raj had led to thousands of resignations of teachers, lawyers, judges and Indian Civil Service officers. There was some resistance in the House, although Congress had a comfortable majority and 34 MPs were in jail, and a few demos on the streets, but nothing to compare with the great protest marches led by the Mahatma, or even with the huge J. P. Narayan demos which had allegedly justified the Emergency. It was not simply that people welcomed the peace and quiet. There was a sense in which Indira *was* India, had represented the nation all her life and could still be trusted to do so now. As Jaffrelot and Anil conclude, 'the Emergency was dictatorship by consent.'[12]

More surprisingly, many foreign observers such as Margaret Thatcher (always an admirer of her fellow Somervillian) and Michael Foot were sympathetic. Foot, having been assured by Indira that she would hold elections as soon as the country had stabilized, urged the British Cabinet to have 'an imaginative understanding of what has been achieved during the Emergency and why these achievements invoke so much popular support'.[13] Which you cannot conceive of him saying if anything similar had been attempted in the United Kingdom. Was there perhaps a concealed neo-colonialism at work here, a sense that Indians didn't really need all that stuff like habeas corpus and freedom of speech?

The Emergency was not simply a matter of locking up without trial something like 110,000 opponents – more even than any British Viceroy had attempted at one go. Those jailed included not only her most prominent political opponents such as Morarji Desai and J. P. Narayan, but also members of the former ruling houses of Jaipur and Gwalior (Lord Mountbatten complained to the Indian High Commissioner at a Buckingham Palace soiree, 'You have locked up all my friends'),[14] trade unionists galore and countless inoffensive ordinary citizens. Jail conditions for the *prominenti* were tolerable, but the lower classes could expect beatings and torture of the sort that were commonplace in Indian jails before and after the Emergency. The death toll in the jails ran into thousands.

Mrs Gandhi followed up the arrests with fierce censorship laws. 253 Indian journalists were jailed, and 40 foreign correspondents deported, including the revered Mark Tully of the BBC. By now she was in a state of full-blown paranoia – 'You do not know the plots against me.'[15]

The constitutional amendments which had enabled her to impose such a draconian shutdown were now followed by three more: the 38th, which safeguarded the declaration of an internal emergency against any legal challenge, and entrenched the President's rule in the states (she used this power to sack non-Congress governments that had come to power in Gujarat and Tamil Nadu); then the 39th, which invalidated the Allahabad judgment against her and swept away the specific 'corrupt practices' clause under which she had been found guilty; and above all, the 42nd, enacted over a year later in November 1976, which gave Parliament the right to amend the previously sacrosanct basic structure of the Constitution. The 42nd also extended the term of the Lok Sabha from five years to six, and made it mandatory for the President to act solely on the advice of the Cabinet, thus making him a total puppet.

These actions may seem tailored to the particular situation in India at the time, but they bear a family resemblance to the actions of all Caesars, Big and Little, in cementing their power. Take, for example, the Five Acts of Boris Johnson: they too restrict judicial review, take the supervision of elections and the definition of electoral malpractice away from the courts, reduce the discretion of the sovereign (King/President), and introduce new restrictions on the right to protest and demonstrate and invent new punishments for infringement. This is no coincidence. These are the things you need to do if you want to impose civic silence. Nor is it a coincidence that Narendra Modi, whose politics might seem to be the polar opposite of Mrs Gandhi's, never speaks ill of her. Hers is, after all, an example that he is strongly tempted to follow when and if he needs to.

Also, the Supreme Court, now a congenially compliant body, confirmed that detention without trial was perfectly legal. Habeas corpus seemed to be a thing of the past. Only one of the justices dared to protest that 'detention without trial is an anathema to all those who love personal liberty.'[16]

Here as elsewhere, federalism mitigated the impact of the Emergency. The further away you lived from the Delhi–Haryana–West United Provinces triangle, the less you were affected; in South India very little at all. In the distant provinces, judges felt able to speak their minds, as did the local papers. Out in the sticks, habeas corpus was not a dead letter.[17]

Elections were postponed under the new law in February 1976, and again in November. Some of Mrs Gandhi's admirers wanted to make this blissful state of affairs permanent. Sanjay's sleazy backer, Bansi Lal, Chief Minister of Haryana, said to B. K. Nehru, Indira's cousin, 'Nehru sahib, get rid of all this election nonsense. If you ask me, just make our sister President for life and there's no need to do anything else.'[18]

These were a truly dreadful crew. But as she later explained, she had come to mistrust the bureaucrats and preferred to let 'her own people' run the show. The bureaucrats had never 'lifted a finger to help me. In the circumstances, am I to blame if I entrust sensitive jobs to men who may not be very bright but on whom I can rely?'

Not very bright, perhaps, but not very honest, certainly. The centralization of power and the degeneration of the country into a barely concealed kleptocracy went hand in hand. And with Sanjay now effectively in control of large parts of the administration, especially in Delhi, trouble inevitably followed. Her wilful younger son had his own five-point plan to complement her 20-point plan. The two key points were family planning and slum clearance.

Sanjay's friend Jagmohan, the vice-chairman of the Delhi Development Authority, fancied himself as India's answer to Baron Haussmann and wanted to sweep away all the rickety old houses, some dating back to the Mughal period, and drive great boulevards out to the new towns he envisioned on the farmland beyond the Jumna River. The Emergency gave the imperious Jagmohan a golden opportunity. Soon the bulldozers were grinding beyond the Turkman Gate, sweeping away everything in their path without legal ado or fair warning to the residents.

At the same time, Sanjay embarked on a vast sterilization programme to stem the population, which had zoomed from 240 million in 1901 to 550 million in 1971 and was still climbing. He started in Maharashtra with compulsory sterilization for men who already had three children. Volunteers for vasectomy received a reward of 120 rupees, a tin of cooking oil or, notoriously, a transistor radio. In the first five months of the Emergency, 3.7 million Indians were sterilized. By the time the campaign was halted, the target of 23 million in three years was well on schedule. The two campaigns interacted to hurt the poor most grievously. They could often hang on to their tenements only by agreeing to be sterilized – under Indian conditions by no means a risk-free procedure. Hundreds died on the operating table or from subsequent infections.

As Sanjay's teams snipped their way across India, there was a growing realization at home and abroad of how far Indira Gandhi had departed from her father's legacy. In the *Spectator* John Grigg remarked that 'Nehru's tryst with destiny seems to have been turned into a tryst with despotism – and by his own daughter.'[19]

Three Congress luminaries, known inevitably as the Triumvirate, floated the idea of building on the Emergency to introduce a more presidential system, but one deliberately designed without the checks and balances of the US Constitution. Their note to Mrs Gandhi spelled out what they were up to:

> The Emergency has helped to convert a soft and politically permissive state into an effective democratic state. The gains of the Emergency have to be consolidated and structural changes in the constitution have to be effected to ensure that the government is not prevented through obstruction or subversion from carrying out the mandate of the majority.
>
> 1. To remove as much as possible the fetters that at present stand in the way of the proper functioning of the prime minister and government.
> 2. To prevent as much as possible judicial interference of essential legislative and executive acts.[20]

Sanjay had been kept out of these discussions. He was in any case contemptuous of the Triumvirate, and his mentors such as Bansi Lal started agitating to set up constituent assemblies in Uttar Pradesh, Punjab and Haryana, but all with much the same objective as the Triumvirate's, to install authoritarian systems that would make the Emergency permanent in a different guise.

All this talk made Mrs Gandhi nervous. 'We cannot but be a democracy,' she told Dhar: 'a secular democracy and a democracy striving steadily to enlarge its socialist contents.'[21] She was also getting cold feet about Sanjay's sterilization programme, as reports of its excesses filtered through to her.

The only way out, as Dhar and the more decent civil servants now pressed her, was to hold elections. Mrs Gandhi retreated into the brooding silences that were becoming a feature. After a time, rather to the surprise even of those who had been urging her on, she gave in. On 18 January 1977, she announced that elections would be held, and sharply too, only two months later. The outside world, which had not been privy to her dithering, was stunned. Why had she done it? The arguments about her motives have continued to this day.

The conventional view is that she believed the sycophants who told her she would win – and win big – and that she had been misled by the poll forecasts from her own intelligence agencies. Dhar denies this. She was given a fairly accurate picture of the political situation. His own view was that, deep down, 'she was not comfortable with the Emergency, and she wanted to get out of it somehow, anyhow.'[22] After all, it was clear to the meanest observer that the Emergency had been much more popular in the early months; from the point of view of electoral advantage, that would have been the time to go to the polls.

Dhar also felt that she was feeling isolated and cut off, and longing for the crowds who had acclaimed her so fervently in 1971. Like many of the leaders we have focused on – Charles de Gaulle, for example – she was at her happiest in the 'bain de foule', bathing in the people's love. Ramachandra Guha adds the thought that the foreign criticism was getting to her. She took the decision to hold the election only a fortnight after Bernard Levin's two long articles in The Times in the first week of January 1977 denouncing her constitutional amendments as designed to emasculate the presidency and the judiciary and confirming the 'transformation of India into a fully authoritarian regime under its seedy dictator, Mrs Indira Gandhi'. These followed two earlier articles by Levin in October 1976, attacking the censorship and the suspension of habeas corpus.[23]

All these motives may have played a part, as may her pledge at the outset that the Emergency would be only a temporary measure. Unlike other successful coup leaders, she seems to have had no game plan for a long-term transformation of the system, and when one was offered to her, by the Triumvirate, she didn't much like the look of it. To put it kindly, we may hazard that she stumbled into her dictatorship, and never quite lost a lingering bad conscience about it. Her father's high-minded advice may still have whispered to her, however faintly.

There is perhaps a simpler explanation. The only legitimation of the Emergency, threadbare though it was, came from a pliant Lok Sabha, but if the Lok Sabha itself ceased to be legitimate, then the dictatorship would be nakedly exposed. At some point, the parliament would have to renew its credentials. There would have to be elections. She had, after all, repeatedly said in interviews that 'we are committed to elections.'[24] If only in formal terms, this was 'a constitutional dictatorship'.

There was also the interesting parallel with the imposition of civil martial law by the British Raj to quell disturbances in 1932. Once the colony had been brought to heel, martial law was lifted and elections were held. The British historian D. A. Low, himself steeped in the Raj from childhood, brilliantly predicted in 1975 that Mrs Gandhi would do the same – and would lose the election.

Yet only a month earlier, the President had signed into law the appalling 42nd Amendment entrenching the Emergency beyond challenge. Why throw it all away now? Jaffrelot and Anil hazard the thought that 'this inconsistency is typical of sultanic regimes, where an atmosphere of arbitrariness permits leaders to indulge themselves.'[25] Part of the sultan's charisma derives from his unpredictability. His thought processes are too deep for ordinary mortals to follow. Indira had startled the outside world by imposing the Emergency. Even Morarji Desai predicted, on the very night that the Emergency was declared, that she would never take the country into a dictatorship. 'She'll never do it – she'd commit suicide first.'[26] Well, she did it, and without a backward glance. Now she startled them all over again.

Anyway, for whatever mixture of reasons, she took the plunge. And she lost. In fact, she was slaughtered. In the northern Hindi provinces, Congress was wiped out, reduced to two seats out of a previous 226, but the party continued to do well in the southern states – showing that it was the impact of the Emergency that did for her. The streets of Delhi had not seen such mass rejoicing since the British departed.

Mrs Gandhi had made much of her pledge that she would 'abide' by the result. Yet soon after the election, there was a strange meeting between Sanjay, his mother and General T. N. 'Tappy' Raina, whom Indira had appointed as Chief of Army Staff. Sanjay told Raina that it would be possible to control India by deploying a mere three or four army divisions. 'The Congress Party, supported by the paramilitary forces and the police, can deal with other administrative details.'[27] In other words, he was inviting Raina to join in a military coup. Raina refused to take the bait, though he agreed that Sanjay's analysis was 'mathematically correct'. Anyway, no more was heard of any such coup. But the incident showed how Sanjay's mind – and his mother's – were working in that frenetic moment. This was not the first time Mrs Gandhi had consulted General Raina on such a question. The day before she declared the Emergency, she summoned him from a golf course in Rajasthan to ask for his support. Tappy reportedly replied (there seems to be no authoritative account of the meeting) that the army could not be used to further her ends and would obey only the orders of 'a legally construed government'.[28] Nonetheless, the Indian Army was a highly visible presence in the early days of the Emergency, with armoured regiments a common sight on the streets of Delhi, contributing to the huge numbers of policemen on parade. Thus the army had given at least tacit consent to the proceedings.

The new Janata government was a ragbag, united only in its opposition to the Emergency and its loathing of Indira Gandhi. The Shah Commission which was set up to enquire into the excesses of the Emergency failed to nail her personal responsibility (even so, she had all the copies of the Commission's report destroyed, at least those she could lay her hands on). And the attempt to intensify her humiliation by arresting her was a fiasco. But the new government did do its job of restoring the Constitution, and with diligence and dispatch. Just before the 1977 election, Morarji Desai complained that the Constitution had been 'vasectomized' during the emergency, and he promised to 'rectify' it.

This election pledge was magnificently fulfilled, largely due to the work of the new Law Minister, Shanti Bhushan. The 44th Amendment undid all the evil effects of the 42nd, and more. The term of Parliament reverted to five years, the Supreme Court regained the right to adjudicate on all election matters (including those relating to the PM), the period of President's Rule in the states was limited, and any state of emergency now had to be approved by a two-thirds majority in Parliament, and had to be renewed every six months, and had to be in response to an 'armed rebellion', rather than a mere 'internal disturbance'.

A model piece of work. And even the authors of the Emergency were no longer in a mood to defend their excesses. When the 44th Amendment was passed with a comfortable majority in December 1978, Mrs Gandhi herself voted for it, for once finding herself on the same side as Morarji Desai.[29] So the Constitution of India was restored to the state in which Nehru and the founding fathers had left it. Nor have subsequent governments dared to tamper with the actual text, although serious threats and alarms have cropped up during the governments of BJP and Narendra Modi.

For Modi and the Hindu nationalists, the Emergency was both a windfall and a lesson. Because they formed the only coherent opposition during the Emergency, they were propelled from the fringes of Indian politics into the mainstream, and their new prominence gave the various factions a strong incentive to unite and learn how to win national elections. At the same time, the Emergency gave them a strong sense of how ready the vast bulk of Indian voters were to accept authoritarian rule and its consequences. This is the indirect, ongoing legacy of Mrs Gandhi.

Unlike the direct suppression of constitutional protections during the Emergency of Indira Gandhi, Modi's government in its first term (2014–19) assaulted the constitution by subtle and oblique routes. Tarunabh Khaitan, Professor of Public Law at Oxford, describes it as 'death by a thousand cuts'.[30] Under the BJP, the Lok Sabha refuses to recognize an official Leader of the Opposition if no opposition party has won more than 10 per cent (55 seats) of the chamber (in 2014 the sadly shrunken Congress Party mustered only 44). In 2018, the government briskly guillotined discussion on the Finance Bill, although there were still weeks available for debate. It has also redefined various Bills as 'money bills', so that, as under the British system, the Upper House has no right to veto them. It has interfered in the appointment of judges, packed the civil service with its own supporters and brought charges of sedition against protesters and journalists. Its legislative and executive actions against the Muslim minority are notorious, but they are only part of a systematic campaign to achieve a one-party Hindu state in all but name. In Assam, the government has deported millions of Muslims who lacked the papers to prove long-term residence, while extending citizenship to recent Hindu immigrants from Bangladesh with the clear intention of transforming the state into a Hindu fortress. All these and many other deliberate and shameless perversions of the spirit, if not the letter, of the Constitution have continued into Modi's second term. Halfway through, the London *Times* summarized the country's present situation thus:

India's once proud if sluggish judiciary no longer functions independently. Instead of working for Asia's most vibrant free press, Indian journalists choose between jail for doing their job or functioning as government mouthpieces. In eight years, Modi has held not a single press conference. Parliamentary debates are routinely truncated and laws are fast-tracked without scrutiny. Having winked at or openly supported vigilantism against India's

200 million Muslims, Modi is increasingly resorting to structural
forms of discrimination, such as the 2019 Citizenship Act, which
could revoke the citizenship of millions of Muslims.[31]

Not surprisingly, the stench of corruption has only deepened, not least
after the Finance Acts of 2016 and 2018, which granted immunity to
the BJP for receiving previously illegal foreign donations. In the first
year of the new rules, the BJP received 2.1 billion rupees in donations,
while the Congress Party got only 50 million. Shanti Bhushan resigned
in disgust from, in succession, the old Congress Party, Janata, and
finally the BJP, to spend the rest of his long life (he is now 96) setting
up anti-corruption pressure groups and parties, in collaboration with
his no less vigilant son Prashant and, for part of the time, with the
legendary activist and Gandhian hunger striker, 'Anna' Hazare (Anna
means father or elder in Marathi). The Aam Aadmi, or Common Man's
Party, has had some success recently in electing Chief Ministers in
Delhi and Punjab. But the corruption, both in Parliament and the
courts, chunters merrily on. All we can say is that it is now monitored
and denounced by a skilled and determined corps of critics.

Yet at least India is clinging on to Nehru's Constitution, more or
less, although Mrs Gandhi's assaults may have softened up opposition
to these more recent incursions. So we are justified, on balance, in
including Mrs Gandhi's Emergency in our selection of coups that
failed. This is not because it was a feeble effort. Not only was the
constitution deliberately and thoroughly degraded, but free speech
was also abolished, and a merciless regime imprisoned without
trial over 100,000 of its citizens, most of them sharing squalid jails
with common criminals. It is a shock, even in India today, to meet
respectable citizens now in late middle age, who speak ruefully of
having been 'jugged by Mrs G'.

But if her Emergency was a repulsive failure, which fully deserves
to be remembered with obloquy, Indira Gandhi herself was not cast
into outer darkness as a result. In 1980, after the Janata government
collapsed under the weight of its contradictions, she returned in
glory, to win her third general election victory. Just as we have argued
that coups do not all follow the same predetermined path, neither do
they succeed or fail for the same reasons, so their authors may suffer
a variety of fates, from being strung up by their heels outside a petrol
station to being returned to power in a fair and free election only
three years later.

Even so, the comeback of Indira Gandhi is one of political history's more remarkable episodes. It can be attributed in equal measure to her superb energies as a campaigner and to the unique place she both inherited and sustained in the nation's story. During the campaign of January 1980, she spent 62 days on the road, addressing 20 meetings a day, and Congress won 301 out of 572 seats in the Lok Sabha. But this was scarcely the old Congress. This was Congress (I), and at least 150 of the new MPs were Sanjay groupies, described by Inder Malhotra as

lumpen young men . . . innocent of . . . parliamentary proprieties, unencumbered by ideology or idealism, short on cerebration and long on . . . muscle power. Sanjay's acolytes looked upon their membership of Parliament and proximity to the centre of power as a short-cut to making the maximum amount of money in the shortest possible time.[32]

Not unlike ambitious young East India Company men in the old days. And the idea of going into politics as the quickest way of making money has stuck. Visitors to India today are regularly amazed by the huge numbers of MPs, often running into the hundreds, who are under investigation for corruption.

And what about their Prime Minister? Was she chastened, had she learnt any sort of lesson? Not exactly. She did not attempt to tamper with the Constitution again; she exploited it as hard as she could. She immediately sacked the nine Janata state governments, imposing President's rule and calling fresh state elections, of which Congress won all but one. In Andhra Pradesh, she changed the Chief Minister no fewer than four times in four years. Like most people who have been in power too long, she also became rather batty, placing increasing reliance on the dodgy Brahmachari, the handsome swami who had been her yoga teacher for 20 years. Like her father, she was sceptical of conventional religion, but she now performed rituals dictated by Brahmachari to ward off the plots against her she descried everywhere. When Sanjay was killed trying to loop the loop in his new aeroplane, Brahmachari told her that the plane had crashed because she had failed to visit all the shrines he had instructed her to. After Sanjay's death, a grieving nation named hydro-electric stations, trains, bus terminals, bridges, dams and streets, schools and hospitals after him.

His death was a relief to the nation, nonetheless, though an irreparable loss to his mother. She retreated further into superstition and paranoia. She saw foreign and domestic enemies everywhere, and could not resist intervening all over the subcontinent to impose her will. In the Punjab, Sanjay's loyalists had backed a violent Sikh holy man called Bhindranwale in the hope of warding off the threat of an independent Sikh state. Bhindranwale and his heavily armed followers holed up in the complex of buildings that comprise the Golden Temple of Amritsar. After a long stand-off, Mrs Gandhi sent in an assault force to winkle them out. Operation Bluestar ended in a worse loss of life than Brigadier Dyer had inflicted in his massacre at Amritsar 60 years earlier. With equally headstrong determination, she tried to get rid of Farooq Abdullah, the Chief Minister of Kashmir, even going so far as to install the appalling Jagmohan as governor of the province to winkle him out. In Sri Lanka, she recklessly supported the Tamil separatist army with terrible consequences. These decisions came home to roost in the most appalling way. In 1984, Indira was assassinated by two of her Sikh bodyguards, and seven years later her elder son Rajiv was killed by a female Tamil suicide bomber. Her murder could have been prevented, if only she had not overruled the advice of her intelligence chief that all Sikhs should be removed from protection duty.

It could be argued that the trouble in these border states was an inevitable consequence of the sprawling diversity of the subcontinent. But when Rajiv succeeded his mother, this good-humoured airline pilot with little political experience managed to secure peace with the Mizos, the Sikhs and the Assamese in a relatively short space of time. In all three cases, he allowed parties or leaders opposed to the Congress to come to power through peaceful means. All that was needed was a modicum of tolerance and goodwill at the centre, qualities for which Mrs Gandhi was not remarkable. She entirely lacked her father's ability to reach out to political opponents.

It's hard to avoid the conclusion that Indira Gandhi was an intemperate and arrogant politician who should never have been allowed to stay in power so long. At the same time, she never ceased to be a bold and brilliant campaigner. Marvellous at getting power, high-handed and short-sighted in exercising it. This, unfortunately, is a not infrequent combination, and not just in India.

The experience of the Emergency is both disheartening and heartening. Disheartening because it shows how easily a popular

Prime Minister with a comfortable majority can subvert the long-standing political arrangements to construct an authoritarian regime. Heartening too, though, because it shows how easily a fresh government can restore those arrangements – to such an extent that, when returned to power, even the original subverter has to respect them. Constitutional democracy is fragile, yes, but even in extremis it can be given the kiss of life, if there's a competent doctor on the premises.

Superman Falls to Earth – the Toppling of BoJo

The United Kingdom left the European Union at 11 p.m. on 31 January 2020. The previous month, in the general election on 12 December, Boris Johnson had secured a majority of 80, streaming far ahead of Labour by more than 10 per cent of the votes cast. This advantage in public opinion was to be sustained for a year and more. In May 2021, the Conservatives scored a remarkable by-election victory in the Labour stronghold of Hartlepool.

What was Johnson to do with this glorious triumph? How was he to lead the nation to the sunlit uplands that were promised as a consequence of Britain leaving the EU? After all the agonies of the Brexit wars, what was to be the reward? As a prelude to the upcoming talks about a free trade deal with our former partners, on 3 February 2020, he gave a sweeping oration in the Painted Hall at Greenwich. It was a splurging hymn to the glories of free trade and the spirit of Adam Smith, almost as baroque as Sir James Thornhill's enormous ceiling fresco with its allegories of Time Exposing Truth and other desirable outcomes. It's a fine piece of Boris bravura, if you overlook the fact that, during the heyday he is hymning, Britain, like many rapidly industrializing countries (the US in the nineteenth century, China today), was ruthlessly protectionist when it suited her, which is just what Adam Smith was complaining about, and he was a Customs Officer himself, so he should know.

Quite early in the text as delivered, there comes a weird, contorted paragraph with an even weirder bit in the middle. 'We are starting,' Johnson claims,

> to hear some bizarre autarkic rhetoric, when barriers are going up, *and when there is a risk that new diseases such as coronavirus will trigger a panic*

and a desire for market segregation that go beyond what is medically rational to the point of doing real and unnecessary economic damage, then at that moment humanity needs some government somewhere that is willing at least to make the case powerfully for freedom of exchange, some country ready to take off its Clark Kent spectacles and leap into the phone booth and emerge with its cloak flowing as the supercharged champion of the right of the populations of the earth to buy and sell freely among each other [*my italics*].

'Coronavirus . . . panic'? Apart from the awkward syntax, what is this interpolation doing in there? We can, I think, with a little imagination reconstruct the scene in No 10. Johnson is brewing up the Greenwich speech, splashing on the saucy metaphors, sprinkling the demotic seasoning, and is interrupted by a briefing from Public Health England or possibly the Chief Medical Officer, or maybe just Dominic Cummings: there is a nasty virus heading this way from China.

So what does our own Superman do? Far from commissioning plans for an emergency response, he swirls his cloak and takes the first available opportunity to denounce the doomsters even before they rear their heads. No doubt his staff cast their eyes over the speech. With a normal PM, they would point out that this coronavirus reference is

a) entirely irrelevant to the free trade theme;
b) conjures up a panic which does not exist; and
c) deters a speedy and rational response to a danger of as yet unknown proportions.

And a normal PM would mutter, 'Oh yes, I see what you mean', and cut it out. But this is not a normal Prime Minister.

A month later, Johnson was still boasting of shaking hands with all and sundry. It was seven weeks to the day before the official lockdown was imposed. Seven weeks. The cost of that delay cannot be nicely calculated, any more than the cost of abandoning any effort to trace and contact the infectors, or to impose any sort of quarantine on people returning from abroad. But we know what wasn't done, and when it wasn't done, and we know the death toll. A year after the Greenwich speech, 100,000 people had died, and thousands more had nearly died, including Johnson himself. It was clear from the start that he was more interested in keeping the economy humming than saving lives. Cummings claimed afterwards that Johnson had disagreed with the first lockdown and said that he would rather 'see bodies pile high' than take the country into a third lockdown.

According to Cummings, Johnson repeatedly argued, after he was pushed into the first lockdown, that 'I should have been like the Mayor in Jaws and kept the beaches open' (ignoring the fact that the shark in the film scored a couple more kills off the crowded beaches). [Cummings's evidence to the Select Committee, May 26, 2021] The Health Minister at the time, Matt Hancock, a fierce enemy of Cummings, recorded in his diary that Johnson couldn't stop talking about COVID FREEDOM DAY and claiming, against all the evidence, that 'the virus isn't really killing many people any more, so "how can we possibly justify the continuing paralysis"'? The Prime Minister's new theory was that 'the virus may be starting to run out of potential victims', and anyway it was only killing old people.[1]

We know too of the hasty attempts to rig the record: the persistent denials, despite clear evidence to the contrary, that the government's original policy was the unlovely 'herd immunity'; Cummings' retrofitting of his blog on the night he returned from Durham to show that he had all along prophesied the dangers of a coronavirus; and so on, ad nauseam.

Johnson's insouciance goes hand in hand with his gargantuan self-confidence. So it is not surprising that his reaction to these embarrassments was to double down. Instead of standing back and letting others better qualified take the next decisions, Clark Kent proposed, according to the *Daily Telegraph* on 3 June, to 'take back control' of the epidemic. So what on earth was he doing before? More generally, we understood that Cummings's spad squads would zoom into every ministerial department to get things done. 'Hub and spokes' was to be the new design for Whitehall, and the spokes could expect to be severely spoken to if they did not do what they were told. When some journalists first remarked on these overweening tendencies, we were told we were being hysterical; No. 10 always behaved like that. The next week, the Chancellor of the Exchequer was told to sack all his advisers and accept Cummings's nominees instead. It is hard to recall a parallel in post-war British politics with the humiliation of Sajid Javid, just as it is hard to recall a parallel with the purging of the 21 liberal Tory MPs. Even Attlee's expulsion of the Bevanites was only temporary.

Since Brexit Day in January, the final EU negotiations were being managed by a new Task Force Europe, led by Johnson's chief negotiator, David Frost, the burly, acerbic diplomat who was one of the few in the Foreign Office who had always loathed the EU. Frost's conversations with Michel Barnier soon became openly bitter and recriminatory, in a way not seen before in all the long years of the talks. Frost was backed up by contemptuous briefings from the No. 10 Press Office, again of an unprecedented rudeness, surpassing even the gruff Bernard Ingham under Thatcher or the venomous Alastair Campbell under Blair. For all Johnson's oily protestations that he wished to see warm and friendly relations with 'our European friends', he only had eyes and ears for the domestic Europhobes who put him where he was. We had moved on from 'Get Brexit done' to 'Get shot of Europe'.

Johnson's policy had always included leaving the single market and the customs union and saying goodbye to the European Court of Justice. But as far as I can see, it was only in the Painted Hall that he fully spelled out what 'deal' meant and did not mean. On trade, on fisheries, on science and culture, on anything in fact, these were to be transient transactions, to be terminated when either side fancied. 'I see no need to bind ourselves to an agreement with the EU.' Any fisheries agreement was to be negotiated annually. What delicious cod wars, what herring hassles, what scallop spats we had to look forward to. As for the fears of business, Johnson blathered on about the marvellous no-quota, no-tariff deals that were just around the corner. But when it came down to it, to use his patent *mot de Cambronne*, 'fuck business'. National sovereignty was to trump commerce every time. This was the art of the deal à la Trump. 'While we will always co-operate with our European friends whenever our interests converge – as they often if not always will – this will not in my view necessarily require any new treaty or institutions, because we will not need them.' No membership of any European institution then, no alignment, no entrenchment, no permanence, no real affection. To re-quote de Gaulle: 'Treaties are like young girls and roses; they last as long they last.' Or of course, Palmerston: 'We have no eternal allies and we have no perpetual enemies. Our interests are eternal and perpetual'.

So goodbye Europe, and more or less, bye-bye world. In Johnson's first year as Prime Minister, I struggle to recall any significant conversation he had with a foreign leader. What would be the net effect of all this, even assuming a tolerable outcome on trade in goods, if not in services? An anxious nation still convalescing from the virus and the economic damage it had caused, unable to distinguish between these ill effects and the effects of leaving the EU; across the Channel a no less anxious EU, bruised by Brexit and by British abuse as well as the pandemic, disinclined, to put it mildly, to do us any favours. And all this as a result of a freely chosen policy. We were not driven to the cliff edge by accident or incompetence. It was always the Brexiteers' destination of choice. It turned out to be a chilly place, in which Britain was regarded by her former partners with a mixture of resentment and contempt.

The first practical question was of course whether the UK could secure even the barest of trade deals that would not affront the susceptibilities of the European Reform Group. As the bargaining reached its climax in December 2020, the Brexotics remained as suspicious as ever. Their leaders, such as Martin Howe QC, a member of Bill Cash's 'Star Chamber', said that Johnson should reject the EU's 'one-sided and damaging trade agreement': 'once the EU has pocketed its huge concessions on goods, with the UK getting almost nothing in return, it becomes impossible to negotiate something better later.'[2] The historian Robert Tombs, a passionate late convert to Brexit, agreed: 'We must not make unreasonable concessions over fish. Even more importantly we must not sign up to one-sided legal obligations – the so-called "level playing field" – keeping us tied indefinitely into the EU system.'[3]

Yet, come Christmas Eve, what happened? After a hasty examination of the terms that had been agreed, the Star Chamber could find no serious flaw in them. Tombs himself exulted that 'the EU knew what it had to lose and backed down.'[4] But what did the 1,246 pages of the Trade and Co-operation Agreement actually say?

At the outset, the European Commission emphasizes that 'the Agreement goes beyond traditional free trade agreements and provides a solid basis for preserving our longstanding friendship and co-operation.' In particular:

> Both parties have committed to ensuring a robust level playing field by maintaining high levels of protection in areas such as environmental protection, the fight against climate change and carbon pricing, social and labour rights, tax transparency and State aid, with effective domestic enforcement, a binding dispute

settlement mechanism and the possibility for both parties to take remedial action.

And all that's before we get on to a fisheries agreement which preserves a huge share of the catch for continental fishermen, and, for Northern Ireland, that pesky border in the Irish Sea. If I were Michel Barnier or Ursula von der Leyen, I would have been quietly pleased with my handiwork.

How, then, did the wizards of the Star Chamber reconcile themselves to this settlement, which, on the surface, would appear to contain most of the things they hate? What they argued was that the TCA enshrined the legal sovereignty of the UK and that a 'robust' UK government could weasel out of anything it found inconvenient. And if the EU protested, then under the TCA we could give 12 months' notice to quit, or wait to renegotiate the whole thing in five years' time. In other words, the main reason for signing up to this agreement was the ease with which we could get out of it. Not exactly a friendly start to what Gove called a new 'special relationship between sovereign equals'.

And how likely was the Star Chamber's scenario to pan out in reality? After all the agony of the past four and a half years, how eager was any UK government going to be to pick a big fight with the EU? Would voters really forgive a renewal of the Brexit war? Besides, as the former Chancellor Philip Hammond has questioned, was this hard-won right to diverge from EU standards going to be much more than notional? The tide was now flowing as strongly in this country as in the EU in favour of protecting the environment and workers' rights, and against the wholesale deregulation that had been the war cry of the Thatcher years.

What was clear was that the next few years would be occupied with filling in the vast gaps in the TCA, by negotiating treaties of mutual recognition on the professions, financial services, insurance and a dozen other fields, as well as working out the things that were already in the TCA, such as the fiendishly complex rules of origin. Was our ultimate destination something like the European Free Trade Association, which was where we had come in 60 years ago? Who knows, by 2030 we might have reached the condition of Norway, still conforming, as an entirely independent country, to the vast corpus of EU law and practice, though it would of course be off limits to mention the *acquis communautaire*. It's a matter of taste whether you choose to call this a state of informal vassalage, to use the Brexiteers' favourite term of abuse.

But for the time being, the subject was agreed to have been settled, or at least safely parked out of the way. Whole debates in the House of Commons would pass without either side daring to mention the B-word. In the right-wing press, any mention of possible downsides to the Brexit agreement was utterly forbidden. Columnists who felt inclined to embark on the subject would feel their editor's hot breath down their necks, not to mention their proprietor's, and would turn to less controversial subjects like transgender rights or climate change. The conspiracy of silence was almost overwhelming.

Tory supporters felt that any potential criticisms of the Johnson regime were now 'priced in'. Yes, Dominic Cummings' breach of lockdown and Johnson's subsequent exculpation of his behaviour, declaring that he had acted 'responsibly, legally and with integrity', had shocked some po-faced moralists, but the damage had not 'cut through' to the overall prospects of the Conservative Party, which had every chance of winning yet another term at the next general election.

At least, that was the general consensus up to the summer of 2021. Then, in a by-election on 17 June, the Liberal Democrats took the rock-solid Tory seat of Chesham and Amersham. Was this merely the usual mid-term blues, or had the Conservative brand suffered some underlying damage from the agony of Covid, despite the arrival of Britain's 'world-beating' vaccine?

Then on 21 October, the Parliamentary Commissioner for Standards found that the leading Brexiteer and former Cabinet Minister, Owen Paterson, MP for North Shropshire, had breached Parliament's paid advocacy rules, by lobbying ministers to secure a £133 million contract for the pharmaceutical company Randox in March 2020 to supply testing kits during the coronavirus pandemic, without any other firm getting a look-in. A further £347 million contract had been awarded to Randox six months later, again without other firms being given a chance to bid. The whole business seemed like a flagrant example of the 'VIP lane', down which Tory friends and donors could secure exclusive access to contracts worth billions for PPE and testing equipment which often turned to be unusable. The Commissioner concluded that 'no previous case of paid advocacy has seen so many breaches or such a clear pattern of behaviour in failing to separate private and public interests.' The Committee on Standards had no hesitation in deciding that Paterson be suspended, which would have triggered a recall petition in his constituency. Johnson, moved by loyalty to his dogged supporter and also by sympathy for the recent suicide of Paterson's wife, put on a three-line whip to delay the suspension and set up a new committee to look at the disciplinary process anew. Paterson showed no sign of remorse. In a TV interview, he declared, 'I wouldn't hesitate to do it again tomorrow.'[5] His mulish behaviour and the government's indulgence towards him created such national outrage that Johnson backtracked and said that there would, after all, be a vote on Paterson's suspension. Paterson forestalled this by resigning, with bitter reluctance, and on 16 December the Tories were crushed in the subsequent by-election.

At about this time, rumours began circulating of another murky aspect of politicians' behaviour during the pandemic. The *Daily Mirror* claimed on 30 November that there had been a convivial gathering of staff at No. 10 during the previous December. Boris Johnson said that the lockdown rules had been followed, and Downing Street denied that any sort of party had taken place. He fatally repeated in the Commons the claim that 'all guidance was followed completely.'[6] Then in January 2022, there was another report of drinks in the No. 10 garden, in May 2020. Johnson admitted attending this one and did apologize. Downing Street also apologized to the Queen for two more events held during the third lockdown on 16 April 2021, on the eve of Prince Philip's funeral. By now Johnson had ordered a Cabinet Office Inquiry to be led by the civil servant Sue Gray. On 22 January, the Met opened its own investigation of potential breaches of Covid-19 regulations. After looking into 12 gatherings, including at least three attended by Johnson himself, the police issued no fewer than 126 fixed-penalty notices to 83 people, including Johnson, his new wife Carrie and the Chancellor of the Exchequer, Rishi Sunak. Sue Gray's report deepened the damage by describing the culture of excessive drinking at multiple events, and the rudeness shown to cleaners and security staff. Dominic Cummings, now pursuing a relentless vendetta against his former patron, blogged more details of these illegal booze-ups. Fatally, it was revealed to ITV News that the Prime Minister's PPS, Martin Reynolds, had sent out an invitation to No. 10 staff to 'socially distanced drinks' in the garden on 20 May, ending, 'Bring Your Own Booze!' Reynolds swiftly became known as Party Marty.[7] The irony is that, as one minister remarked, 'Boris doesn't even particularly like parties.' Like many egotists, he seems ill at ease in social gatherings at which he is not the designated speaker.

The anger aroused across the nation was provoked not simply by the cynical disregard shown by ministers and their personal staff for the rules they had themselves drafted to shut down everyone else's lives, but also by the way the truth had had to be dragged out of them through a screen of obfuscation and outright lies. After Partygate, as it was fatefully dubbed, pressure began to build for a vote of no confidence in Johnson. The threshold for calling one was passed without much difficulty and the vote held on 6 June. Johnson won the vote with 211 in favour and 148 against. It wasn't only Keir Starmer who drew the conclusion that this was 'the beginning of the end'.

By now, the Tories were lagging far behind Labour in the polls. In by-elections on 23 June, Labour regained Wakefield and the Lib Dems overturned the enormous Conservative majority in Tiverton and Honiton. BoJo's reputation as an infallible election-winner was beginning to look shaky. Had it really been such a brilliant triumph to wallop a Labour Party led by Jeremy Corbyn? At the same time, the old doubts about Johnson's character were being thrust in the nation's face.

What became apparent in the late spring and early summer of 2022 was how few real friends Johnson had in the House of Commons. He had always trod a lonely path there, and now he was paying for it. When the by-elections went so badly wrong and when he was booed by the crowds outside St Paul's for the Platinum Jubilee service on 3 June, his principal attractions – that he was popular in the country and that he was an election winner – began to look shaky. As one rebel minister mused, 'when your support is that transactional, it can just fall away.'[8]

One final scandal tipped the scales irrevocably. Chris Pincher, the Deputy Chief Whip, was found to have been persistently groping young men. He resigned on 30 June and had the party whip removed. Johnson denied that he had known of any specific allegations against Pincher before appointing him. Then it emerged that he had in private referred to him as 'handsy' and 'Pincher by name, Pincher by nature'. Eventually on 5 July Johnson was forced to say sorry on the BBC for having ignored the warnings about Pincher.

You don't have to look back far to see what a dreadful falling off in the standards of behaviour expected from MPs was shown by Partygate and the Owen Paterson and Chris Pincher affairs. As recently as 2017, three senior ministers had had to resign instantly when they were found to have misbehaved: Damian Green as Mrs May's Deputy Prime Minister for lying about pornography found on his computer, Michael Fallon as Defence Secretary over allegations of sexual harassment, and Stephen Crabb as Work and Pensions Secretary for sending sexually explicit texts to a girl he had interviewed. None of them was allowed to hang on for a moment. Now it seemed that the Prime Minister of the day would instinctively excuse every instance of misbehaviour, including his own.

Johnson's apology, abject though it was, did not work. Minutes after it was broadcast, Sajid Javid, the Health Secretary, resigned. Then, ten minutes later, Rishi Sunak resigned as Chancellor (apparently without any co-ordination with Javid). Johnson responded in private with a torrent of four-letter words. The next morning, Wednesday, 6 July, other ministers started resigning, one after the other. It was a serial bombardment, compounded by the damning critiques of Johnson's leadership which accompanied the resignations. Again and again, the PM's former admirers lamented the loss of 'integrity, decency, respect and professionalism', to quote the Prisons Minister, Victoria Atkins, in her resignation statement.[9]

At 10.25 that morning, Michael Gove popped into Johnson's office to say, 'Boss, I'm really sorry to say this, but I think you should announce you're standing down today.' To which a furious BJ retorted: 'I'm going to fight, they're going to have to prise me out of here.'[10] On and on the resignations went, with the occupants of what they themselves dubbed the Bunker desperately trying to plug the gaps in the ministerial ranks. One minister who did not resign was Gove himself. Late that evening, he returned a call from No. 10 and asked Johnson if he was retiring, to which he received the venomous comeback: 'No, Mikey mate, I'm afraid you are.'[11] For his second stab in the back, Gove was not to be forgiven.

There had now been more than 40 resignations of ministers, more than ever recorded in a single day, not to speak of dozens of backbenchers who had expressed no confidence in their leader. One of the last to resign was Michelle Donelan, who had been appointed Education Minister only two days earlier, the shortest tenure on record for any minister. Ministers were handing in their cards from all over Westminster. Charles Moore, former editor of the *Daily Telegraph* and an old comrade of Johnson, who had just ennobled him (he had also campaigned passionately to save Owen Paterson), was strolling through the park and saw Simon Hart, the Welsh Secretary, sitting on a park bench tweeting away. 'Oh, Simon,' inquired Moore, 'what are you up to this evening?'

'If you wait 15 seconds,' Hart replied, 'I'm literally resigning.'[12] Somehow no other image conjures up so sharply the forlorn, chaotic dissolving of the British government on the evening of Wednesday, 6 July.

Sir Graham Brady went to see the PM at 6.15 that evening to warn him that they planned to elect a new executive of the 1922 Committee. The new executive was almost certain to change the rules to permit another confidence vote, and 'it is fairly obvious you would lose it.'[13]

Even Johnson himself began to see the impossibility of reconstructing his government from the remaining available duds and rejects. After hearing one particularly implausible name, he told the other inmates of the Bunker, 'It's not fair on the nation to give them a D-List government,' implying, as most impartial observers had already agreed, that the government he had presided over was no better than a C-List. At about 10.30 p.m., he announced to his fellow inmates: 'I can't do this, it's all too ghastly, it's not me.'[14] And with that final flash of egocentricity, it was all over. The final downfall had been breathtakingly quick. At 6 p.m. on 5 July, Javid had gone. In less than 48 hours Superman was gone too.

Boris Johnson's farewell speech at the Downing Street lectern.

There has been no more humiliating exit in British political history. Johnson was thrown out not because of some great policy difference, or after some grim setback in war like Asquith and Chamberlain, or because he had simply lost an election. In fact, he never lost an election, except for his first outing in a hopeless seat in North Wales. He was thrown out because — let us use his own demotic here — he was a shocker, a rotter, a stinker. He remained unrepentant and unapologetic, bidding the public au revoir and certainly not farewell. He ended his last PMQs with the words, 'Hasta la vista, baby' — characteristically taken from Arnold Schwarzenegger's Terminator 2. And in his parting speech behind that infernal lectern, he put on his toga and declared that 'like Cincinnatus, I am returning to the plough,' leaving the clear implication that, like Cincinnatus, he would be ready to return to save the nation in its hour of need. To nobody's surprise, he decided less than two months later that the hour of need had already arrived, flying back from the West Indies to offer himself as the ideal replacement for his successor. He even managed to drum up 100 MPs to support his return. Incorrigible to the last, both Johnson and his eternal stooges.

The epilogue to his eviction had been no less painful and wincingly brief. Liz Truss, a former Remainer, had risen in the Tory hierarchy by adopting the rhetoric of the Brexiteers. It was clear to most people who knew her that she lacked the capacity for any high office, and certainly the highest. If Johnson was, as Cummings maintained, like a shopping trolley veering from side to side in a shopping mall (he borrowed the metaphor from Johnson's description of his own progress towards Brexit),[15] Truss was widely known to be mercurial, dogmatic and not very bright. But I don't think anyone predicted quite how reckless she would be. The mini-budget she cooked up with the arrogant Kwasi Kwarteng not only panicked the bond markets; it also destroyed the nation's financial credibility.

The record of ministerial turnover in these desperate months is like a serial car crash: five Prime Ministers in six years, six Chancellors in three years, seven Secretaries of Education in four years. And finally a Prime Minister who lasted 49 days, the shortest term in the history of the UK.

Far from the UK now being free to take advantage of Brexit, the country was now irremediably shackled to the bond markets, and doomed to pursue the most gruelling economic stringency as far as the eye can see. How distant now seemed the glorious scenario of the Painted Hall.

As Superman was finally grounded – along with the nation's economic prospects – we need to note one interesting fact: the conspiracy of silence over Europe seemed to be coming to an end. It's unsettling when the Great Unsayable suddenly becomes sayable – taken for granted, in fact, as if it were part of the conventional wisdom, the sort of thing people have been saying for years. I had this weird feeling when I saw the headline in the *Daily Telegraph* of 15 October 2022: 'Project Fear Was Right All Along.' Jeremy Warner, the paper's garlanded economic columnist, went on to say that 'Downbeat projections by the Treasury and others on the economic consequences of leaving the EU, contemptuously dismissed at the time by Brexit campaigners as "Project Fear", have turned out to be overwhelmingly correct.' If anything, he says, they have 'underestimated both the calamitous loss of international standing and the scale of the damage that six years of policy confusion and ineptitude has imposed on the country'.

I can't think of anything quite so shocking being said in public since Lytton Strachey used the word 'semen' in front of the Miss Stephenses in their Bloomsbury drawing room in 1907. Right up to this moment, the slightest hint that Brexit had any downside was *strengstens verboten* in the pages of the *Telegraph*, the *Daily Mail*, the *Daily Express*, the *Sun*, or indeed round the Cabinet table in No 10.

Almost as remarkable is the way in which Jeremy Warner places the damage in a six-year continuum. Only now is it becoming *salonfähig* to declare that Brexit has not been neatly 'delivered', like a parcel or a baby, but goes on being an unholy mess, bringing down Prime Ministers in shoals (Warner correctly predicted that Liz Truss could not survive – she resigned five days later), making the UK a subject of global derision and life intolerable for fruit and veg farmers, hospitals and care homes, bars and bistros, none of whom can get the staff, now that we have 'taken back control of our borders'. It was Truss's belated recognition that her beloved agenda of economic growth could not get off the ground without letting in more unskilled migrants that detonated Suella Braverman's explosive resignation as Home Secretary. In her short first tenure, Ms Braverman was well on the way to making her predecessor Priti Patel look like Martin Luther King. Now I come to think of it, Suella too declared that 'I have a dream', only hers was of seeing a flight packed with illegal migrants taking off for Rwanda. The obscure airline which volunteered for this mission soon pulled out, finding it too distasteful.

Truss's mini-budget which turned into a maxi disaster was similarly driven by the urge to break out of the low-growth fiscal rectitude she inherited from Rishi Sunak and which Boris Johnson had been trying to undermine throughout his misbegotten years in power. Economic policy under the past three short-term Prime Ministers has been a desperate search to demonstrate the concrete benefits brought by leaving the EU. Poignantly, even in her blink-and-you-missed-it resignation speech, Truss was still mourning the failure of her vision that 'would take advantage of the freedoms of Brexit'.

There have been other leaders of politics and business clearing their throats. Simon Wolfson, a keen Brexiteer and Chief Executive of Next, pleaded for a relaxation to immigration rules to address the severe worker shortages. 'We have got people queuing up to come to this country to pick crops that are rotting in fields, to work in warehouses that otherwise wouldn't be operable, and we're not letting them in,' said Lord Wolfson. 'In respect of immigration, it's definitely not the Brexit that I wanted, or indeed, many of the people who voted Brexit wanted.'[16] George Eustice, Boris Johnson's former Environment Secretary, revealed that he thought the trade deal that Liz Truss negotiated with Australia was 'not actually a very good agreement. The UK gave away far too much.'[17] Jonathan Jones, former head of the government legal service, denounced the Retained EU Law (Revocation and Reform Bill) which started its passage through Parliament in the autumn of 2022 as 'a very, very bad way to change and make law'.[18] It created huge uncertainty about which EU laws were to be retained and which replaced, even assuming that the civil service could cope with the 2,400 EU laws that are still on the statute book. Former members of the Bank of England's monetary policy committee have been frank about the long-term damage caused by Brexit — a 4 per cent hit to GDP, and a 15 per cent loss to trade both ways with the EU, according to the OBR and other forecasting bodies. Andrew Bailey, the Bank's Governor, has not sought to conceal the damage either.

Yet Rishi Sunak is still stuck in a catatonic state, as much the prisoner of the Europhobes as Truss and Johnson were. When *The Sunday Times* reported[19] that the government was now contemplating a Swiss-style deal with the EU, the Brexiteers exploded with instant outrage at this betrayal of Brexit, and Rishi Sunak scurried to deny any such intention. Any sensible halfway accommodation with the EU looks a long way off.

The political nation remains in denial, reinforced by the Labour Party's terror of allowing any substantial debate on the issues. For all the attention given to it in the House of Commons, the European Union might as well not exist. These days, the faraway country of which we know little seems to be France. It is impossible to imagine any previous Prime Minister who, when asked whether they regarded the President of France as a friend, would reply, 'The jury's out.' Liz Truss's defenders excused this as a joke, but it was a joke intended to tickle the fancy of her Europhobe audience during the tense moments of a leadership campaign. Boris Johnson certainly earned his honorific as 'the Britain Trump' by his reluctance to engage with any leaders in Western Europe, though he had a weakness for Viktor Orbán, the Hungary Trump. His prickly English nationalism was made embarrassingly plain by his refusal during the pandemic to work with the First Ministers of Scotland and Wales. The Johnson years were a time not so much of 'Splendid Isolation' as of sociopathic diplomacy. The self-styled Spartans of the European Research Group have been calling the shots out of all proportion to their numbers – at least Leonidas had 300 men with him at Thermopylae.

The whole interminable farce has been, largely if not wholly, of Johnson's own making. It is the ripest example of bad governance in Britain since the war. Nor should we forgive or underplay the brutality with which he has got his own way. I don't mean simply by destroying the governments of Cameron and May, but by his sacking half a dozen Permanent Secretaries who might have spoken truth to power, and by purging 21 of his leading pro-European MPs, not to mention his high-handed legislation to weaken the Royal Prerogative, take control of the Electoral Commission, restrict judicial review and the votes of the poor and the right to demonstrate. His behaviour has been uniquely chaotic – we are all aware of that – but many people have still not hauled in his personal unpleasantness. Never has a *faux bonhomme* fooled so many for so long. It's an indication of the deranged state of the Tory party that so many of its MPs and supporters should have contemplated for a nanosecond his return only three months after he was disgraced and booted out in a way that no other British Prime Minister has ever suffered, or deserved to suffer. To the last, he remained a bully, trying to arm-twist Rishi Sunak and Penny Mordaunt, the two final contenders, into supporting his return as Prime Minister. People may claim that Liz Truss was the worst PM in history, but she was only a Boris Johnson tribute act.

Donald Trump and the March on the Capitol

Standing on the dais behind the new President, George W. Bush uttered the definitive judgment on Donald Trump's speech: 'That's some weird shit.'[1] Trump's first, and so far only, inaugural is remembered mostly for his proclamation: 'From this day forward, it's going to be only America First, America First.' But what struck its hearers more at the time was Trump's aggrieved and truculent tone on an occasion that traditionally aspires to be cheering and uplifting. This was partly due to the aggrieved and truculent nature of Steve Bannon, the President's short-lived Svengali, who wrote the shocking description of 'American carnage'. The speech depicted the state of the nation as

> Mothers and children trapped in poverty in our inner cities, rusted-out factories scattered like tombstones across the landscape of our nation, an education system flush with cash, but which leaves our young and beautiful students deprived of all knowledge, and the crime and the gangs, and the drugs that have stolen too many lives and robbed our country of so much unrealized potential.

This was not a speech designed to make Americans feel good about themselves, certainly not when it was delivered in Trump's most menacing and grumpy tone, with the scowl of a golfer who has just sliced his drive out of bounds. 'I do bring rage out,' Trump himself once reflected. 'I always have. I don't know if it's an asset or a liability.'

It is of course both. His graceless tirades have horrified millions of his countrymen, but they have spoken to millions more. Trump professes contempt for 'losers', but losers are his core audience, and a carefully targeted one too. He rejoices in the support of those whom

Hillary Clinton so foolishly included in her 'basket of deplorables'. By contrast, Trump declares, 'I love the poorly educated.' When a foreign model asked him during a plane trip the meaning of 'white trash', he replied: 'They're people just like me, only they're poor.'[2]

Steve Bannon saw in his master echoes of earlier populist stump orators, like William Jennings Bryan, who could rage against bankers to rural audiences for hours on the trot. Bannon prepped Trump for his inauguration by telling him tales of his predecessor Andrew Jackson, whose inauguration had drawn to Washington thousands of his obstreperous supporters, who drank the capital dry and outstayed their welcome (shades of what was to come four years later, and on a more violent and terrifying scale).

Trump's critics, and his fans too, preferred to think of him as an unprecedented irruption into American history. But Bannon was right in thinking that most of his instincts and his policies have roots going way back. Before the aviator Charles Lindbergh founded the America First Committee to keep the US out of the Second World War, Woodrow Wilson had used the slogan in his doomed 1916 pledge to keep America out of the Great War. Before him again, the press baron William Randolph Hearst had used 'America First' during his tilt for the Democratic nomination in 1904, in which he also played up the threat of Chinese immigration, 'the Yellow Peril'. Orson Welles's film, *Citizen Kane*, based on Hearst, is Trump's favourite film.[3] In the 1920s, the Ku Klux Klan took up the slogan, and as late as 2016 David Duke, former Grand Wizard of the Klan, ran for a Louisiana senate seat as an America First candidate.

For Trump, 'America First' has meant withdrawing from every possible international organization. At one time or another as President, he demanded that the US withdraw from NATO, from the North American Free Trade Agreement, the World Health Organization, the Paris climate accords and the World Trade Organization. He was equally hostile to bilateral agreements with other nations, such as South Korea and Iran. This isolationism also has plenty of precedents, going back to the failure of the US Senate in the 1920s to ratify the Treaty of Versailles and join the League of Nations, under the influence of such implacable America-aloners as Senator William Borah of Idaho.

Isolationism is closely connected with 'nativism', which goes back to the early days of the Republic and the limitations on immigration imposed by the Alien and Sedition Acts of the 1790s. 'Native

American' parties did pretty well in the 1840s and 1850s – 'native' here meaning descendants of the original colonists, not American Indians, who did not enter the political equation at all. The 'Know-Nothing' or 'American' Party of the 1850s was especially hostile to the immigration of Irish Catholics. Ex-President Millard Fillmore accepted the nomination of the Know-Nothing Party for the 1856 election, and finished third. Ex-President Trump is unlikely to have to stoop to such an undignified resort, retaining as he does such an iron grip on the official Republican Party, a grip not significantly weakened until the midterm elections of November 2022. Hostility to the Irish later mutated into hostility to German arrivals and, later again, to the ongoing loathing of the Mexican influx. As late as 2002, no less a figure than the famous diplomat George F. Kennan warned against recklessly trashing American culture 'in favour of a polyglot mishmash'.

Not all isolationists have also been nativists, but quite a few, including Trump, have been both. After the First World War, for example, the famous patrician Senator Henry Cabot Lodge helped to scupper any prospect of the US joining the League of Nations: 'I have loved but one flag and I cannot share that devotion and give affection to the mongrel banner invented for a league.' At the same time, he was hot on the restriction of immigrants from southern and Eastern Europe by imposing literacy tests which would help to keep out 'races with which the English-speaking people have never hitherto assimilated, and who are most alien to the great body of the people of the United States'. All these sentiments live and breathe today in the person of Donald J. Trump, only he puts it more roughly: 'Why are we having all these people from shithole countries come here? Why not more Norwegians?'[4] Almost his first major action as President was to impose the travel ban on immigrants from most Muslim nations.

In economic terms, America First naturally expresses itself in a flinty protectionism, most conspicuously and repeatedly by tariffs on foreign steel – a traditional remedy going back to Alexander Hamilton and resorted to by half a dozen presidents. Again and again, economists have protested that such tariffs hurt American consumers. Yes, they give a temporary boost to steel producers, but at the expense of the far larger number of steel-consuming firms. In 1930, 1,000 economists protested against the Smoot–Hawley Bill which had such a catastrophic effect throughout the 1930s. But again and again, the political pressures have proved too strong to resist, even for self-proclaimed free-traders such as George W. Bush. The only difference is that Trump really is a convinced protectionist, for whom the word 'globalist' is about the worst insult in the political dictionary.

On other issues too, Trump's instincts are in line with traditional right-wing attitudes. Like many Republicans before him, he runs against Washington and the 'pointy-head' bureaucrats who ruin the lives of ordinary hard-working Americans. It was Ronald Reagan who first promised 'to drain the swamp' of DC; it was Richard Nixon who claimed to be speaking for 'the silent majority' – Calvin Coolidge used the phrase first in his 1920 campaign. But it was Donald Trump who first took such slogans seriously, being the only President ever to come into office with zero experience of public service in any field, civil, political or military. It was to turn out that his interest in the processes and institutions of government was pretty near zero, too. His only noticeable legislative achievement was a fairly orthodox tax bill, which lowered taxes on corporations and the better off, in much the same style as Reagan and the younger Bush.

If he had not lost control of Congress in the mid-term elections, like so many presidents before him, he might have done more. But his lack of enthusiasm for working with Congress and his personal contempt for most Congressmen and -women suggest otherwise. There were just too many members of Congress, he complained. How could he be expected to remember their names? In any case, they were mostly people of no account: 'men's shoe salesmen', 'flyovers' (meaning provincials from the states you only fly over, the people who are of course the bedrock of Trump's support).[5] This contempt for elected representatives is typical of Caesars. Witness de Gaulle's distaste for the parliamentary struggle in which he would be criticized every day 'by men whose only claim is to have had themselves elected in some small corner of France'.

Trump never fulfilled his dearest dream of repealing Barack Obama's health reforms, although he did manage to knock out the 'mandate' which penalized workers who failed to pay their insurance dues under the scheme. Nor could he ever persuade the Congress to vote funds to build his beloved wall along the Mexican border. The resulting stand-off led to the longest shutdown of government in US history. Even after the bitter row was patched up, Trump still felt compelled to declare a 'National Emergency concerning the Southern Border of the United States' (15 February 2019, Proclamation No.

9844). The idea was to transfer $8 billion already voted for military construction towards building the Wall. This was unprecedented; none of the other previous 58 emergency declarations had involved bypassing Congress to divert money for purposes it had expressly refused to approve. All through 2019, there were suits in the courts to declare 9844 unconstitutional, but Trump renewed it for a further year in February 2020 and again at his last gasp, on 18 January 2021. Three days later, Joe Biden terminated 9844, which he declared unconstitutional in the first place.

Trump was not alone among modern Presidents in governing largely by executive order in face of a hostile Congress. But most of Trump's EOs were remarkably short-lived. On day one of his presidency, Joe Biden signed 15 EOs and two agency directives, among other things rejoining the Paris climate accords and the World Health Organization and repealing the Muslim travel ban. Ironically, the most controversial of Biden's early acts was to accelerate the timetable for withdrawing US troops from Afghanistan – something Trump had been urging throughout his presidency, against the strenuous opposition of his senior advisers.

THE CAMPAIGN THAT NEVER ENDS

So Trump's instincts, and his policies, are not random eruptions, bracing or menacing according to your taste. They fit neatly within the traditional spectrum of right-wing policies clustered within the Republican Party and spilling over into the far Right. America First, isolationism, nativism and strict immigration control, protectionism and a low-tax, law-and-order, minimal state: these have been standard fare on the Right, off and on, ever since the founding of the USA. There's nothing odd or hetereogeneous about them.

In cultural terms, the Trumpsphere is not really a new phenomenon either. It is the America of the cowboy rather than the Puritan, of Huckleberry Finn lighting out for the Territory to avoid being civilized by Aunt Sally, of the grizzled rancher in the movie who says, 'We don't cotton to strangers around here.' Trump woos the same audiences and by the same techniques as Elmer Gantry and Buzz Windrip did in the 1930s novels of Sinclair Lewis. Indeed, Trump's appearance on the scene immediately reminded several commentators of *It Can't Happen Here*. He is the inheritor of Ronald Reagan and Andrew Jackson, but with a harsher, more vengeful edge, and a pawky, demotic language which can be traced back to the deliberately misspelled monologues of the nineteenth-century humorist Artemus Ward.

What, then, was new, odd, even unique, in American history about the Trump experience and the Trump Presidency? Two elements, I think, distinct but closely linked: Trump's relentless non-stop campaigning and his chaotic style of government. The combination has produced indignation and uproar among his opponents, but its aggressive irreverence has also generated a seemingly unbreakable loyalty in his core supporters.

The way Trump has campaigned remains unforgettable. Those huge rallies in which the candidate would enrapture his audience for hours in his rambling, looping, derisive, flattering style, blasting his opponents with baseless slanders and teasing them with endlessly repeated nicknames – Crooked Hillary, Sleepy Joe, Pocahontas. These monologues, alternately sardonic and sentimental, have often bewitched liberal reporters who came to sneer. They run on so seductively. It's a kind of white rap.

And what a lot Trump puts into them. He takes endless trouble over the lighting, the music, the placing of the audience. How painfully this compares with his slapdash impatience with the business of actually governing, his unwillingness to read even the shortest briefing paper.

Even more remarkable was his addiction to Twitter. In the eight years before he became President, he issued nearly 35,000 tweets – about 12 every 24 hours, and pumped out deep into the night and the early morning. These sassy, often abusive little messages came straight off the top of his head. By contrast, Hillary Clinton's tweets were often composed by her campaign committee. The text of one issued in her name allegedly took nine hours to agree. There was no spontaneity. Her messages, like the tweets of most other politicians on both sides of the Atlantic, do no more than record sentiments proper to the occasion, like the cards of condolence left by Victorian ladies. They haven't got the hang of the medium at all.

Twitter's limit of 140 characters in a single tweet suited Trump's slam-bang, in-your-face style. When Twitter doubled its limit to 280, he welcomed the opportunity to flesh out his thoughts, but added, 'It's a bit of a shame, because I was the Ernest Hemingway of 140 characters.'[6] A rare reference to any literary figure. Trump read little or nothing outside politics as well as inside. It is said he hasn't even read all of his own book, *The Art of the Deal*, ghosted for him by Tony Schwartz.

It was to his Twitter followers that he confided his frustrations, with foreign leaders, with the recalcitrant Congress, with his own advisers. The Twitter audience are often the first to hear that he has sacked a staffer or Secretary of State. The tweet may even be the first the victim himself hears of their dismissal.

From the start, Trump was entranced by the new medium and instantly grasped its possibilities: 'I love Twitter . . . it's like owning your own newspaper – without the losses.'[7] The directness was the thing. 'This is my megaphone. This is the way I speak directly to the people without any filter. Cut through the noise. Cut through the fake news. That's the only way I have to communicate. I have tens of millions of followers. This is bigger than cable news.'[8] Once in the White House, he was clear about his debt: 'Without social media, number one, I wouldn't have won, and number two, you know, I'm number one on Facebook.'[9] Trump also claimed to be number one on Twitter. In fact, he was some way down the pecking order on both.

But he did not disdain cable news either. In fact, Fox News became his personal channel. One of its anchors, Sean Hannity, told people that he was staying at Fox only 'to fight for Donald J. Trump'. The other two, Tucker Carlson and Laura Ingraham, combined with Hannity to form a sort of brains trust for Trump, who would spend several hours a week on the phone to them.

All this provided Trump with unmediated access to his core voters, a closeness that probably hadn't been available since ancient Greeks and Romans crowded into the Agora and the Forum to hear it straight from Demosthenes and Cicero. The new media of the twentieth century had never been properly exploited by the Democratic politicians of the day, partly out of nervousness and a certain pudeur. Compare FDR's fireside chats – only 30 of them over his 12 years as President – with Trump's tens of thousands of tweets. When Roosevelt's aides and the public clamoured for more, he said, no, these talks should be confined to major events.[10] Trump had no such compunction.

His critics expected that at least this obsessive tweeting might tail off after the extraordinary event of his election, by all accounts as unexpected by him as by most of the pundits. Trump would become more presidential; he simply would not have the time for such idle chatter. You campaigned in poetry, you governed in prose.

Not a bit of it. Once installed in the White House, Trump simply carried on a permanent campaign, rather in the sense that Chairman Mao aspired to carry on a permanent revolution. This was reflected in Trump's working habits. He would come down to the Oval Office at 11 a.m. or even 11.30, barely having glanced at the briefing book he had been given the night before.[11] He had no appetite for prolonged policy discussion in any case. His eyes would glaze over. Sometimes he would simply get up and leave the room. Instead, he would spend five or six hours of the day watching TV, surfing the channels. The TV was not just his prime relaxation, after golf; it was his echo scanner, recording the vibes from his fan base, their reactions to every passing political breeze.

He governed as he campaigned, in brief, fiery messages. Typical was his announcement to his appalled aides, without any previous discussion: 'I want an executive order withdrawing the US from NAFTA and I want it on my desk by Friday.'[12] When nothing happened, he returned to the attack in spades: 'We've talked about this ad nauseam. Just do it. Just do it. Get out of NAFTA. Get out of KORUS [the free trade agreement between the US and South Korea]. And get out of the WTO. We're withdrawing from all three.'[13]

This refusal to govern in the accepted way began with the transition into his presidency – a painstaking mechanism now prescribed by law – or rather with Trump's refusal to bother with any such thing. He told Chris Christie, the former Governor of New Jersey, who had been appointed head of the transition team, 'I don't want a transition. I'm shutting down the transition. I told you from day one it was just an honorary title. You're jinxing me. I'm not going to spend a second on it.'[14] Or spend a dollar either – he became obsessed with the cost of the transition, and fired Christie. As a result, his presidency started in chaos. It finished that way too.

THE DEEP STATE HITS BACK

As often as not, his aides managed to argue him off his more dangerous impulses, but not always. During the Trump Presidency, the US did withdraw from the Paris climate accords, and hobbled the World Trade Organization by refusing to appoint fresh judges to resolve trade disputes. At the height of the Covid pandemic, Trump also withdrew funding from the World Health Organization.[15] Quite often, though, Trump's top aides succeeded in frustrating him by devious methods.

In early September 2017, Gary Cohn, former President of Goldman Sachs and now the President's chief economic adviser, chanced upon a letter lying on Trump's desk in the Oval Office. The letter was a one-page draft from Trump to the President of South Korea, terminating the US–Korea free trade agreement known as KORUS. Trump had been threatening this for months, arguing that KORUS was a huge waste of money, while his staff had been protesting that it was the foundation of a hugely profitable trade relationship, a crucial military alliance and a no less crucial shared intelligence operation in the region.

Cohn simply removed the draft from the desk. The President failed to notice that it had gone and temporarily forgot about the whole thing.[16] KORUS endures to this day. Trump's Staff Secretary, Rob Porter, pulled a similar trick by deftly removing from the Resolute Desk a draft statement withdrawing from the Paris accords, which Trump was about to have read out to the press.[17] As we have seen, the withdrawal did in the end take place, but only after proper discussion. Another such episode took place just after the 2020 election, on 11 November, when Kash Patel, a mysterious figure who had somehow crept on to the National Security Council, slid a one-page memo across the table to General Mark Milley, chairman of the Joint Chiefs of Staff, directing him to withdraw all US forces from Afghanistan and Somalia. This was a long-held aim of Trump's, but he had never managed to get it past his advisers. And he didn't now. Milley took the memo to the National Security Adviser, Robert O'Brien, and got it withdrawn.[18]

Trump did not surround himself entirely with right-wing goons. Cohn and Porter were men of intelligence and achievement, as were the generals on his staff, H. R. McMaster and James Mattis. All of them spent much of their time trying to block or at least dilute the President's impulses, and all soon fell foul of him and were eased out or brutally fired. The President's only loyalty was to his core voters, in whom he confided as other presidents have confided in their wives. Rex Tillerson, the formidable long-serving CEO of Exxon, had a particularly torrid time after being hired as Secretary of State. First, Trump undermined him on Twitter, writing of Tillerson's diplomatic overtures towards North Korea's mercurial despot Kim Jong-Un that he was 'wasting his time trying to negotiate with Little Rocket Man. Save your energy, Rex.' He then changed his tune completely. The North Korean leader was no longer Little Rocket Man, but Trump's best friend, and they wrote effusive letters to each other, without any discernible result. Trump was so proud of this correspondence that after he left office he took the letters, quite illegally, with him down to his private Florida estate, Mar-a-Lago. In any case, Tillerson had to go, because it leaked out that he had called Trump 'a fucking moron'. He was fired, without warning, by tweet.

If the President had constantly undermined his advisers, they had tirelessly conspired to undermine or 'work around' his dearest wishes. This was not unprecedented. James Schlesinger, Defense Secretary in August 1974, had issued an edict to military leaders not to follow orders that came directly from President Nixon, who was facing impeachment, without first checking with him and his JCS chairman, General George Brown. It was feared that Nixon might try to evade his fate by ordering a nuclear strike. 'Pulling a Schlesinger' became shorthand for senior officials conspiring with each other to prevent an unhinged President from taking some appalling step. Milley actually invoked this precedent two days after 6 January 2021, when he summoned the senior officers from the National Military Command Center and told them to follow the established procedures and consult him if they should receive orders from the President to launch a nuclear missile.

Here, then, we have clear examples of the 'Deep State' doing precisely what its right-wing enemies, such as Steve Bannon, accused them of: frustrating the will of an elected President. And as often as not, a good thing too. In military matters, David Rothkopf argues in *American Resistance – The Inside Story of how the Deep State Saved the Nation* (2022),

> Had the most dangerous of Trump's impulses, biases and misunderstanding translated into action, alliances would have crumbled, enemies would have benefitted, wars would have been fought, war crimes would have been committed, and the military would have in the end become the enforcement arm of an authoritarian government.[19]

THE BIG STEAL AND THE BIG LIE

Suspicions that Trump would not take defeat lying down had been circulating for months in the summer of 2020, ever since he began lagging in the polls. We saw earlier how he had tweeted defiance in the early hours after Obama's victory in 2012. As far back as 2016 his long-time ally and original campaign manager, Roger Stone, had registered the domain name 'Stop the Steal', in case Trump might lose either the Republican primary or the Presidential election that year. Trump had already shown his total lack of scruple about breaking the law, most notoriously in his phone call to the newly elected President of Ukraine, Volodymyr Zelensky, threatening to withhold $400 million in aid unless Zelensky came up with some dirt on Presidential candidate Joe Biden's son Hunter's dealings in Ukraine. For this blatant blackmail, he was impeached but not convicted. Why should he be fearful of the vengeance of the law, so long as the Republicans held half the Senate?

As early as March, Trump had been obsessed with the idea that the Democrats were somehow going to steal the election from him. On 20 July, he even toyed with the idea of postponing the elections on the ground that the Covid pandemic (whose seriousness he had previously pooh-poohed) posed a national emergency.[20] And at 2.30 a.m. on the morning after the election, far from conceding defeat, he came out with a rambling speech, demanding that the counting of mail-in votes be stopped: 'This is a fraud on the American public. This is an embarrassment to our country. We were getting ready to win this election. Frankly, we did win this election.'[21] He did not of course mention that it was Republican officials who, in state after state, had arranged that mail-in votes, which were predominantly Democrat votes, be counted later, precisely to give the impression that Trump was winning. A few days later, he was ranting: 'People have got to know this was stolen. This was taken from us. It wasn't even a close election. We won by a landslide.' In fact, he had lost the popular vote by seven million votes. In the electoral college he lost by 232–306, precisely the same margin by which he had defeated Hillary Clinton. If a few thousand votes in five or six states had gone the other way, he would have won, but that quirk of the system would have produced a similar upset in other post-war elections, such as Nixon–Kennedy and Bush–Gore. There was no genuine reason to quarrel with the joint verdict of the election security groups, including CISA, the Department of Homeland Security's Cybersecurity and Infrastructure Security Agency, that 'the November 3rd election was the most secure in American history . . . There is no evidence that any voting system deleted or lost votes, changed votes, or was in any way compromised.'[22]

Trump's reaction was to fire CISA's chief Chris Krebs – by tweet, of course.

By early December, 50 lawsuits challenging the results had failed in states across the Union, in most cases being thrown out with contempt by the judges.[23] Trump's early fantasy about seizing the voting machines had melted into oblivion. None of the targeted state assemblies – Pennsylvania, Arizona, Wisconsin, Michigan, Georgia – would listen to the arguments of Trump's lead lawyer, the increasingly frantic Rudy Giuliani, why they should not certify their electors. None of these bodies was willing even to convene a formal hearing.[24]

Giuliani's next gambit was to propose that when the Senate met on 6 January to ratify the elections results, the Vice-President should reject the slate of electors formally offered to him.[25] The egregious California academic lawyer, John Eastman, asserted that Vice-President Pence had the discretion to replace Biden electors with Trump electors, or he could send the Biden electors back to the Republican-controlled states, where they could be replaced.[26] Trump loved the idea, but everyone else thought this was barmy, including the otherwise loyal Pence, who could find no respectable lawyer to endorse the Eastman thesis. He told Trump repeatedly that he had no such discretion: 'I'm just there to open the envelope.'[27] From that position he did not budge, however much Trump derided him for being a weakling and a pussy and no patriot.

Pence was by no means the only high official Trump badgered to overturn the result. On 2 January Trump phoned Georgia's Secretary of State, Brad Raffensperger, urging him to find 11,780 votes for him, which was the margin he lost the state by. Luckily, Raffensperger recorded the whole loopy conversation, which went on for an hour and was as futile as it was scandalous:

> We think that if you check the signatures – a real check of the signatures going back in Fulton County – you'll find at least a couple of hundred thousand of forged signatures of people who have been forged. And we are quite sure that's going to happen . . . So look. All I want to do is this. I just want to find 11,780 votes, which is one more than we have because we won the state.[28]

Raffensperger gave him the brush-off. So did Rusty Bowers, Republican Speaker of Arizona's House of Representatives, when Trump and Giuliani called him to announce that they had found 200,000 illegal immigrants and 6,000 corpses who had voted in Arizona. Instead of providing evidence for this absurd claim, Trump and Giuliani went on to declare that there existed an arcane law in Arizona that would permit Bowers and the Republicans, who controlled the legislature, to chuck out Biden's electors and replace them with Trumpers. Bowers would be subjected to a continued barrage right up to 6 January, including a call from the appalling Eastman. He had no difficulty in resisting these ridiculous suasions. For his pains, though, he was swiftly ejected from his post by Trump loyalists. Election-deniers have now swept the board in Arizona.

None of these legal setbacks deterred Trump and his acolytes from whipping up the storm that broke on 6 January at the Capitol. Back on 19 December, in a tweet announcing that it was 'statistically impossible' for him to have lost the election, he had summoned his followers to Washington in order to obstruct the congressional certification of the electoral college: 'Be there, will be wild.' Ten days later, he tweeted from Mar-a-Lago: 'JANUARY SIXTH SEE YOU IN DC.'[29]

In his blow-by-blow account of the events of 6 January, *The Storm is Here* (2022), the *New Yorker* reporter Luke Mogelson points out that this was by no means the first mass demo in Washington since the election. On 14 November, thousands of Trumpers had marched through Black Lives Matter Plaza on their way to Freedom Plaza, the rallying point for what was billed as the Million MAGA March. Alex Jones, ally of Roger Stone and a notorious conspiracy theorist,[30] was there, yelling, 'Start getting out your rope, it's time to make a noose.'[31] He had organized a 'Stop the Steal' caravan to travel all the way from Texas to the Capitol.[32] The procession stretched back from the top of Capitol Hill for more than a mile.[33] As the march passed the headquarters of the FBI, Jones chanted, 'Down with the Deep State.'[34]

On 12 December, the day after the Supreme Court rejected the motion to invalidate every vote from the five swing states, another MAGA March had been held. The Proud Boys, America Firsters and Groypers (a white nationalist group named after a frog-like cartoon character) gathered in their thousands round the Washington Monument to denounce the treachery of the Supreme Court, whose reinforced conservative majority had so signally failed to live up to expectations. The marchers then marauded their way through central Washington, shouting obscene slogans against the police and Black Lives Matter. Nicholas Fuentes, leader of the Groypers, spelled out the message: 'Our Founding Fathers would get into the streets, and they would take this country back, by force if necessary. And that is what we must be prepared to do.'[35]

These huge marches on 14 November and 12 December gave the authorities every reason to expect something just as bad, and probably worse, on 6 January. Indignation among Trumpers was boiling up rather than dying down; millions of dollars were still pouring into his re-election campaign, more millions after he had lost than before. Nor was actual physical interference with the electoral process any sort of novelty. In 2000, at the end of the Presidential election, Roger Stone had helped organize the notorious Brooks Brothers Riot in Miami, in which a mob of Republicans wearing Brooks Brothers suits had stormed the Board of Elections, assaulting staff and banging on windows, forcing the recount to be called off, thus sealing George W. Bush's paper-thin victory over Al Gore in Florida and giving him the Presidency.[36] The same disreputable crew were still at work 20 years later. Who was to say they would not somehow pull off a repeat? Whatever the mixture of reasons – the undoubted sympathy among Washington police officers for the Trump cause, or simply complacency – security around the Capitol was derisory, especially when you compared it with the huge and brutal display of force to control the Black Lives Matter protests. 'How is it possible,' wonders Luke Mogelson, who had witnessed all the earlier riots, 'that the perimeter of the US Capitol, on this day, could be so poorly defended and breached with such shocking speed and ease? Where was the militarized and vastly disproportionate force that had been marshaled to "dominate" racial justice protesters in Minneapolis and Portland?'[37]

But of course the prime responsibility for the terrifying mayhem of 6 January rests with the actions of Donald J. Trump, culminating in the extraordinary venomous ramble he delivered at noon to the huge crowd of his supporters at the Ellipse, the park just south of the White House fence. We must quote a few snatches to convey how deliberately he geed them up with his flood of phoney statistics, rancorous insults and dark prophecies:

> Our country has had enough. We will not take it any more and that's what this is all about. And to use a favourite term that all of you people really came up with: We will stop the steal. [As though Trump and Stone had not crafted the slogan themselves]. Today I will lay out just some of the evidence proving that we won this election and we won it by a landslide . . .

You're the real people, you're the people that built this nation. You're not the people that tore down the nation . . . And you have to get your people to fight. And if they don't fight, we have to primary the hell out of the ones that don't fight . . .

But we look at the facts and our election was so corrupt that in the history of this country we've never seen anything like it . . .

Now it is up to Congress to confront this egregious assault on our democracy. And after this, we're going to walk down, and I'll be there with you, we're going to walk down, we're going to walk down . . .

Because you'll never take back our country with weakness. You have to show strength and you have to be strong . . .

If you don't do that, that means you will have a President for four years, with his wonderful son. You will have a President who lost all of these states . . . You will have an illegitimate President. That's what you will have. And we can't let that happen . . .

We won in a landslide. This was a landslide. They said it's not American to challenge the election. This was the most corrupt election in the history, maybe of the world . . .

And we fight. We fight like hell. And if you don't fight like hell, you're not going to have a country any more.

Trump speaking outside the White House at the 'Save America' March, 6 January 2021.

Trump's defenders cling to the injunction he also gave 'to peacefully and patriotically make your voices heard'. But the thrust of the speech is about fighting to save the nation from the worst criminal fraud in American history. The repeated instruction to march down with him to the Capitol is anything but pacific, even if he has no intention of actually marching himself, rather than watching the whole thing on television back in the White House. He is there with them only in spirit, but the spirit is fierce and unforgiving.

This is, after all, the third stage in Trump's relentless campaign to overturn the result and get himself installed for a second term. The first was his denouncing the result as a fraud, in the small hours of the morning after the election. This segued into a denunciation of all the official bodies which had monitored the election and certified the outcome as fair and valid.

The next stage was the series of active manoeuvres to get the result officially overturned, personally masterminded by Trump and Giuliani. These were clearly criminal acts of attempted suborning, as shown by the testimony of Rusty Bowers in Arizona and the wonderful taped conversation between Trump and Brad Raffensperger in Georgia, and of course the repeated arm-twisting of Mike Pence to make him commit an illegal act no previous Vice-President had dreamed of. Then finally comes this incitement to riot on 6 January.

All of which clearly amounts to a slow-motion coup d'état, beginning in the small hours of the election morrow and finally snuffed out by Pence two months later. That the coup was as ludicrous as it was cynical does not remove the permanent stain it leaves on the otherwise tranquil history of the American Constitution. Even if Trump fails to make a comeback, his example can only encourage some other unscrupulous operator to try it on again, either at state or national level. As we have seen, almost exactly two years later Bolsonaro's followers tried an exact replay in Brasília.

We must pay tribute to the public officials who did their duty and frustrated Trump's criminal intentions: first, the officials who oversaw the count, then the checkers who oversaw the overseers, then the prominent figures like Bowers, Raffensperger and Pence who had to block the President, their President, head on. These people – and there were hundreds of other men and women who performed similar roles with the same scrupulosity – cannot be caricatured as part of the Deep State. On the contrary, they are the proud representatives of the Visible State.

THE AMERICAN DISTRUST

There remain, though, deep problems with the body politic in America. The first is the continuing popularity of Donald Trump, with his huge base inside the Republican Party and beyond its farthest shores. As Michael Wolff puts it at the end of his superb trilogy on the Trump presidency:

> The fact that all the modern standards of opprobrium, obloquy, disgrace, public mortification and general measures of accountability did not bow him was at the core of liberal rage and frustration. His ability to stand up to the moral wrath of the liberal community seems also to be at the core of the continuing awe and devotion of so many others.[38]

On 21 May 2022, after Trump's second impeachment, a poll found that 73 per cent of Republican primary voters wanted him to run again in 2024.[39] A Trump rally in Ohio on 26 June 2022 drew 10,000 fans.[40] Attempts to load the electoral scales in favour of the Republicans continue apace. More than 400 bills to restrict voting have been introduced across the US since the election. Nearly 20 new laws have been enacted, and dozens more were pending in state legislative chambers.[41]

Trump's threat on 6 January 'to primary the hell out of the ones who don't fight' is being amply fulfilled. In primary races across the country, Trump-supported candidates have mostly romped home, while those who dared to stand up to him, like Rusty Bowers and Liz Cheney, have usually been thrown out by huge margins.

The midterm elections of 2022 undoubtedly dented Trump's popularity and loosened his grip on the Republican machine. But only for a time. By the beginning of 2024, he was steaming back into favour, breathing fire and vengeance, the numerous court cases against him only enhancing his self-image as the embattled crusader to Make America Great Again. He won the first Presidential primaries by miles and continued to poll well against Joe Biden. His setbacks have not altered the underlying world view of conservative Republicans and much of the wider American public. Many candidates Trump backed were defeated, but hundreds of Trump-loving election deniers were elected, and those ambitious hopefuls who now disavow Trump as their leader do not disavow Trumpism. Millions of Americans remain incurably suspicious of government in general, and of Washington in particular. There is a pervasive disbelief that public officials, those 'pointy-head bureaucrats', can play any serious part in improving the lives of ordinary Americans. Still ringing in the ears of many

Americans is the wisecrack of Ronald Reagan: 'The top nine most terrifying words in the English language are: I'm from the government and I'm here to help you.' Or as Reagan again put it more bluntly in 1981: 'Government is not the solution to our problem, government is the problem.'[42] Drain the swamp in DC, and all will be well.

It is to counteract this unshakeable prejudice that Michael Lewis wrote his attractive little book, *The Fifth Risk*. Lewis confronts the know-nothing arrogance of the Trump inner circle, which refused to bother with the mechanism, now laid down in statute, for ensuing a smooth and efficient transition to a new presidency. Then he gently guides the reader (and Donald Trump too, if he ever bothered to read anything) through the ways in which government protects and promotes all sorts of desirable things, ranging from the health of poultry to the forecasting of tornados and the improvement of search-and-rescue techniques at sea. Technical innovation is rarely the sole preserve of private business. John MacWilliams, chief risk officer at the Department of Energy, points out that government has always played a major role in innovation, all the way back to the founding of the country: 'Early-stage innovation in most industries would not have been possible without government support.'[43] In energy as elsewhere, the private sector steps in and deploys its remarkable ingenuity only once the Department of Energy, through its multifarious agencies, has shown that the new gizmo can work.

In *American Resistance: The Inside Story of How the Deep State Saved the Nation*, the political scientist David Rothkopf offers a feisty defence of the Deep State, in particular of the roles we have seen senior officials playing in diverting or diluting Trump's most dangerous impulses and cloth-headed caprices. But he ends with a sharp warning that more than a year after being turfed out of the White House Trump was still on the warpath. In a speech in Florence, South Carolina, in March 2022, for example, the ex-President declared that 'we will pass critical reforms making every executive branch employee directly fireable by the President of the United States. The Deep State must and will be brought to heel.'[44] Miles Taylor, the young Chief of Staff at the Department of Homeland Security who turns out to have been the famous 'Anonymous' who penned a ferocious critique of Trump in *The New York Times*, believes that if there had been a second Trump term, 'more than half the Cabinet would have been in "acting" roles from the get-go' – the point being that acting officials do not need to be confirmed by Congress, which enables the President to appoint any old crony who would not stand a hope in hell of gaining confirmation.[45]

THE DEEP STATE AND THE SHALLOW STATE

The idea of the 'Deep State' had been hovering around the margins of political debate for several decades. It was first applied mostly in relation to new or newish nation-states, such as Turkey and Pakistan. In these insecurely rooted political systems, the army, the intelligence services and the police were said to be in cahoots with one another, and able to undermine, or pull the strings of, or actually replace, the regime. In the US, and later the UK, the idea was redeployed by right-wingers who had become convinced that the Establishment at all levels was frustrating the policies they had been elected to 'deliver' – an increasingly popular term, suggesting that the policies in question were like so many parcels to be dumped unopened on the nation's doorstep, rather than careful reworkings of this or that complex set of political arrangements. This Establishment was depicted as a more or less deliberate combination, amounting to a conspiracy, of senior civil servants, the military, intelligence chiefs, the mainstream media and other hidden influencers, as well as avowed Democrat (or Labour) officials and politicians.

In the US, this obsession was first promoted with brio by Steve Bannon and his inner circle, notably Corey Lewandowski, Trump's early campaign manager. Lewandowski co-published a book called *Trump's Enemies: How the Deep State is Undermining the Presidency* (2018). There was a degree of cynicism attached to the whole operation: Bannon told Sara Carter, the designated ghostwriter, 'You do realize that none of this is true?'[46] It was only as his Presidency wore on that Trump himself placed the blame for his frustrations in office squarely on the Deep State. On 7 September 2018, for example, he declared that 'unelected, deep state operatives who defy the voters to push their own secret agendas are truly a threat to democracy itself.' Lewandowski's book centres on the allegations of Russia's collusion with the Trump campaign, which it denounces as a total hoax, manufactured by Hillary Clinton's supporters as a revenge for her humiliating defeat. David Rothkopf in *American Resistance* in turn declares that 'the hoax was itself a hoax, a disinformation campaign designed to provide cover for the President's long history of dubious relations with Russia and of pursuing policies favourable to it,'[47] notably Trump's approval of Putin's ambitions to take over the Crimea and then the whole of Ukraine, a country Trump has always disliked.

But the more general target of the Trumpers' attack is the Deep State itself, which Lewandowski claims 'has spread like a cancer, and it's become impossible to get rid of'. Strategically placed throughout the bureaucracy, these hidden Democrats 'work hard for liberal presidents like Obama and Bill Clinton, then white-knuckle it through eight years of a Republican, slow-rolling and obstructing their agenda at every turn.'[48] This, so the conspiracy theory runs, has created a permanent branch of government for one political party – one that never changes and can't be voted away. Thus, 'between the lines of the Constitution, agents of the deep State have penciled in an infallible system to keep themselves in power for ever.'[49] Clearly, the only answer is to give the President sweeping powers to drain the swamp from top to bottom.

In the UK, Boris Johnson's Svengali, Dominic Cummings, during his brief reign of terror in Whitehall, was convinced that nothing could be achieved unless the Deep State was purged of Johnson's opponents. We have seen how many Permanent Secretaries he managed to get rid of, an unprecedented purge. Even after his downfall, Cummings continued to warn Johnson (for whom he now had nothing but contempt) that the Deep State was still out to get him. 'Deep State will wreak revenge in 2/3 years before election,' he tweeted on 12 May 2022. Johnson seems himself to have come to subscribe to this analysis, musing in his speech on the Commons vote of no confidence of 18 July 2022: 'Some people will say as I leave office that this is the end of Brexit, oh, yes, and the Leader of the Opposition and the Deep State will prevail in its plot to haul us back into alignment with the EU as a prelude to our eventual return.'

The Deep State accusation reveals more about the mindset of the accusers than about the reality of politics. After all, the 'depth' of any state is surely a measure of its *strength*, an index of its likely durability, the rationality of its behaviour, the justice of its actions. A successful state requires officials and institutions who are impartial, incorruptible, professionally qualified and experienced, and can be relied on to act in accordance with established laws and rules of conduct. To perform their duty, they must exercise independence of judgement and, in extreme cases, be prepared to put their jobs on the line when speaking truth to power. If they are convinced that the intentions of the President or Prime Minister are ill-informed or rash or damaging to the nation's interests, or even downright illegal, it is their duty to speak out. If of course the President or Prime Minister has sufficient energy and a long enough attention span to face down the opposition and convert his or her impulses into concrete policies, then it is their duty to carry those policies through, or else resign. That is how the system works, and how it is intended to work. Rothkopf tells us that several of his sources objected to being described as part of the Deep State and to his calling his book *American Resistance*.[50] They had not set out to be part of any resistance, but simply to do their job properly as they saw it.

Luckily, one of the things Trump and Johnson have in common is an inability to persist. Where they did persist, as they did with Brexit or with leaving the Paris climate accords, their orders were followed. If Johnson had carried on with his more spectacular wheezes – building an airport in the Thames Estuary, or a bridge from Scotland to Northern Ireland – in the end, the Deep State might have knuckled down and got on with 'delivering', but God knows at what a cost.

There is ultimately something fraudulent about the Deep State scare. Lewandowski ends his book[51] with a triumphant list of Trump's achievements in his first two years: all the bothersome regulations swept away, all the tariff walls erected against foreign manufactures, all the international deals and treaties abandoned, all the deplorable immigrants kept out – just the things that the agents of the Deep State are said to loathe. So these sinister conspirators don't seem to be very effective in blocking changes of which they disapprove. The truth is that the whole scare is a device for inflaming public paranoia. It is, for want of a better phrase, fake news.

Trump's extraordinary threat in March 2022 that, if returned to power, he would seek powers to fire every employee of the federal government is in one sense laughable. No conceivable US Congress would pass such a law. But it shows clearly his prevailing itch: to abolish a government based on laws and substitute a government which simply expresses the unhampered will of the President, what you might call a Shallow State. A state in which the only voice is the voice of Caesar. Which is only another way of saying 'a totalitarian state'.

In the Shallow State, politics becomes a play of surfaces, a dialogue of tweets and banner headlines, in which Fox News reflects the President, and the President reflects Fox News. The Shallow State is insistently self-important; it struts and frets its hour upon the stage, impatient and resentful of competition or critique. For its believers, the Shallow State is the only reality, and they themselves its only citizens. As Donald Trump told his fans at the Ellipse on 6 January, 'you're the real people.'

VIRUS, WHAT VIRUS?

Failures by government are of course numberless, and often flagrant and catastrophic. These failures may result from the usual human failings of myopia and complacency. But no less frequently they follow from the failure to follow the sensible and rigorous rules that have been laid down by previous administrations. In other words, they result not from too much government, but from not enough. The most spectacular disaster of public policy in recent years was the failure of the financial regulators across the Western world to supervise their banks. It will be a long time before Ed Balls, then Britain's Minister for the City, lives down his boast in 2006 that 'today our system of light-touch and risk-based regulation is regularly cited as one of our chief attractions.'

Reading Patrick Radden Keefe's classic study of the opioid epidemic, *Empire of Pain*, you are struck to start with by the insatiable greed and commercial dynamism of the Sackler brothers and their descendants. But then you cannot help noticing the crucial failures of the Food and Drug Administration to check more carefully the blithe claims of Big Pharma that first Librium and Valium and then, more disastrously, OxyContin, were not addictive. The crucial sentence featured on the Purdue company's packaging of OxyContin was: 'Delayed absorption, as provided by OxyContin tablets, is believed to reduce the abuse liability of the drug.'[52] Believed by whom? Radden Keefe enquires. There had been no clinical trials, no historical evidence to support this comforting assertion, which fooled both the FDA and the millions who swallowed the tablets and whose lives were ruined or cut short. There is no doubt that close liaison between Purdue and the FDA and staff interchanges between the two lulled the FDA into a criminal complaisance.

When Donald Trump in his inaugural address included the opioid epidemic in his catalogue of 'American carnage', it is unlikely he was thinking that the whole ghastly tragedy could have been avoided by tighter regulation of the drug companies. Throughout the Covid pandemic, in fact, he was egging on Dr Stephen Hahn at the FDA to approve a vaccine more quickly. In August 2020, he tweeted: 'The deep state, or whoever, over at the FDA, is making it very difficult for drug companies to get people in order to test the vaccines and therapeutics. Obviously, they are hoping to delay the answer until after November 3rd.'[53] In other words he was accusing the FDA of delaying the release of the vaccine in order to prevent him from being re-elected. In mid-December, he tweeted: 'While my pushing the money drenched but heavily bureaucratic FDA saved five years in the approval of NUMEROUS great new vaccines, it is still a big, slow old turtle. Get the dam vaccines out NOW, Dr Hahn. Stop playing games and start saving lives!!!' [sic][54]

But from the start, Trump had minimized the danger of the virus. 'It's going to disappear,' he said on 27 February 2020. 'One day – it's like a miracle – it will disappear.'[55] On 6 April he tweeted, 'LIGHT AT THE END OF THE TUNNEL'.[56] Four days later, he predicted that the eventual death toll would be 'substantially' lower than the 100,000 predicted by the government task force.[57] By 9 August 2022, the death toll had reached over a million, almost the highest in the world. He did accede, reluctantly, to the pleas of Dr Tony Fauci, who had been director of the National Institute of Allergy and Infectious Diseases for the unheard-of span of 36 years, and ordered a 15-day lockdown, followed even more reluctantly by a 30-day extension. Throughout, though, he was obsessed by the slogan 'Reopen America' – which he thought crucial to his prospects of re-election. Accordingly, he began to undermine the extension by tweeting 'Liberate Minnesota', 'Liberate Michigan', 'Liberate Virginia', not only subverting his own guidelines, but also pushing responsibility away from himself out to the states, many of whom, as Fauci kept pointing out, lacked the federal government's resources to control the virus and distribute the vaccine.[58] As the pandemic raged on, Trump belittled, by word and personal example, every single precaution – social distancing, wearing masks, even the vaccine itself. 'This is going to go away without a vaccine,' he told Republican members of Congress on 8 May.[59] Unlike Joe Biden, he never sat down with Fauci for a proper tutorial on how the virus worked.[60] Fauci swiftly came to the conclusion, shared by most Trump observers with half a brain, that 'his sole purpose is to get re-elected.'[61] It is poor consolation that Trump's mishandling of the pandemic turned out to be the prime cause of his defeat in 2020.

Jamie Raskin, member for Maryland in the House of Representatives, helped write the articles for Trump's second impeachment. He is also a professor of constitutional law, and he argues that 'the current shape of presidential power is a total prostitution of the constitutional design. And Trump tried to compound that, to make it even worse.'[62] The original intention of the Founders was that almost all the important powers should be vested in the Congress as the elected representatives of the people. The core job of the President was merely to take care that the laws should be faithfully executed; he was meant to be an add-on, just to keep the wheels of government rolling. But now the whole system has been turned on its head, and 'the President is somehow deemed to be something like a king of the world.'[63] And that is how the rot sets in. 'The history of authoritarianism is always the story of a would-be dictator or tyrant trying to step outside of the official constitutional structure and instead create a parallel shadow government.'[64]

There was a makeshift gallows in the middle of the Washington Mall, near the statue of Ulysses S. Grant, writes Luke Mogelson:

> Beside the gallows, a woman held up a sign that read 'THE STORM IS HERE.'
> 'Keep pushing!'
> 'Shoot the politicians!'
> 'Get those fucking cocksucking Commies out!'
> 'Hang Mike Pence!'
> 'There's a fucking million of us out here, and we are listening to Trump, your boss,' a large man in a Make America Great Again hat shouted at the officers blocking his path.[65]

Luke Mogelson remembered that he had seen the large man taking part in the Patriot Prayer violent counter-attack against the BLM protests in Portland, Oregon a fortnight earlier. He recognized others as they swept past him over the flimsy barricades and up on to the great marble terrace of the Capitol, then into the central rotunda, and on through the narrow passage leading to the Senate. There was Alex Jones, the conspiracy theorist and Roger Stone's henchman, whom we met before on the 14 November MAGA March. There was Leo Bozell, grandson of Brent Bozell, the brother-in-law of William F. Buckley and ghostwriter of *Conscience of a Conservative* by Barry Goldwater, the Arizona Senator who was the darling of American conservatives and in 1964 ran unsuccessfully for the White House. His father Leo Bozell III, a Fox News regular, had just co-signed an open letter declaring Trump 'the lawful winner of this election' and exhorting Republicans in the swing states to 'appoint clean slates of electors to the Electoral College', as Professor John Eastman had urged. Thus had American conservatism degenerated from a reverence for Edmund Burke into unashamed illegality.

QAnon Shaman Jacob Chansley inside the US Senate Chamber
on 6 January 2021.

There too, most unforgettably, was Jacob Chansley, who calls himself
the Q Shaman, the spearhead of the apocalyptic QAnon movement,
which believes that an occult society of Satanist cannibals, including
Barack Obama, the Clintons and George Soros, is taking over the United
States. The good news is that the Trump Presidency is destined to save
the world from these fiends. Trump himself indulges QAnon because
its members are his most fervent supporters. As Chansley strode along
the Mall, he was carrying a spear and wearing a fur headdress with
horns. His face was painted red, white and blue. 'We got 'em by the
balls, baby,' he said to Mogelson *en passant*, 'and we're not letting go!'[66]

By the time the rioters got to the Senate Chamber, the senators had
all been hustled out, some from under their desks where they had
been sheltering, and taken to various places of safety.[67] The Chamber
was empty. The Trumpers wandered around for a bit, then began to
rifle the senators' desks, pulling out speech notes and briefing papers.
A witless wonder descended on them. What to do next? What exactly
were they there for? Some went on peering at the ring binders and
sheaves of paper, one of them muttering, 'There's gotta be something
in here we can use against those scumbags.' Others started putting the
papers back, fearful of being arrested for stealing. From the gallery,
another Trumper yelled down: 'Take everything, take all that shit!'

'No,' said an older man in body armour, 'we do not take anything.' This, Mogelson recognized, was Larry Rendall Brock Jr, a retired air force lieutenant-colonel, still sporting the wrist patches of the 706th Fighter Squadron on his flak jacket. When a Groyper in a red MAGA hat climbed up and sat in the leather Speaker's chair, recently vacated in a hurry by Vice-President Pence, and started spouting, 'Donald Trump is the Emperor of the United States . . .' another man in cowhide work gloves and a hunting jacket said in a Southern accent, 'Hey, get out of that chair.' And Lt-Col Brock added, 'We can't be disrespectful.'[68]

Hard to imagine any greater disrespect than smashing your way into the Capitol, into the very Chamber where the Senate was due to be certifying the electoral college. Yet behind the intoxication of the headlong rush, there was a curious mixture of confusion and resentment, even the faintest blush of shame.

At this moment, the Q Shaman strides into the Senate Chamber, looking around him and grinning: 'Fucking A, man!' He then climbs on to the dais, horns and all, and announces, 'I'm gonna take a seat in this chair, because Mike Pence is a fucking traitor.' Handing his smartphone to a henchman, he adds, 'I don't usually take pictures of myself, but in this case, I think I'll make an exception.'[69] And this is the photo that whizzes round the Twittersphere, the apotheosis of social media.

After a while, most of the remaining Trump supporters grow bored and amble out of the chamber. Mogelson stays behind to watch a pudgy young police officer gently chivvy the rest. 'Any chance I could get you guys to leave the Senate wing?'

'We will,' says the Southerner in the cowhide gloves. 'I been making sure they ain't disrespectin' the place.'

'OK,' says the officer. 'I just want to let you guys know: this is, like, the sacredest place.'

PART IV

THE SACREDEST PLACE

In Luke Mogelson's unrivalled first-hand account of the whole extraordinary day, this is the most telling passage. It has a resonance that reaches back into one of the most profound disagreements in political philosophy. According to the classic theory on which the United States is founded, the pudgy police officer was absolutely correct. He was in fact uttering the doctrine laid down three centuries ago in John Locke's *Second Treatise*, which is perhaps the founding document of the Founding Fathers. In Locke's formulation, after men have moved out of the state of nature into civil society, they gather together in an Assembly, or what he calls a 'Legislative', to sort out their differences and agree on the rules by which they will live together. This body accordingly becomes supreme, and, yes, sacred:

> Civil Society, being a State of Peace, among those who are of it, from whom the State of War is excluded by the Umpirage, which they have provided in their Legislative, for ending all Differences, that may arise amongst any of them, 'tis in their Legislative, that the Members of a Commonwealth are united, and combined together into one coherent living Body. This is the Soul that gives Form, Life, and Unity to the Commonwealth.[1]

It doesn't matter that they don't agree on everything. In fact, there are bound to be important things on which they disagree, in view of 'the variety of Opinions, and contrariety of Interests, which unavoidably happen in all collections of Men'.[2] And when they disagree, they may have to take a vote, after which the decision of the majority becomes the rule. This is the essential: that the losers in the vote as well as the winners should agree to be bound by the decision. Loser's consent is crucial. Donald Trump, please note. Or, as Locke puts it:

> And thus every man, by consenting with others to make one body politic under one government, puts himself under an obligation, to every one of that society, to submit to the determination of the majority, and to be concluded by it; or else this original compact, whereby he with others incorporates into one society would signify nothing, and be no compact, if he be left free, and under no other ties than he was in before in the state of nature.[3]

There really is no good alternative to this kind of arrangement, Locke says. All very well to submit yourself the rule of a single pre-eminent excellent man. But what happens when the excellent ruler is succeeded by a less excellent ruler? Then people begin to see that their properties, perhaps even their lives, are no longer secure, and they realize that they

> could never be safe nor at rest, nor think themselves in Civil Society, till the Legislature was placed in collective Bodies of Men, call them Senate, Parliament, or what you please. By which means every single person became subject, equally with other the meanest Men, to those Laws, which himself, as part of the Legislative had established.[4]

They are imperfect institutions, these Senates or Parliaments: often undignified, noisy, sadly corruptible, endlessly fallible. But they are the least bad alternative. As Machiavelli argued even earlier than Locke in his *Discourses on Livy*:

> Good laws may arise from those tumults that many inconsiderately damn. To me, it appears that those who damn the tumults between the nobles and the plebs blame those things that were the first cause of keeping Rome free, and that they consider the noises and the cries that would arise in such tumults more than the good effects that they engendered.[5]

I have taken these quotations and much else from Jeremy Waldron's marvellous 1996 Seeley lectures at Cambridge, republished as *The Dignity of Legislation* (1999). Waldron argues that 'legislation and legislatures have a bad name in legal and political philosophy'[6] – there seems something disreputable about the clamour and the catcalling, the filibusters and the scramble for votes. By comparison, how serene and unchallenged is the dictator orating from his balcony, the judge uttering his *obiter dicta* in the hushed courtroom, or the President tweeting in the wee small hours.

Lawyers tend to be rather patronizing about statutes. They prefer the common law, handed down to us in an unbroken stream through the ages, and deplore with Sir William Blackstone how 'the Common Law of England has fared like other venerable edifices of antiquity, which rash and unexperienced work-men have ventured to new-dress and refine, with all the rage of modern improvement'.[7] What a ghastly thought it is, too, that the latest batch of laws may be chucked out when the other lot gets into power. Thomas Hobbes found it particularly repulsive:

It follows hence, that when the legislative power resides in such convents as these, the Laws must needs be inconstant, and change, not according to the alteration of . . . states of affaires, nor according to the changeableness of mens mindes, but as the major part, now of this, then of that faction, do convene; insomuch as the Laws do flote here and there, as it were upon the waters.[8]

Auguste Romieu and indeed Adolf Hitler felt much the same about the deplorable mutability of parliamentary majorities.

But for us, the thought that the minority may one day – perhaps quite soon – become the majority holds no fears. That the decisions of Parliament are perpetually correctible is not the defect but the glory of the system. This correctibility extends to everything about the House: its qualifications for membership by age and sex, its electorate (ditto), its rules and procedures. It is as mutable as human life, but because those rules, once established, are to be scrupulously observed, it is a steady ship. This is the only way to steer a course through the disagreements that are part of life.

In parliamentary government, the minority are not excluded or disregarded, let alone ostracized. Their arguments are recorded; so are their votes. They have had their say, and their say remains part of the ongoing debate and may in time come to persuade or at least influence the majority. The Leader of the Opposition is an official post supported by public funds. He or she is a Prime Minister-in-waiting.

Often the incoming government adopts or does not overturn the measures of the previous government which it fiercely opposed at the time. Churchill in 1951 did not try to dismantle the National Health Service or undo the nationalizations of the Attlee era. Tony Blair in 1997 did not try to reverse the trade union laws and the privatizations of the Thatcher era. Reluctantly or not, a new settlement emerges, for the time being at least. We stand together upon what Michael Oakeshott called 'a new platform of understanding'.

Wouldn't it be so much nicer if we could all agree, at least on the basics? Why don't we try to discover what Rousseau called 'the general will', which, once agreed on, would provide an essentially unchanging set of arrangements? What we needed, Rousseau thought, was a godlike Legislator, or, as Stalin called it, 'an engineer of human souls': a caudillo, a *duce* – in short, a Caesar who would cut short the argument. Rousseau does call for some sort of national assembly, chosen by periodic and fair elections, but he wishes to discourage protracted argument in its sessions: 'long discussion, dissensions and uproar proclaim the ascendancy of private interests and the decline of the State.'[9]

Even modern philosophers of a liberal cast of mind hanker for this delicious unanimity, this haven of certainty. John Rawls in his celebrated *Theory of Justice* defines 'a well-ordered society' as a society in which its members share a common view about justice. The work of agreeing on these common assumptions about what is to count as fair is meant to be done in the first of Rawls's four-stage sequence towards a just society. So the representatives are to have agreed on these basics before they actually meet as a legislature.

But, as Waldron points out so forcefully, this isn't how the world works, or is ever likely to work:

> In the United States, in Western Europe, and in all other democracies, every single step that has been taken by legislatures towards making society safer, more civilized, and more just has been taken against a background of disagreement, but taken nevertheless in a way that managed somehow to retain the loyalty and compliance (albeit often grudging loyalty and compliance) of those who in good faith opposed the measures in question.[10]

The dismantling of segregation, the prohibition of child labour, the liberation of women, the universal adult franchise – all of these reforms, and many more, were achieved after strenuous political conflict, not by anything resembling the consensus that Rawlsians regard as essential.

There's a similar misunderstanding in another popular remedy for 'doing politics better'. In 'deliberative democracy', a group of well-intentioned people get together for an exhaustive discussion of some knotty social problem – income tax rates, abortion, nuclear power, anything. At the end of the discussion in this 'citizens' assembly', as it is called, this earnest conclave is expected to come up with a unanimous answer. Here the fallacy is, as Waldron says, the belief that there must be something wrong with the motivations of the participants if they cannot agree, or, heaven forbid, have to resort to a vote. They must be arguing on the basis of narrow self-interest or sectarian prejudice. If they sincerely addressed the common good, they would surely be bound to find common ground in the end? Well, no, they wouldn't.

We can see a typical example in the demo staged by Extinction Rebellion on 2 September 2022. Fifty of its supporters broke into the Palace of Westminster, and a selected handful of them superglued themselves to the Speaker's Chair in the Commons, holding up big placards saying 'LET THE PEOPLE DECIDE' and 'CITIZENS ASSEMBLY NOW'. The assumption being, of course, that this citizens' assembly would discover the People's Will, or the General Will as Rousseau would put it, in a fashion superior to any decision any Parliament could reach. And the assumption behind this assumption is that the People's Will would be for an all-out war against climate change, involving draconian new regulations. The views of any minority opposing such measures would then be erased. But supposing the citizens' assembly was unable to reach any such conclusion – supposing, perhaps, the assembly recommended only very mild action or no action at all? Don't imagine that the Extinction Rebels would meekly accept any such decision. They would carry on campaigning twice as hard. No loser's consent for them.

Disagreement is inevitable in human affairs. And it is a good thing to explore it thoroughly and, if need be, passionately. To call Parliament 'a mere talking shop' (which is, after all, what the word means) is not an insult, but the highest of compliments. It is the mark of Caesars and would-be Caesars that they itch to cut short the debate. It is noticeable, indeed, how uncomfortable modern Caesars are in private conversation and public debate. As we have seen, senior advisers to Donald Trump found it impossible to engage him in a sustained policy discussion. His eyes would glaze over, or he would simply get up and walk off. Similarly, Boris Johnson at the dinner table will weary of chatting with his neighbours and jump up to make a speech. In the House of Commons, he was always abrupt and ill at ease, spending as little time as was decent in the Chamber. For the Caesar, Parliament is a rival for public attention, a place to be bypassed, neutered, prorogued or actually closed down. He feels, above all, the need to put an end to the prating, or rather other people's prating – he himself is unstoppable in full flow.

So if a free society is to flourish, the freedom of parliamentary debate has to be protected. Parliamentary privilege is not a silly shibboleth, a piece of pompous flummery. It is the keystone of the defence against Caesarism. When they are under pressure, the first reaction of the Caesar and the Caesarists is to attack the immunity of Parliament. By smashing down the doors, tramping up the aisle with guns, parading obscenities and funny hats, the Caesarists hope to shatter the legislators' air of invulnerability, break their aura, intimidate them into impotence.

The two most memorable episodes in British political history both concern a breach of those privileges. I began by describing Cromwell's dismissal of the Rump. But only a decade earlier, there had been an equally startling irruption into the Chamber. In both cases, the Speaker in the chair was William Lenthall, who was Speaker for most of the 20 years of the Long Parliament. Contemporaries and later historians alike have had their criticisms of Lenthall, writing him off as a weak time-server mostly out for himself. He was certainly as avaricious as any other politician of the day, and he did now and then sway with the wind during the long agonies of the 1640s and 1650s, but he was always concerned to rescue some shreds of constitutional stability from the mayhem, to bring in the return, not so much of the monarchy (though he did in the end go along with it), but of civil peace. I cannot think entirely ill of any man who writes in his will that he wants to be buried under a plain stone slab, bearing only the inscription 'Vermis sum' – I am a worm. Certainly on 4 January 1642 his behaviour earned him a sort of immortality. It is the same kind of immortality we have seen earned by otherwise obscure officials who dared to stand up to would-be Caesars: Lucius Caecilius Metellus in ancient Rome, Shanti Bhushan in Mrs Gandhi's India, Brad Raffensperger and Rusty Bowers in Trump's America, and the first Tory MPs who dared to jump from Boris Johnson's runaway train.

Charles I was desperate to arrest the five MPs he thought were plotting against him – John Pym, John Hampden, Denzil Holles, Arthur Hazelrig and William Strode. Allegedly egged on by the Queen – 'Go, you poltroon, go and pull those rogues out by the ears, or never see my face again' – Charles set off for the House of Commons in person, accompanied by no fewer than 400 armed men. He had sent an advance warning to the Lord Mayor, forbidding him to send men to protect Parliament.

At about 3 p.m., the Five Members received warning via the French ambassador that Charles was on his way. They slipped out of the House and took a waiting barge down to the City. Charles took about 80 of his soldiers into the precincts of Parliament and left them in the lobby, with the door propped open so that the MPs could see them fiddling with their swords and pistols. The King then walked up to Lenthall and said, 'Mr Speaker, I must for a time make bold with your chair.' Lenthall politely vacated the Chair. Charles then called out for Pym. Total silence. Then for Holles. Dead silence. And so on. Where were they? the King asked Lenthall.

At which the Speaker courteously fell to one knee and gave the legendary brush-off: 'May it please your Majesty, I have neither eyes to see, nor tongue to speak in this place, but as this House is pleased to direct me, whose servant I am here.'

'I see that all my birds are flown,' muttered the King, and left the Chamber, pursued by shouts of 'Privilege! Privilege!' The next day, Charles rode to Guildhall, again in person, to demand that the Five Members be surrendered to him. Not merely did he meet with another blank refusal, but he was pursued through the streets by crowds shouting, 'Privileges of Parliament!' – surely one of the most cumbersome slogans ever shouted at a demo, but one that showed the cause was not some arcane thing but one that carried real public resonance.

Charles I attempts to arrest the Five Members, 4 January 1642.

By 10 January, Charles had decided that the capital had become too hot to hold him, and he decamped to Hampton Court, then on to Windsor, never to see London again until he was brought back there to be tried for his life and executed seven years later.

The King's two failed attempts to collar the Five Members were only the most vivid of his humiliations in the lead-up to the Civil War. London had already been in tumult for months. And the Long Parliament was on the warpath to reclaim and enlarge its powers. It had passed the Triennial Act, which ensured that Parliament should meet every three years, whether the King chose to summon it or not. It had pronounced Ship Money illegal, affirming that no plea of public danger could justify the King in raising taxes without Parliament's consent. It declared convictions imposed by the Star Chamber illegal and freed some of the victims of the repressive actions of Archbishop Laud. Charles even grudgingly relinquished his prerogative to dissolve Parliament; henceforth it could only dissolve itself, by an Act of Parliament. He did, however, draw the line at giving up command of his armed forces. Most provocative of all, John Pym and others had drawn up the Grand Remonstrance, a bizarre catalogue of all the grievances, oppressions, blunders and breaches of the law that had piled up since Charles had come to the throne 15 years earlier. In other words, the Long Parliament had already set itself on the road to a parliamentary supremacy of the sort we still enjoy.

Lenthall's words still ring in our ears. As a common subject like any other, he gladly bends his knee to his King. But as Speaker, he has to remain deaf to whatever Charles may ask of him. The House of Commons is a world unto itself, whose proceedings cannot be 'impugned' in any outside court, or even by the King. 'This little room is the shrine of the world's liberties', Churchill claimed in 1917, in the darkest days of the Great War. It is certainly the political heart of the United Kingdom. Attempts to bypass Parliament (or the US Congress) by executive order or administrative fiat, or to cut short its proceedings by illegal prorogation or dissolution are grievous injuries to the body politic. Parliamentary privilege is the prime antidote to Caesarism.

In order to make its enormous pretensions a practical reality, Parliament has to insist on its physical immunity. Its boundaries (and its members when they are about their business) have to be sacrosanct, just as the *pomerium*, the sacred girdle round ancient Rome prescribed all sorts of laws that applied within it and proscribed armed forces and all sorts of undesirables from entering it.

It is also the-stock-in-trade of Caesars and wannabe Caesars to work up a rhetoric against the pretensions of Parliament and its members. The elites 'inside the Beltway' or 'the Westminster bubble' are contrasted with the 'real' hard-working citizens outside the metropole. The 'voice of the people' is boomed out in the popular media, on Fox News and Twitter, by those politicians identifying themselves as outsiders who dare to speak out.

The huge claims that Parliament makes for its privileges also impose on its members correspondingly huge responsibilities. They have to provide effective oversight of their own rules, and monitor the conduct of their fellows. The idea that the Committee on Privileges, for example, should suspend its enquiry into the conduct of Boris Johnson after his resignation was absurd, and shocking.

But Parliament's duties of oversight go far beyond its own internal activities. It must also provide effective ongoing supervision of all the quangos and corporations it has set up over the years: the railways, the water industry, the building trade, the nuclear power stations, the City of London, the National Health Service, to name but a few. The abolition of the Audit Commission was one of the most reckless acts of recent Tory governments. Perhaps the most egregious aspect of the Brexiteers was their boast to be restoring the sovereignty of Parliament, while doing their damnedest to prevent Parliament from scrutinizing the terms of Britain's exit – with catastrophic results for small exporters, fruit and veg farmers, care homes and a dozen other sectors. The cry for deregulation *per se* and a 'bonfire of the quangos' is as thoughtless a slogan as can be imagined. The liberties and licences that Parliament has conferred have to be kept under examination by Parliament. Ultimately the responsibility has to come back where it started, to the Chamber. It cannot be hived off or farmed out, without some meaningful recourse to the original source of its authority. Such meticulous scrutiny is possible only if Parliament is left free to pursue its inquiries down to the most detailed questions, such as the safety of the cladding on tower blocks or the addictive properties of opiates. The welfare of the poorest depends not on the pressure of the mob but on the most minute examination of what is actually happening on the ground in care homes and social security offices.

Whether it be Charles I on 4 January 1642 or Donald Trump and the QAnon Shaman on 6 January 2021, the insult to the integrity of

Parliament always takes much the same form. And it always has to be resisted. If Parliament and the Senate are not the sacredest places, then nothing much else is sacred.

The intrusion of Charles I generated, or helped to generate, the famous ceremonial which is still performed at each State Opening of Parliament: Black Rod, the major-domo of the House of Lords, is sent from the Upper House to summon MPs to hear the King's Speech from the Throne. The door of the Commons is slammed in Black Rod's face, to symbolize the independence of the House of Commons. He (or at present she) bangs three times on the door with the rod, the door is opened, and the MPs then follow the Speaker and Black Rod back to the Upper House. It is not, I think, an official part of the tradition that the MPs should be jabbering loudly to each other as they walk through the Central Lobby, but this shows a proper spirit of irreverence, the reverence on this occasion being entirely directed toward the House of Commons. Unlike many supposedly ancient traditions that were only devised in Victorian times, this one really does go way back. Thomas Duppa, deputizing as Black Rod in 1679, recounts the instructions he received for an almost identical ceremony.[11] The only difference is that he is told to knock four or five times.

I used to think that the whole performance was the kind of mummery we didn't need any more. But now I think we need it more than ever.

Further Reading

A

Abbott, Frank Frost, *A History and Description of Roman Political Institutions*. Boston: Ginn and Co, 1901

Abbott, W.C. ed., *The Writings and Speeches of Oliver Cromwell*, 4 vols. Cambridge, Mass.: Harvard University Press, 1937–47

Adamson, John, ed., *The English Civil War: Conflicts and Contexts 1640–1649*. London: Bloomsbury Academic, 2008

Appian, *The Civil Wars*, tr. John Carter. Harmondsworth: Penguin, 1996

B

Bear, Ileen, *Adolf Hitler*. London: Alpha Editions, 2016

Beard, Mary, *SPQR: A History of Ancient Rome*. London: Profile, 2015

Bell, David A., *Men on Horseback*. New York: Farrar, Straus and Giroux, 2020

Bew, John, *Castlereagh: Enlightenment, War and Tyranny*. London: Quercus, 2011

Bower, Tom, *Boris Johnson: The Gambler*. London: WH Allen, 2021

Brogan, Hugh, *Alexis de Tocqueville: A Life*. London: Profile, 2009

Bromwich, David, *The Intellectual Life of Edmund Burke*. Cambridge, Mass.: The Belknap Press, 2014

Burleigh, Michael, *The Third Reich: A New History*. London: Pan, 2000

C

Caesar, Julius, *The Civil Wars*, tr. A. G. Peskett. London: Heinemann, Loeb Library, 1928

Caesar, Julius, *The Gallic War*, tr. H. J. Edwards. London: Heinemann, Loeb Library, 1917

Canfora, Luciano, *Julius Caesar: The Life and Times of the People's Dictator*. Berkeley: University of California Press, 2007

Carlyle, Thomas, ed., *Oliver Cromwell: Letters and Speeches*, 3 vols. London: Chapman and Hall, 1845–6

Carlyle, Thomas, *On Heroes, Hero Worship and the Hero in History*. London: James Fraser, 1841

Cicero, *De Oratore: The Speeches In Catilinam*, tr. Louis E. Lord. Cambridge Mass.: Harvard University Press, Loeb Library, 1946

Cicero, *Letters to Atticus*, tr. E. O. Winstedt, 3 vols. London: Heinemann, Loeb Library, 1912–18

Clark, J. C. D., *English Society 1688–1832*. Cambridge University Press, 1985

Condorcet, Nicolas de, *Esquisse d'un Tableau Historique des Progrès de l'Esprit Humain*. Paris: Agasse, 1795

Coward, Barry, *The Cromwellian Protectorate*. Manchester University Press, 2002

Cust, Richard, *Charles I: a Political Life*. Harlow: Longman, 2005

D

Dale, Iain, *The Dictators: A Warning from History*, (forthcoming). London: Hodder & Stoughton, 2024

De Las Cases, Emmanuel, *Journal of the Private Life and Conversations of the Emperor Napoleon at Saint Helena*, 4 vols. London: Henry Colburn, 1824

Dhar, P. N., *Indira Gandhi, the 'Emergency' and Indian Democracy*. New Delhi: Oxford India, 2000

Dio, Cassius, *Roman History*, tr. H. B. Foster, 9 vols. Cambridge Mass.: Harvard University Press, Loeb Library, 1914

Duppa, Sir Thomas, *Sir Thomas Duppa's Commonplace Book*, ed. Alasdair Hawkyard and J. C. Sainty. Chichester, Sussex: Wiley Blackwell, 2015

Dwyer, Philip, *Napoleon: The Path to Power*. London: Bloomsbury, 2007

Dwyer, Philip, *Napoleon: Citizen Emperor*. London: Bloomsbury, 2013

Dwyer, Philip, *Napoleon: Passion, Death and Resurrection 1815–1840*. London: Bloomsbury, 2018

E

Edwards, Francis, *The Gunpowder Plot*. London: Folio Society, 1973

F

Fest, Joachim, *Hitler*, tr. Richard and Clara Winston. New York: Harcourt Brace Jovanovich, 1974

Firth, Sir Charles, 'Oliver Cromwell', *Dictionary of National Biography*, 1885–1900

Fischer, Fritz, *Germany's Aims in the First World War*. London: Chatto, 1967

Frank, Katherine, *Indira: The Life of Indira Nehru Gandhi*. London: HarperCollins, 2001

Fraser, Antonia, *Cromwell, Our Chief of Men*. London: Weidenfeld & Nicolson, 1973

Fraser, Antonia, *Mary Queen of Scots*. London: Weidenfeld & Nicolson, 1969

Fraser, Antonia, *The Gunpowder Plot: Terror and Faith in 1605*. London: Weidenfeld & Nicolson, 1996

Fukuyama, Francis, *The End of History and the Last Man*. New York: Free Press, 1992

G

Gardiner, S. R., *What Gunpowder Plot Was*. London: Longman, 1897

Gatrell, Vic, *Conspiracy on Cato Street: A Tale of Liberty and Revolution in Regency London*. Cambridge: Cambridge University Press, 2022

Gerard, John, *What Was the Gunpowder Plot?*. London: Osgood, McIlvaine & Co., 1897

Gibbon, Edward, *The History of the Decline and Fall of the Roman Empire*, 12 vols. London: W. Allason, 1821

Gimson, Andrew, *Boris Johnson: The Rise and Fall of a Troublemaker in Number Ten*. London: Simon & Schuster, 2022

Goldsworthy, Adrian, *Caesar: Life of a Colossus*. London: Weidenfeld & Nicolson, 2006

Goodhart, David, *The Road to Somewhere: The Populist Revolt and the Future of Politics*. London: Penguin, 2017

Guha, Ramachandra, *India After Gandhi*. London: Macmillan, 2007

H

Haffner, Sebastian, *Defying Hitler: A Memoir*, tr. Oliver Pretzel. London: Weidenfeld & Nicolson, 2002

Hancock, Matt, *Pandemic Diaries: The Inside Story of Britain's Battle against Covid*. London: Biteback Publishing, 2022

Haynes, Alan, *The Gunpowder Plot*. Stroud: Sutton Publishing, 2005

Heffer, Simon, *Moral Desperado: A Life of Thomas Carlyle*. London: Weidenfeld & Nicolson, 1995

Hennessy, Peter, *Cabinet*. Oxford: Wiley-Blackwell, 1986

Hill, Christopher, *God's Englishman: Oliver Cromwell and the English Revolution*. London: Weidenfeld & Nicolson, 1970

Hilton, Boyd, *A Mad, Bad and Dangerous People? England 1783–1846*. Oxford: Clarendon Press, 2006

Hitler, Adolf, *Mein Kampf*, tr. Ralph Manheim. London: Hutchinson, 1969

Holland, Tom, *Rubicon: The Triumph and Tragedy of the Roman Republic*. London: Little, Brown, 2003

Horace, *Odes*, tr. James Michie. London: Hart-Davis, 1963

Hugo, Victor, *Napoléon le Petit*. Amsterdam, 1853

Hutton, Ronald, *The British Republic 1649–1660*. London: Macmillan, 2000

J

Jackson, Julian, *A Certain Idea of France: The Life of Charles de Gaulle*. London: Allen Lane, 2018

Jaffrelot, Christophe, & Anil, Pratinav, *India's First Dictatorship: The Emergency 1975–1977*. London: Hurst, 2020

K

Keefe, Patrick Radden, *The Empire of Pain:The Secret History of the Sackler Dynasty*. London: Picador, 2021

Kershaw, Ian, *Hitler 1889–1936: Hubris*. London: Allen Lane, 1998

Kidd, Colin, and Rose, Jacqueline, eds., *Political Advice: Past, Present and Future*. London: I.B. Tauris, Bloomsbury, 2021

Kundu, Apurba, *Militarism in India:The Army and Civil Society in Consensus*. London: Tauris Academic Studies, 1998

L

Lay, Paul, *Providence Lost:The Rise and Fall of Cromwell's Protectorate*. London: Head of Zeus, Bloomsbury 2020

Lee, Alexander, *Machiavelli, His Life and Times*. London: Picador, 2020

Lewandowski, Corey R., & Bossie, David N., *Trump's Enemies: How the Deep State is Undermining the Presidency*. NewYork: Center Street, 2018

Lewis, Michael, *The Fifth Risk: Undoing Democracy*. London: Allen Lane, 2018

Lieven, Dominic, *In the Shadow of the Gods:The Emperor inWorld History*. London: Allen Lane, 2021

Locke, John, *Two Treatises of Government*. London: Awnsham Churchill, 1690

Lucan, *Pharsalia*, or *De Bello Civili*, tr. J. D. Duff. Cambridge Mass.: Harvard University Press, Loeb Library, 1928

M

Machiavelli, Niccolò, *The Discourses*, tr. Leslie J.Walker and Brian Richardson. London: Penguin Classics 2013

Machiavelli, Niccolò, *The Prince*, tr. Tim Parks. London: Penguin Classics, 2011

Mack Smith, Denis, *Mussolini*. London: Granada, 1981

Mansfield, Harvey C., *Machiavelli'sVirtue*. Chicago: Chicago University Press, 1996

Marx, Karl, *The Eighteenth Brumaire of Louis Bonaparte*, 1852, tr. Eden and Cedar Paul. London: Allen & Unwin, 1926

McKinstry, Leo, *Rosebery: Statesman inTurmoil*. London: John Murray, 2005

Meier, Christian, *Caesar*, tr. David McLintock. London: HarperCollins, 1995

Mill, John Stuart, *Considerations on Representative Government*. London: Parker, Son and Bourn, 1861

Mill, John Stuart, *On Liberty*. London: John W. Parker, 1859

Mogelson, Luke, *The Storm is Here: America on the Brink*. London: Riverrun, 2022

Morgan, George Blacker, *The Identification of theWriter of the Anonymous Letter to Lord Monteagle in 1605*. London: Good Press, 2019

Morrill, John, 'Oliver Cromwell', *Dictionary of National Biography*, 2008
Morrill, John, ed., *Oliver Cromwell and the English Revolution*. Harlow: Longman, 1996

N

Nicholls, Mark, *Investigating Gunpowder Plot*. Manchester: Manchester University Press, 1991
Nietzsche, Friedrich, *The Will to Power*, tr. Michael A. Scarpitti and R. Kevin Hill. London: Penguin Classics, 2017

O

Oborne, Peter, *How Trump Thinks: His Tweets and the Birth of a New Political Language*. London: Head of Zeus, Bloomsbury, 2017
Oborne, Peter, *The Assault on Truth*. London: Simon & Schuster, 2021
Oborne, Peter, *The Rise of Political Lying*. London: Free Press, 2005
Omrani, Bijan, *Caesar's Footprints: Journeys to Roman Gaul*. London: Head of Zeus, Bloomsbury 2017

P

Parakash, Gyan, *Emergency Chronicles: Indira Gandhi and Democracy's Turning Point*. New Jersey: Princeton University Press, 2019
Payne, Sebastian, *The Fall of Boris Johnson: The Full Story*. London: Macmillan, 2022
Payne, Stanley G., *A History of Spain and Portugal*, 2 vols. Madison: Wisconsin University Press, 1973
Plato, *The Republic*, tr. Benjamin Jowett, 2 vols. Oxford: Clarendon Press. 1908
Pliny, *Natural History*, tr. H. Rackham, W. H. S. Jones and D. E. Eichholz, 10 vols. Cambridge Mass.: Harvard University Press, Loeb Library, 1938–62
Plutarch, *Parallel Lives*, tr. Bernadotte Perrin, 11 vols. Cambridge Mass.: Harvard University Press, Loeb Library, 1914–26
Pocock, J. G. A., *The Machiavellian Moment: Florentine Political Thought and the Atlantic Republican Tradition*. New Jersey: Princeton University Press, 1975
Poole, Robert, *Peterloo: The English Uprising*. Oxford: Oxford University Press, 2019
Popper Karl, *The Open Society*, 2 vols. London: Routledge, 1945
Popper, Karl, *The Poverty of Historicism*. London: Routledge, 1957

R

Roberts, Andrew, *Napoleon: A Life*. London: Penguin, 2015
Romieu, François-Auguste, *L'Ère des Césars*. Paris, 1850
Rothkopf, David, *American Resistance: The Inside Story of How the Deep State Saved America*. New York: PublicAffairs, 2022
Rousseau, Jean-Jacques, *The Social Contract*, tr. H. J. Tozer. London: Swan Sonnenschein, 1895

S

Sallust, *Bellum Catilinae, The War with Catiline*, tr. J. C. Rolfe. Cambridge Mass.: Harvard University Press, Loeb Library, 1921

Santos, Luis Gorrochategui, *The English Armada: The Greatest Naval Disaster in English History*. London: Bloomsbury, 2018

Séguin, Philippe, *Louis-Napoléon le Grand*. Paris: Grasset, 1990

Sharpe, Kevin, *The Personal Rule of Charles I*. New Haven: Yale, 1992

Smith, Adam, *The Wealth of Nations*. London: William Strahan, 1776; Everyman Edition, 1975.

Spengler, Oswald, *The Decline of the West*, tr. C. F. Atkinson, 2 vols. New York: Knopf, 1926, 1928

Spengler, Oswald, *The Hour of Decision*, 1934, English tr. New York: Knopf, 1963

Suetonius, *The Lives of the Twelve Caesars*, ed. Joseph Gavorse. New York: Random House, 1931

Syme, Ronald, *Sallust*. Oakland: University of California Press, 1964

T

Tarlo, Emma, *Unsettling Memories: Narratives of the Emergency in India*. London: Hurst, 2003

Thomas, Hugh, *The Spanish Civil War*. London: Eyre & Spottiswoode, 1961

Thompson, E. P., *The Making of the English Working Class*. London: Gollancz, 1963

Thorpe, D. R., *Selwyn Lloyd*. London: Cape, 1989

Tocqueville, Alexis de, *Memoir, Letters and Remains*, ed. Gustave de Beaumont, 2 vols. Cambridge: Macmillan, 1861

Treitschke, Heinrich von, *Treitschke's History of Germany in the Nineteenth Century*, 1879–2005, tr. Eden and Cedar Paul, 7 vols. London: Jarrold & Sons, 1915–19

Trevor-Roper, Hugh, *Europe's Physician: The Various Life of Sir Theodore de Mayerne*. New Haven: Yale, 2006

W

Waldron, Jeremy, *The Dignity of Legislation*. Cambridge: Cambridge University Press, 1999

Weber, Max, *Economy and Society*, ed. Guenther Roth and Claus Wittich. New York: Bedminster Press, 1968

Weber, Max, *Max Weber on Charisma and Institution Building*, ed. S. N. Eisenstadt. Chicago: Chicago University Press, 1968

White, R. J., *Waterloo to Peterloo*. London: Heinemann, 1957

Wolff, Michael, *Fire and Fury: Inside the Trump White House*. London: Little, Brown, 2018

Wolff, Michael, *Landslide: The Final Days of the Trump Presidency*. London: Little, Brown, 2021

Wolff, Michael, *Siege: Trump Under Fire*. London: Little, Brown, 2019

Woodward, Bob, *Fear: Trump in the White House*. London: Simon & Schuster, 2018

Woodward, Bob, *Rage*. London: Simon & Schuster, 2020

Woodward, Bob, and Costa, Robert, *Peril*. London: Simon & Schuster, 2021

Woolrych, Austin, *Britain in Revolution 1625–1660*. Oxford: Oxford University Press, 2002

Worden, Blair, *Roundhead Reputations: The English Civil Wars and the Passions of Posterity*. London: Allen Lane, 2001

Z

Zamoyski, Adam, *Napoleon: A Life*. London: Collins, 2018

Notes

CHAPTER 1 – WHY IS HE THERE?

1 W. C. Abbott, ed., *The Writings and Speeches of Oliver Cromwell*, vol II, Boston: Ginn and Co, 1939, pp. 640–44
2 Austin Woolrych, *Britain in Revolution 1625–1660*. Oxford: Oxford University Press, 2002, p. 688
3 Antonia Fraser, *Cromwell, Our Chief of Men*. London: Weidenfeld & Nicolson, 1973, p. 64
4 Abbott, ed., *Writings and Speeches*, vol II, p. 319
5 Woolrych, *Britain in Revolution*, p. 624
6 Christopher Hill, *God's Englishman: Oliver Cromwell and the English Revolution*, London: Weidenfeld & Nicolson, 1970, p.198
7 Ibid., p. 199
8 John, Morrill, 'Oliver Cromwell', DNB, 2004
9 Philip Dwyer, *Napoleon: The Path to Power*. London: Bloomsbury, 2007, p. 494

CHAPTER 2 – THE HERO WORSHIPPER

1 Thomas Carlyle, *On Heroes, Hero Worship and the Hero in History*. London: James Fraser, 1841, p. 21
2 Carlyle, *On Heroes*, p. 317
3 Thomas Carlyle, *Oliver Cromwell: Letters and Speeches*, vol I, London: Chapman and Hall, 1845–6, p. 1
4 Carlyle, *On Heroes*, p. 367
5 Julian Jackson, *A Certain Idea of France*. London: Allen Lane, 2018, pp. 754–5
6 Simon Heffer, *Moral Desperado*. London: Weidenfeld & Nicolson, 1995, p. 220
7 Carlyle, *On Heroes*, p. 383
8 Carlyle, *On Heroes*, p. 388
9 Carlyle, *On Heroes*, p. 345

10 Carlyle, *Letters and Speeches*, p. viii

11 Blair Worden, *Roundhead Reputations*. London: Allen Lane, 2001, p. 290

12 Carlyle, *Letters and Speeches*, p. 296

13 Heffer, *Moral Desperado*, p. 222

14 *The Times*, 15 November 1899

15 Leo McKinstry, *Rosebery*. London: John Murray, 2005, pp. 429, 434

16 Woolrych, *Britain in Revolution*, pp. 588, 779; Barry Coward, *The Cromwellian Protectorate*. Manchester University Press, 2002, pp. 174–6

17 Hugh Trevor-Roper, *Europe's Physician*. New Haven: Yale, 2006, pp. 306–11

18 Kevin Sharpe, *The Personal Rule of Charles I*. New Haven: Yale, 1992, p. 608

19 Woolrych, *Britain in Revolution*, p. 310

CHAPTER 3 – AUGUSTUS AND AUGUSTE – AND ADOLF

1   Heffer, *Moral Desperado*, p. 232

2   François-Auguste Romieu, *L'Ère des Césars*. Paris, 1850, pp. 189–90

3   Ibid., p. 6

4   Ibid., p. 99

5   Ibid., p. 81

6   Ibid., p. 13

7   Ibid., p. 28

8   Ibid., p. 129

9   Ibid., p. 29

10 Ibid., pp. 37, 39

11 Ibid., p. 5

12 Ibid., pp. 132–3

13 Philippe Séguin, *Louis-Napoléon le Grand*. Paris: Grasset, 1990, p. 68. Séguin was a prominent and obsessive neo-Gaullist, briefly leader of the Gaullist RPR, who saw parallels between the greatness of the two men.

14 Romieu, p. 40

15 Ibid., p. 41

16 Edward Gibbon, *The History of the Decline and Fall of the Roman Empire*. London: W. Allason, 1821, chapter 3

17 Romieu, p. 49

18 Ibid., p. 75

19 Ibid., p. 93

20 Ibid., pp 123–4

21 Ibid., p. 157

22 Hugh Brogan, *Alexis de Tocqueville*, London: Profile, 2006, pp. 519–20

23 Alexis de Tocqueville, *Memoir, Letters and Remains*, ed. Gustave de Beaumont. Cambridge: Macmillan, 1861, 'Extract from Mr Senior's Journal, December 31, 1851'

24 Ian Kershaw, *Hitler: 1889–1936: Hubris*. New York: W. W. Norton & Company, 2000, p. 33

25 Oswald Spengler, *The Decline of the West*, 2 vols. New York: Knopf, 1963, II, p. 416. In fact, just as Spengler's second volume was published, Lloyd George was about to be ousted from power for ever.

26 Ibid.

27 Ibid., p. 464

28 Adolf Hitler, *Mein Kampf*, tr. Ralph Manheim. London: Hutchinson, 1969, pp. 71–2

29 Ibid.

30 Ibid., p. 74

31 Ibid., p. 78

CHAPTER 4 – THE COMFORTING ILLUSION

1 Karl Popper, *The Poverty of Historicism*. London: Routledge, 1957, p. 3

2 Popper, *Poverty*, p. 118

3 Popper, *Poverty*, ii. pp. 62–3

CHAPTER 6 – THE INVENTION OF CHARISMA

1 Max Weber, *Economy and Society*, ed. Guenther Roth and Claus Wittich, vol 3. New York: Bedminster Press, 1968, p. 1452

2 Dwyer, *Path to Power*, p. 407

3 Weber, ibid., p. 222

4 David A. Bell, *Men on Horseback*. New York: Farrar, Straus and Giroux, 2020, p. 4

5 Max Weber, *Max Weber on Charisma and Institution Building*, ed. S. N. Eisenstadt. Chicago: Chicago University Press, 1968, pp. 21, 53

6 Leon Edel, *Henry James: A Life, Vol V, The Master*, p. 525

7 Christian Meier, *Caesar*, tr. David McLintock. London: HarperCollins, 1995, pp. 92, 136

8 Bell, ibid., p. 192

9 Dwyer, *Path to Power*, p. 166

10 Ibid., p. 197

11 Adam Zamoyski, *Napoleon: A Life*. London: Collins, 2018, p. 168

CHAPTER 7 – THE TIMING

1 Plutarch, *Parallel Lives*, tr. Bernadotte Perrin. Cambridge Mass.: Harvard University Press, Loeb Library, 1914–26, vol VII, 'Caesar', p. 32

2 Tom Holland, *Rubicon*. London: Little, Brown, 2003, pp. xx, xxi

3 Plutarch, *Parallel Lives*, p. 32

4   Ibid.

5   Ibid.

6   Meier, *Caesar*, pp. 365–6

7   Pliny, *Natural History*, VII. pp. 91–2

8   Plutarch, *Parallel Lives*, 'Cato the Younger', p. 51

9   Luciano Canfora, *Julius Caesar*. Berkeley: University of California Press, 2007, p. 121

10   Cicero, *Second Philippic*, 8.116

11   Meier, *Caesar*, p. 363

12   Holland, *Rubicon*, pp. 315–16; Meier, *Caesar*, pp. 379–80; Plutarch, *Parallel Lives*, 'Caesar', p. 35; Appian, *The Civil Wars*, tr. John Carter. Harmondsworth: Penguin, 1996, pp. I.33, and 2.41; Adrian Goldsworthy, *Caesar: Life of a Colossus*. London: Weidenfeld & Nicolson, 2006, pp. 396–7

13   Cassius Dio, *Roman History*, xli.17

14   Julius Caesar, *The Civil Wars*, tr. A. G. Peskett. London: Heinemann, Loeb Classical Library, 1928, I.33

15   Julian Jackson, *A Certain Idea of France: The Life of Charles de Gaulle*. London: Allen Lane, 2018, p. 384

16   Ibid., p. 381

17   Ibid., p. 423

18   Ibid., p. 401

19   Ibid., p. 423

20   Ibid., p. 476

CHAPTER 8 – THE ART OF NOBLE LYING

1   Jackson, *A Certain Idea*, p. 326

2   Ibid., p. 326

3   Ibid., p. 707

4   Ibid., p. 758

5   Emmanuel de las Cases, *Journal of the Private Life and Conversations of the Emperor Napoleon at Saint Helena*. London: Henry Colburn, 1824, I, 2, p. 3

6   Dwyer, *Path to Power*, p. 506

7   Ibid., pp. 497–8

8   Dwyer, *Citizen Emperor*, p.121

9   Dominic Lieven, *In the Shadow of the Gods*. London: Allen Lane, 2021, pp. 129, 133

10   Ibid., p. 100

11   D. R. Thorpe, *Selwyn Lloyd*. London: Cape, 1989, pp. 264–5

12   Ibid.

13   Ibid., pp. 266–7

14 Ibid.

15 Peter Oborne, *Rise of Political Lying*, pp. 191, 193

16 Ibid., pp. 216–17

17 *Republic* 414b, Popper I, p. 140

18 Karl Popper, *The Open Society*. London: Routledge, 1945, I, p. 142

19 Niccolò Machiavelli, *The Discourses*, tr. Leslie J. Walker and Brian Richardson. London: Penguin Classics, 2013, I, 11

20 Niccolò Machiavelli, *The Prince*. London: Penguin Classics, 2011, p. 18, in Tim Parks's rip-roaring translation.

21 Ibid.

22 Friedrich Nietzsche, *The Will to Power*, tr. Michael A. Scarpitti and R. Kevin Hill. London: Penguin Classics, 2017, p. 536

23 Ibid., p. 539

24 Peter Oborne, *How Trump Thinks*. London: Head of Zeus, Bloomsbury, 2017, p. xix

25 *Slate*, March 2016

26 Peter Oborne, *The Assault on Truth*. London: Simon & Schuster, 2021, pp. 63–4

27 *Washington Post*, 24 January 2021

28 *Rolling Stone*, 2 April 2022; *Independent*, 3 April 2022

29 Oborne, *How Trump Thinks*, p. 87

30 *Independent*, 25 March 2021

31 *Spectator*, 29 June 2019

32 Oborne, *Assault on Truth*, p. 18

CHAPTER 9 – THE RESISTIBLE RISE OF BORIS JOHNSON

1   Jackson, p. 18

2   Tom Bower, *Boris Johnson: The Gambler*. London: WH Allen, 2021, p. 17

3   Ibid., p. 18

4   Ibid., p. 79

5   Ibid., p. 32

6   Ibid., p. 69

7   Ibid., p. 77

8   Ibid., pp. 75–6

9   Ibid., p. 245

10 Ibid., p. 266

11 Ibid., pp. 273–4

12 Ibid., p. 285

13 Ibid., p. 290

14 Ibid., p.340

15 Ibid., p. 353

16 Ibid., p. 366
17 David Bromwich, *The Intellectual Life of Edmund Burke*. Cambridge, Mass: The Belknap Press, 2014, p. 136

CHAPTER 10 – THE LECTERN

1 Peter Oborne, *The Rise of Political Lying*. London: Free Press, 2005, p. 256
2 Colin Kidd and Jacqueline Rose, eds., *Political Advice*. London: Tauris Academic Studies, 1998, p. 115
3 *The Times*, 2 April 2021
4 *The Times*, 20 May 2022
5 Oborne, *Rise of Political Lying*, p. 151
6 Andrew Roberts, *The Chief*. London: Bloomsbury, 2022, p. 61

CHAPTER 11 – THE FIVE ACTS

1 OpenDemocracy website

CHAPTER 12 – THE ENEMY AT THE GATES

1 Meier, *Caesar*, p. 446
2 Meier, *Caesar*, pp. 448, 464
3 Christopher Hill, *God's Englishman*, p. 20
4 *The Times*, 22 January 2022
5 *The Times*, 17 May 2022
6 *The Times*, 28 May 2022

CHAPTER 13 – CATILINE ON THE RUN

1 Sallust, *Bellum Catilinae, The War with Catiline*, tr. J. C. Rolfe. Cambridge Mass.: Harvard University Press, Loeb Library, 1921, p. 5
2 Plutarch, *Parallel Lives*, 'Cicero', p. 10
3 Ibid.
4 Suetonius, *The Lives of the Twelve Caesars*, ed. Joseph Gavorse. New York: Random House, 1931, p. 7; Sallust, *Bellum Catilinae*, p. 18
5 Ronald Syme, *Sallust*. Oakland: University of California Press, 1964, pp. 91–6
6 Horace, *Odes*, tr. James Michie. London: Hart-Davis, 1963, vol III, 1, pp. 33–7
7 Sallust, *Bellum Catilinae*, pp. 12–13
8 Sallust, *Bellum Catilinae*, p. 37
9 Plutarch, 'Cicero', 10
10 Syme, *Sallust*, p. 258

11 Syme, *Sallust*, p. 21
12 Cicero, *De Oratore: The Speeches in Catilinam*, tr. Louis E. Lord. Cambridge, Mass.: Harvard University Press, Loeb Classical Library, 1946, I
13 Ibid.
14 Ibid.
15 Sallust, *Bellum Catilinae*, p. 31
16 Cicero, *In Catilinam*, II, iii
17 Ibid., II, xii
18 Ibid., III, vii
19 Sallust, *Bellum Catilinae*, p. 46
20 Cicero, *De Oratore: Pro Sulla*, XV, 42
21 Cicero, *In Catilinam*, III, vi
22 Ibid., III, vii
23 Ibid., IV, iii
24 Ibid., IV, vii
25 Ibid., IV, x
26 Plutarch, 'Cicero', 22
27 Sallust, *Bellum Catilinae*, p.55
28 Ibid.
29 Ibid., p. 58
30 Mary Beard, *SPQR: A History of Ancient Rome*. London: Profile, 2015, pp. 318–19

CHAPTER 14 – GUNPOWDER, TREASON AND PLOT(?)

1 Antonia Fraser, *The Gunpowder Plot: Terror and Faith in 1605*. London: Weidenfeld & Nicolson, 1996, p. 172
2 Alan Haynes, *The Gunpowder Plot*. Stroud: Sutton Publishing, 2005, p. 78
3 Fraser, *Gunpowder Plot*, p. 149
4 Ibid., p. 150, spelling and punctuation modernized
5 Ibid., p. 151
6 S. R. Gardiner, *What Gunpowder Plot Was*. London: Longman, 1897, p. 67
7 Ibid.
8 Haynes, *Gunpowder Plot*, p. 86
9 Gardiner, *What Gunpowder Plot Was*, p. 2
10 Ibid., p. 70
11 Haynes, *Gunpowder Plot*, pp. 85–6
12 Fraser, *Gunpowder Plot*, p. 168
13 Ibid., p. 169
14 Ibid., p. 155
15 George Blacker Morgan, *The Identification of the Writer of the Anonymous Letter to Lord Monteagle in 1605*. London: Good Press, 2019, passim

16 Fraser, *Gunpowder Plot*, p. 285

17 Mark Nicholls, *Investigating Gunpowder Plot*. Manchester: Manchester University Press, 1991, pp. 36–9

18 Antonia Fraser, *Mary Queen of Scots*. London: Weidenfeld & Nicolson, 1973, pp. 483–4

19 Ibid., p. 180

20 Gardiner, *What Gunpowder Plot Was*, p. 21

21 Haynes, *Gunpowder Plot*, pp. 98–9

22 Ibid., p. 81

CHAPTER 15 – THE DINNER PARTY THAT NEVER WAS

1 Vic Gatrell, *Conspiracy on Cato Street*. Cambridge: Cambridge University Press, 2022, p. 349

2 E. P. Thompson, *The Making of the English Working Class*. London: Gollancz, 1963, p. 539

3 Gatrell, p. 193

4 Ibid., p. 203

5 Ibid., p. 263

6 Adam Smith, *The Wealth of Nations*. London: William Strahan, 1776; Everyman Edition, 1975, I, 10

7 Gatrell, p. 170

8 Ibid., p. 269

9 Ibid., p. 168

10 Ibid., p. 232

11 John Bew, *Castlereagh: Enlightenment, War and Tyranny*. London: Quercus, 2011, p. 473

12 Ibid., p. 474

13 Gatrell, p. 348

14 Ibid., p.214

15 Ibid., p.41

16 Ibid., p.347

17 R. J. White, *Waterloo to Peterloo*. London: Heinemann, 1957, p. 92

18 Gatrell, p. 56

CHAPTER 16 – THE BEER HALL PUTSCH

1 Hitler, *Mein Kampf*, tr. Ralph Manheim. London: Hutchinson, 1969, p. xi

2 Joachim Fest, *Hitler*, tr. Richard and Clara Winston. New York: Harcourt Brace Jovanovich, 1974, p. 179

3 Fest, *Hitler*, p. 14

4 Ibid., p. 90

5   Hitler, *Mein Kampf*, p. 51
6   Ian Kershaw, *Hitler 1889-1936: Hubris*. London: Allen Lane, 1998, pp. 50–1; Fest, *Hitler*, pp. 36–7; Hitler, *Mein Kampf*, p. 52
7   Hitler, *Mein Kampf*, p. 20
8   Fest, *Hitler*, p. 47
9   Ibid., p. 113
10 Ibid., p. 52
11 Ibid., p. 62
12 Hitler, *Mein Kampf*, p. 150
13 Kershaw, *Hitler*, p. 122
14 Ibid.
15 Ibid., p. 122
16 Ibid., p. 167
17 Fest, *Hitler*, p. 187
18 Kershaw, *Hitler*, p. 133
19 Ibid., pp. 148–9
20 Fest, *Hitler*, p. 177
21 Ibid., p. 182
22 Ibid., p. 183
23 Kershaw, *Hitler*, p. 208
24 Ibid., p. 377
25 Ibid., p. 111
26 Kershaw, *Hitler*, p. 217
27 Fest, *Hitler*, p. 191
28 Ibid., p. 192
29 Ibid., p. 747
30 Hitler, *Mein Kampf*, p. 598
31 Ibid., p. 41, Hitler's italics
32 Fest, *Hitler*, p. 129
33 Ibid., p. 595
34 Hitler, *Mein Kampf*, pp. 163–9

CHAPTER 17 – MRS GANDHI'S EMERGENCY

1   Katherine Frank, *Indira: The Life of Indira Nehru Gandhi*. London: HarperCollins, 2001, p. 290
2   Ibid., p. 434
3   Ibid., p. 296
4   Ibid., p. 120
5   Ibid., p. 164
6   Ibid., p. 318

7   Christophe Jaffrelot & Pratinav Anil, *India's First Dictatorship: The Emergency 1975–1977*. London: Hurst, 2020, p. 284

8   Frank, *Indira*, p. 328

9   P. N. Dhar, *Indira Gandhi, the 'Emergency' and Indian Democracy*. New Delhi: Oxford India, 2000, p. 310

10 Ramachandra Guha, *India After Gandhi*. London: Macmillan, 2007, p. 504

11 Jaffrelot, *India's First Dictatorship*, p. 330

12 Ibid., p. 356

13 Guha, *India After Gandhi*, p. 384

14 Jaffrelot, *India's First Dictatorship* p. 418

15 Frank, *Indira*, p. 385

16 Guha, *India After Gandhi*, pp. 499–500

17 Jaffrelot, *India's First Dictatorship* p. 110

18 Frank, *Indira*, p. 383

19 *Spectator*, 21 August 1976

20 Dhar, *Indira Gandhi*, p. 339

21 Ibid., p. 337

22 Ibid., p. 351

23 Guha, *India After Gandhi*, p. 519

24 Jaffrelot, *India's First Dictatorship*, p. 404

25 Ibid., p. 405

26 Ibid., p. 229

27 Ibid., p. 430

28 Ibid., p. 114; see also Apurba Kundu, *Militarism in India: The Army and Civil Society in Consensus*. London: Tauris Academic Studies, 1998

29 Guha, *India After Gandhi*, pp. 541–2

30 See *Law and Ethics of Human Rights*, pub. De Gruyter, August 2020

31 *The Times*, 13 August 2022

32 Frank, *Indira*, p. 215

CHAPTER 18 – SUPERMAN FALLS TO
EARTH – THE TOPPLING OF BOJO

1   Matt Hancock, Isabel Oakeshott, *Pandemic Diaries: The Inside Story of Britain's Battle Against Covid*. London: Biteback Publishing, 2022, pp. 248, 249, 261–2

2   *Spectator*, 20 October 2020

3   *Spectator*, 14 December 2020

4   *Spectator*, 24 December 2020

5   Sebastian Payne, *The Fall of Boris Johnson: The Full Story*. London: Macmillan, 2022, p. 18

6   House of Commons, 1, 8 December 2021; Payne, ibid., pp. 21, 30, 109
7   Ibid., p. 53
8   Ibid., pp. 137, 147
9   Ibid., p. 190
10 Ibid., pp. 192–3
11 Ibid., p. 217
12 Ibid., pp. 219–20
13 Ibid., pp. 204–5
14 Ibid., p. 221
15 Ibid., p. 21
16 Guardian, 11 November 2022
17 The Times, 15 November 2022
18 Observer, 23 October 2022
19 The Sunday Times, 20 November 2022

CHAPTER 19 – DONALD TRUMP AND THE MARCH
ON THE CAPITOL

1   Michael Wolff, Fire and Fury: Inside the Trump White House. London: Little, Brown, 2018, p. 44
2   Ibid., p. 23
3   Oborne, How Trump Thinks, p. xv
4   Bob Woodward, Fear: Trump in the White House. London: Simon & Schuster, 2018, p. 320
5   Michael Wolff, Siege: Trump Under Fire, London: Little, Brown, 2019, p. 113
6   Woodward, Fear, p. 207
7   10 November 2012
8   Woodward, Fear, p. 205
9   Bob Woodward, Rage. London: Simon & Schuster, 2020, p. 247–8
10 Woodward, Rage, pp. 390–1
11 Woodward, Fear, p. 230
12 25 April, 2018; Woodward, Fear, pp. 155–6
13 25 August, 2018; Woodward, Fear, p. 264
14 Woodward, Fear, p. 42
15 Woodward, Rage, p. 305
16 Woodward, Fear, pp. xvii–xix
17 Woodward, Fear, pp. 190–1
18 Bob Woodward & Robert Costa, Peril. London: Simon & Schuster, 2021, pp. 156–8
19 David Rothkopf, American Resistance: The Inside Story of How the Deep State Saved America. New York: PublicAffairs, 2022, p. 87

20 Michael Wolff, *Landslide: The Final Days of the Trump Presidency.* London: Little, Brown, 2021, pp. 23, 25

21 Wolff, *Landslide*, p. 62

22 Woodward & Costa, *Peril*, p. 159

23 Wolff, *Landslide*, p. 148

24 Ibid., p. 131

25 Ibid., p. 136

26 Ibid., p. 161

27 Woodward & Costa, *Peril*, p. 229

28 Wolff, *Landslide*, pp. 184–5

29 Woodward & Costa, *Peril*, p. 206

30 Jones was said to be making $800,000 a day out of his businesses peddling a huge variety of conspiracy theories (David Aaronovitch, *The Times*, 25 August 2022). According to reports, he has since been effectively bankrupted by the civil suit provoked by his denial of the Sandy Hook massacre

31 Luke Mogelson, *The Storm is Here: America on the Brink.* London: Riverrun, 2022, p. 177

32 Ibid., p. 177

33 Ibid., p. 178

34 Ibid., p. 181

35 Ibid., p. 194

36 Ibid., p. 171

37 Ibid., p. 230

38 Wolff, *Landslide*, p. 289

39 Woodward & Costa, *Peril*, p. 397

40 Ibid., *Peril*, p. 416

41 Ibid., p. 374

42 Rothkopf, *American Resistance*, p. 3

43 Michael Lewis, *The Fifth Risk, Undoing Democracy.* London: Allen Lane, 2018, p. 64

44 Rothkopf, *American Resistance*, p. 237

45 Ibid., p. 239

46 Wolff, *Siege*, p. 108

47 Rothkopf, *American Resistance*, p. 134

48 Corey R. Lewandowski & David N. Bossie, *Trump's Enemies.* New York: Center Street, 2018, pp. 161–2

49 Ibid.

50 Rothkopf, *American Resistance*, p. 18

51 Lewandowski, *Trump's Enemies*, pp. 268–72

52 Patrick Radden Keefe, *The Empire of Pain: The Secret History of the Sackler Dynasty.* London: Picador, 2021, p. 195

53 Woodward & Costa, Peril, p. 113
54 Ibid., p. 184
55 Woodward, Rage, p. 271
56 Ibid., p. 311
57 Ibid.
58 Ibid., p. 353
59 Ibid., p. 325
60 Ibid., p. 287
61 Ibid., p. 354
62 Rothkopf, American Resistance, pp. 232–3
63 Ibid.
64 Ibid., p. 241
65 Mogelson, The Storm, p. 235
66 Ibid., p. 229
67 Ibid., pp. 245–6
68 Ibid., pp. 249–50
69 Ibid., pp. 254–5

PART IV – THE SACREDEST PLACE

1 John Locke, Two Treatises of Government. London: Awnsham Churchill, 1690, II, 212
2 Ibid., II, 98
3 Ibid., II.97
4 Ibid., II, 94
5 Machiavelli, The Discourses, I, 6.16
6 Jeremy Waldron, The Dignity of Legislation. Cambridge: Cambridge University Press, 1999, p. 1
7 Ibid., p. 9
8 Ibid., p. 128
9 Jean-Jacques Rousseau, The Social Contract, tr. H. J. Tozer. London: Swan Sonnenschein, 1895, p.167
10 Waldron, The Dignity of Legislation, p. 155
11 Sir Thomas Duppa's Commonplace Book, ed. Alasdair Hawkyard and J. C. Sainty. Chichester, Sussex: Wiley Blackwell, 2015, pp. 19–20

Picture Credits

Page 13 *Res Gestae Divi Augusti* © Seth Schoen, CC BY-SA 2.0 <https://creative-commons.org/licenses/by-sa/2.0>, via Wikimedia Commons

Page 14 President Donald J. Trump in hard hat © Mark Makela/Getty Images

Page 19 Statue of Oliver Cromwell outside Westminster Hall © Marc-Andre_LeTourneux/Getty Images

Page 27 Thomas Carlyle © Elliott & Fry, Public domain, via Wikimedia Commons

Page 39 French troops on the streets of Paris during Prince Louis-Napoleon Bonaparte's coup d'état of 1851 © Universal History Archive/Universal Images Group via Getty Images

Page 40 The eviction of the judges of the High Court of Justice, whilst making provision for the impeachment of Louis-Napoleon during his coup d'état of 1851 © Universal History Archive/Universal Images Group via Getty Images

Page 49 Napoleon's remains are delivered by the small ship *La Dorade*, which took him to Courbevoie, a suburb of Paris © Henri Félix Emmanuel Philippoteaux, Public domain, via Wikimedia Commons

Page 55 A propaganda poster depicting the dictator António Salazar as Afonso I, the first king of Portugal. The motto says: 'Everything for the nation, nothing against the nation' © Silvestre.85, CC BY-SA 4.0 <https://creativecommons.org/licenses/by-sa/4.0>, via Wikimedia Commons

Page 72 Bust of Gaius Julius Caesar (Vatican Museum) © Musei Vaticani (Stato Città del Vaticano), Public domain, via Wikimedia Commons

Page 77 Picture dated 8 May 1945 showing French general Charles de Gaulle dropping a wreath of flowers off at the Arc de Triomphe as Parisians gathered around to celebrate the unconditional German capitulation at the end of the Second World War © AFP via Getty Images

Page 81 Napoleon Bonaparte on the bridge at Arcole © Antoine-Jean Gros, Public domain, via Wikimedia Commons

Page 81 Napoleon Bonaparte crossing the St Bernard Pass, May 1800 by Jacques-Louis David (1748–1825) © Leemage/Corbis via Getty Images

Page 97 Prime Minister Boris Johnson gestures prior to boarding his General Election campaign trail bus on 15 November 2019 in Manchester, England © Frank Augstein-WPA Pool/Getty Images

Page 112 Enemies of the People © Daily Mail

Page 128 Migrants sit in a dinghy illegally crossing the English Channel from France to Britain on 15 March 2022 © Sameer Al-Doumy/AFP via Getty Images

Page 145 Cicero in the Senate denouncing Catiline, by Cesare Maccari (1840–1919), fresco from Palazzo Madama, Rome © Photo by DeAgostini/ Getty Images

Page 155 Undated illustration entitled, 'The Gun Powder Conspiracy,' depicting the Guy Fawkes conspirators: Thomas Bates, Robert Winter, Christopher Wright, John Wright, Thomas Percy, Guido Fawkes, Robert Catesby and Thomas Winter © Bettmann/Getty Images

Page 172 The arrest of the Cato Street conspirators © http://www. slangon.com/blog/, Public domain, via Wikimedia Commons

Page 197 Adolf Hitler, Hermann Göring, Julius Streicher and the doomed Max Scheubner-Richter lead the Nazi march to the War Ministry, 9 November 1923 © Keystone/Hulton Archive/Getty Images

Page 207 Mrs Indira Gandhi, Prime Minister of India from 1966 until 1977 and from 1980 until 1984, the daughter of Jawaharlal Nehru, who was independent India's first Prime Minister © Michael Ochs Archives/ Getty Images

Page 230 Outgoing British Prime Minister Boris Johnson gives a final speech outside 10 Downing Street before travelling to Balmoral to meet Queen Elizabeth II and officially resign as Prime Minister © Wiktor Szymanowicz/Anadolu Agency via Getty Images

Page 249 US President Donald Trump speaks at the 'Save America March' rally in Washington DC on 6 January 2021 © Tayfun Coskun/Anadolu Agency via Getty Images

Page 259 QAnon Shaman Jacob Chansley inside the Senate Chamber after the US Capitol was breached by a mob during a joint session of Congress on 6 January 2021 in Washington DC © Win McNamee/Getty Images

Page 268 The attempted arrest of the 'Five members' by Charles I in 1642, painting in the Lord's Corridor, Houses of Parliament, by Charles West Cope © Charles West Cope, Public domain, via Wikimedia Commons

Acknowledgements

Some of the material and the arguments in this book were first aired, in one form or another, in the pages of the London Review of Books, the New York Review of Books, Prospect and The Times Literary Supplement. I am lastingly grateful to the editors of these journals for the delicious opportunities they have given me over the years and their brilliant advice, in particular to Mary-Kay Wilmers, Tom Crewe, Alice Spawls, Ian Buruma, Julie Just, Sameer Rahim, David Horspool and Toby Lichtig. At Bloomsbury, I am no less grateful for the sage encouragement of Robin Baird-Smith and the vigilant and acute editing of Graham Coster and Sarah Jones.

What I have found in trying to trace the motives and tactics of Caesars and would-be Caesars down the ages is that general social, political and economic histories, however intelligent, can take you only so far. There is no substitute for the detailed insights and revealing anecdotes to be found in the best biographies, both ancient and modern. It is the Caesar's Life that gives life to his project. I owe more than I can say to those historians and reporters whom I have quoted here, often at larcenous length, prime among them: Mary Beard, Tom Bower, Philip Dwyer, Katherine Frank, Antonia Fraser, Vic Gatrell, Ramachandra Guha, Tom Holland, Julian Jackson, Ian Kershaw, Luke Mogelson, Peter Oborne, Sebastian Payne, David Rothkopf, Jeremy Waldron, Michael Wolff, Bob Woodward, Blair Worden and Adam Zamoyski.

Index

Note: page numbers in *italic* indicate illustrations.